Television at the Crossroads

Also by George Wedell

BROADCASTING AND PUBLIC POLICY

STRUCTURES OF BROADCASTING (*editor*)

STUDY BY CORRESPONDENCE (*with R. Glatter*)

BROADCASTING IN THE THIRD WORLD (*with Elihu Katz*)

MEDIA IN COMPETITION: The Future of Print and Electronic Media in 22 Countries (*with George Michael Luyken*)

EUROPE 2000: What Kind of Television? (*editor*)

MAKING BROADCASTING USEFUL: The African Experience (*editor*)

RADIO 2000: The Opportunities for Public and Private Radio Services in Europe (*with Philip Crookes*)

MASS COMMUNICATIONS IN WESTERN EUROPE: An Annotated Bibliography (*with George Michael Lukyen and Rosemarie Leonard*)

Also by Bryan Luckham

THE LIBRARY IN SOCIETY

READING CHOICE IN MANCHESTER AND MISKILC (*with Istavan Kamaras*)

STUDIES ON RESEARCH IN READING AND LIBRARIES (*co-editor*)

First published 2001 by
PALGRAVE
Houndmills, Basingstoke, Hampshire RG21 6XS and
175 Fifth Avenue, New York, N.Y. 10010
Companies and representatives throughout the world

PALGRAVE is the new global academic imprint of
St. Martin's Press LLC Scholarly and Reference Division and
Palgrave Publishers Ltd (formerly Macmillan Press Ltd).

ISBN 0–333–71646–9

This book is printed on paper suitable for recycling and made from fully managed and sustained forest sources.

A catalogue record for this book is available from the British Library.

Library of Congress Cataloging-in-Publication Data
Wedell, E. G. (Eberhard George), 1927–
   Television at the crossroads / by George Wedell and
   Bryan Luckham ; with cartoons by Miroslav Barták.
      p. cm.
   Includes bibliographical references and index.
   ISBN 0—333-71646-9 (cloth)
   1. Television broadcasting—Great Britain. I. Luckham,
Bryan. II. Title.
   PN1992.3.G7 W37 2001
   384.55'0941—dc21
                                                        00–068190

10   9   8   7   6   5   4   3   2
10   09   08   07   06   05   04   03   02   01

Printed and bound in Great Britain by
Antony Rowe Ltd, Chippenham, Wiltshire

Television at the Crossroads

George Wedell

and

Bryan Luckham

with cartoons by Miroslav Barták

To our better halves

Contents

Part III   The Future

List of Tables and Figure

Foreword

This book is the outcome, at several years' remove, of an Emeritus Fellowship of the Leverhulme Trust which I held from 1994 to 1996, and which I acknowledge again here with gratitude. The Trust's Fellowships for Professores Emeriti were created to allow university professors who have recently retired to complete work on which they were engaged while in office. In my case the help afforded to me was valuable in enabling me to prepare a follow-up volume to the book I wrote in 1966–68.

I moved to my Manchester chair directly from a period as the Secretary of the Independent Television Authority. The Authority was created in 1955 to appoint and supervise, under the terms of the Television Act 1954, the commercial television companies providing a second television channel for the United Kingdom. The volume *Broadcasting and Public Policy*[1] was the first attempt to describe and compare the BBC as the original public service broadcasting organisation created in 1927 with the independent television system launched in 1955. I looked at the two organisations essentially as instruments for the provision of information, education and entertainment. It emerged that the two channels had experienced a large measure of convergence around the public service model even though they were divergent in origin and structure.

Thirty years later it has seemed important to look again at the British system, by now altered almost beyond recognition, and to consider how it now corresponds to the public interest. By 1994 I had retired from the chair of Communications Policy in the University, and from the directorship of the European Institute for the Media, founded in Manchester in 1983, and moved to Düsseldorf in 1992. At the beginning of the project I decided to consult a group of people working in television. Lord Thomson of Monifieth, chairman of the Independent Television Authority from 1981 to 1988 and by then chairman of the Leeds Castle Foundation in Kent, invited us to hold a meeting at the Castle, at which some of the key issues as they were seen in 1994 could be discussed. I am much obliged to Lord Thomson and his fellow trustees for making the meeting possible.

Those attending the meeting included: Mr Manuel Alvarado, Professor Jay Blumler, Mr Robert Boyle, Mr Michael Bukht, Dr Richard

Collins, Mr David Elstein, Mr Peter Fiddick, Ms Liz Forgan, Mr David Glencross, Mr Michael Pilsworth, Professor Vincent Porter, Mr Anthony Pragnell, Mr Colin Shaw, Ms Janet Street-Porter, Lord Thomson of Monifieth, Ms Janice Turner, Mr Brian Wenham and Mr Will Wyatt. I want to acknowledge here the help I received from the participants at the time and since then.

During my tenure of the Emeritus Fellowship two urgent missions diverted a part of my attention. The first was a request from the director-general of UNESCO to undertake an inquiry into media relations between Iran and the ex-Soviet states of Central Asia. The second was an assessment of the role of television in the development of democracy in Africa south of the Sahara, which the Commission of the European Union asked my colleague Professor André-Jean Tudesq of Bordeaux and myself to undertake.

When I was able to resume intensive work on the manuscript Mr Bryan Luckham, a colleague of long standing in the University of Manchester and the European Institute for the Media, agreed to join me as co-author. This made feasible the completion of the manuscript in 1999. I am much indebted to him for this help.

Others to whom I am much indebted include: Mr Graham Allen MP, Mr Martin Bell MP, Professor Dorothy Emmet, Mr Peter Heinze, Sir Jeremy Isaacs, Mr Martin Jackson, Mr David Lowen, Lady (Brenda) Maddox, Mr David Plowright, Professor Ronald Preston, Mr Barry Reeve, Mr Raymond Snoddy and Baroness Warnock, in this country; and Ms Cindy Brown, Mr Wilson P. Dizard Jr, Mr Charles Firestone, Professor George Gerbner, Mr Jack N. Goodman, Mr Robert M Pepper and Mr Douglas Rivlin, in the United States of America. But I must emphasize that the opinions expressed in the book are those of my co-author and myself.

During my tenure of the Leverhulme Fellowship Mrs Olivia Henley acted as research assistant and laid the foundation for the work that was completed some years later. I thank her warmly for this work. My friend Mr Anthony Pragnell, formerly director-general of the Independent Television Authority, has throughout been most supportive. He read the manuscript with care and saved us from errors and omissions, both general and particular. We are grateful.

Mr Wolfgang Lehr, the retired director-general of Hessischer Rundfunk in Frankfurt, Germany, and a fellow governor of the European Institute for the Media, drew to my attention the brilliant cartoons of the Czech artist Miroslav Barták. These express better than any others I know the essential ambivalence of television. I am grateful to Mr Barták for permission to use the cartoons at the head of each chapter, and I hope their dry wit cheers my readers as much as it cheers me.

My secretary Mrs Ena Dilley has taken responsibility for turning an untidy manuscript into elegant typescript conforming to the requirements of the publisher. Both Mr Luckham and I are most grateful to her.

GEORGE WEDELL
Manchester

Part I
The Framework

1
Moving the Goalposts

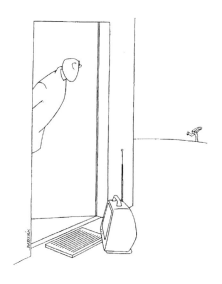

'The programmes on British television are a product of the interaction of supply and demand: Discuss.' The short answer to this examination question is 'Yes and no.' There have only been three years in the history of broadcasting in this country during which the answer would have been an unequivocal 'yes'. Those were the years from 1922 to 1925 when, subject to a licence from the Postmaster General to broadcast, the infant radio companies around the country began to supply radio signals over the air in order to see whether there would be any demand for them. Demand amounted to about 5000 receivers or, at $2\frac{1}{2}$ people per set, to 12 500 listeners.

About 70 years later 99.4 per cent of the United Kingdom has access to five terrestrial television channels as well as access either to direct-to-home satellite services or cable services. An average of about 20 million viewers watched television by one or another of these modes of reception, disposed as shown in Table 1.1.

The three-quarters of a century between the launch of radio in the early 1920s and the establishment of multichannel television in the 1990s cover the rise and fall of broadcasting in the UK as an instrument of social and cultural policy. At the beginning of the period the goalposts were planted in the soil of the public corporation. As Professor W. A. Robson[1] has pointed out, the BBC was not, in fact, the first public corporation:

> Prior to the 1914–18 war there were only one or two public corporations charged with operating public utilities. The Port of London Authority, established in 1908, was an exceptional example. But in 1919 there started to flow that stream of public bodies beginning with the Forestry Commission.

Nor was the idea of a public corporation Lord Reith's. As Asa Briggs[2] recounts,

> Many writers and politicians dwelt on the advantages of public corporations at this time – notably Herbert Morrison, Sir Henry Bunbury and W. A. Robson. American visitors came from the United States of Franklin D. Roosevelt to learn what 'public corporations' were. They went on conducted tours of the Central Electricity Board, the London Passenger Transport Board and the BBC to see how large scale institutions behaved when they were called upon to act as 'trustees for the national interest'.[3]

Table 1.1 Television audiences in multichannel homes in the 1990s (audience shares as percentages)

A	Terrestrial channels	1999 Jan.–Aug.	1996 Year	1993 Year
	BBC1	20.6	23.6	24.5
	BBC2	6.7	6.5	6.5
	BBC total	27.3	30.1	31.0
	ITV	24.6	26.5	30.5
	Channel 4 / S4C	6.9	6.9	7.2
	Channel 5 (since March 1997)	4.1	–	–
	ITV total	35.5	33.4	37.7
	Totals	62.8	63.5	68.7
B	*Non-terrestrial channels*	*1999 Jan.–Aug.*	*1993 Year*	*1993 Year*
	Sky 1	4.1	4.7	7.0
	Sky News	1.1	1.1	1.3
	Sky Movies	4.0	7.0	8.6
	Sky Sports (includes small amount of non-sport until Oct. 1996)	4.5	5.4	3.3
	Bravo (from Nov. 1993)	0.4	0.7	–
	Cartoon Network (includes TNT before 1998)	2.1	2.8	–
	Discovery/Home and Leisure	1.3	1.3	–
	Disney (Oct. 1995)	1.1	1.1	–
	Eurosport (Feb. 1994)	0.8	1.1	–
	Granada Plus (Oct. 1996)	0.7	–	–
	Living (Sept. 1993)	1.2	1.1	–
	MTV	1.2	0.7	1.4
	Nickelodeon (Sept. 1993)	1.6	1.8	–
	UK Gold	2.3	2.1	2.8
	VH-1 (Sept. 1994)	0.8	0.7	–
	Totals	37.2	36.5	31.3

Source: Audience data BARB 1993–99 compiled by William Phillips, *The Journal of the Royal Television Society*, October 1999, p. 33.

But there is no doubt that Reith was one of the most ardent and determined protagonists of the principle, and that he regarded his own work at the BBC as the crucial example of its application:

after all the system was introduced into this country more or less while the watchmen slept. By a side door, and by someone of no account. Odd sort of muddle-up it was thought to be; neither one thing nor the other; not worth bothering about; wait to see what a mess there would be. The side door was a Royal Charter; I was the person of no account – but with something like a Royal Commission behind me. And the thing worked; against almost all expectation it worked; I saw to that; jealously planned and watched its development and safeguarded the essentials of its establishment; date 1 January 1927; subject (or product) broadcasting.[4]

This conflation of the concepts of the public interest and, at the time radio broadcasting, came about as a result of the work of one of the first of the many committees that have deliberated on broadcasting matters since the 1920s. Following the report of the Committee on Broadcasting of 1925 under the chairmanship of the Earl of Crawford and Balcarres,[5] the content of broadcasting was declared to be definitely a matter of public interest, and a suitable object of government regulation under rules approved by Parliament. It is sobering to recall that section 15 of the Committee's report recommended that 'a moderate amount of controversy should be broadcast, provided the matter is of high quality and distributed with scrupulous fairness'. Accordingly the BBC licence of 1927 made it a requirement that the public should be protected from partisan information. As we all know, arrangements to ensure this have taken up a great deal of time of broadcasting managers from that day to this.

But it is not only the interests of the listeners and viewers which have preoccupied governments. The economic effects of the new media on the life of the country have never been far behind. Already in 1925 Sir William Boosey, managing director of the Queen's Hall in London, claimed in his evidence to the Crawford Committee that broadcasting would ruin the concert business.[6] Again, complicated rules were devised to ensure that a more or less level playing field was maintained between the promoters of concerts and the growing musical activities of broadcasters.

When the monopoly of the BBC in television matters was broken in 1954 the government, having supported the commercial lobby of Mr Selwyn Lloyd and his friends despite the objections of Lady Violet Bonham-Carter and her friends, suffered similar pangs to those of the Crawford Committee in 1925. What would the commercial television operators do to the audience? Would they give the viewers what they wanted? Perish the thought. So, in the course of the debate on the Television Bill of 1954 the emphasis once again began to shift towards regulation. Television viewers, the government held, needed to be protected from unbridled commercialism such as that rampant in American television. Viewers were entitled to receive good television programmes, irrespective of whether these were paid for by the licence fee or by the revenue from spot advertising inserted in the ITV schedules. In the event, therefore, the conditions under which the commercial companies came to operate were similar, if not identical, to those established eight years before for BBC television. And these, in turn, with surprisingly few modifications, derived their legitimation from the rules developed for BBC Radio in 1927.

After the 1980s when the then government's doctrine on market forces was applied to broadcasting, quite a strong tide is flowing once again in favour of the public interest. The government's Green Paper of May 1995[7] states boldly that 'government has a responsibility both to promote diversity and choice for consumers and to set the right framework for industry to flourish'.[8] More surprisingly, in a departure from the views prevailing during the Thatcher era, the paper went on to claim that 'television, radio and the press have a unique role in the free expression of ideas and opinion, and thus in the democratic process. The main objective must therefore be to secure a plurality of sources of information and opinion, and a plurality of control over them.'[9] The background to these uncompromising statements seemed to be a renewed willingness in the new Department of Culture, Media and Sport to recognise that there is a public interest in broadcasting reaching beyond the market place. 'The government has an explicit responsibility', we were told, 'to see that the country has a well educated and informed citizenry.'[10]

That was all very well, but it turned out to be too late to close the stable door. The horse of largely unfettered private interest had bolted during the deregulatory 1980s, spurred on by the explosion in information technology. Any householder on the cable system or with a satellite dish was by the 1990s able to receive a plethora of different television programmes, many of which were outside public control since they originated outside the country.

Attempts to regain an element of control have taken two forms. The first has been the development of European Union legislation to harmonise standards for television programmes originating in the member states of the Union. The compromises made to achieve the first European Directive, *Trans-frontier Television*, in 1989 drew attention to the difficulty of legislating on a European scale in the field of cultural policy. It remains to be seen when the proposed revision of the 1989 Directive intended, among other matters, to remove ambiguities in the definitions for quotas of material of European origin, will find its way on to the European statute book. The other attempt at regaining control has been unilateral. Although the government cannot prevent undesirable satellite programmes from being beamed at the United Kingdom, it can make it unlawful to buy the decoding equipment needed to view them, or for British advertisers or sponsors to buy time on such programmes. The order announced by the Secretary of State on 14 November 1995 in respect of a satellite programme uplinked in Sweden is an example. Such unilateral action is, of course, not always wise or practicable.

The combination of the explosion in the number of channels, the arrival of digital transmission and the expansion of broadcasting beyond national frontiers has moved the goalposts. The regulation of the public interest in broadcasting as traditionally understood is no longer practicable. Just as it is no longer practicable for a man with a red flag to walk in front of a motor car, so many of the constraints and safeguards with which broadcasting used to be hedged about no longer command general consent. Even those constraints and safeguards that *are* necessary may no longer be susceptible to attempts at control. On the other hand new constraints may be envisaged arising from technological advances. It may be that an entirely new concept of the public interest needs to be developed which is capable of encompassing new opportunities and hazards. We discuss the evolving role of regulation in greater detail in Chapter 9.

Strategic issues in broadcasting policy

Here we are concerned with strategic issues in broadcasting policy. In discussing the public interest in broadcasting we need to distinguish between:

(a) the strategic considerations which should govern the conduct of a country's affairs according to the principles of civilisation and democracy; and

(b) the tactical considerations arising from the circumstances, technological, political, social and economic, in which broadcasting systems are conducted at any one time.

There is understandably, a tendency for those working in the broadcasting industry to concentrate on (b) at the expense of (a), on the assumption that the broad strategic principles are fixed and can be

taken for granted by the broadcasters. In practice the strategic considerations no longer, everywhere and at all times, go without saying. At a
time when governments withdraw from areas in which they were traditionally active, it is as well to remind ourselves that the original objective of broadcasting policy was to protect the citizen from exploitation
by *ex parte* political and commercial interests.

Fundamental challenges faced those countries in which a broad consensus on the nature of democratic societies was not well established.

> It took the experience of dictatorships and the second world war for
> the basic anti-totalitarian attitude of liberalism, as well as of democ-
> ratic socialism and of Christian democratic ideas to find common
> ground and create a more lasting basis for cooperation between
> individualistic and communitarian ideas. This generalising of liber-
> alism, its integration into all democratic parties, turned a concept
> that had often been declared dead (in authoritarian countries) into
> the foundation of the revived liberal parliamentary democracy of
> the West.[11]

This analysis by K. D. Bracher, the distinguished contemporary histo-
rian at the University of Bonn, illustrates that arguments which are
taken for granted here do have to be spelt out in some other European
countries. Bracher continues by describing the component of freedom
within a democratic framework, not only in terms of basic rights but
also of pluralism:

> The notion of democracy as the agreement simultaneously to toler-
> ate and restrain different opinions and ambitions, signals more
> clearly than more formal constitutions the difference that sets
> democracy apart from all forms of dictatorship. The common will is
> based on, and determined by, the readiness to set voluntary bound-
> aries on the plurality of ambitions and forces. Only where this basic
> agreement is accepted can the democratic state grant the multitude
> of aspirations full play without endangering itself.[12]

The notion of the state 'granting the multitude of aspirations full play'
implies a doctrine of the primacy of 'the state' which we have traditionally rejected. Freedom should be the natural condition of citizens
except in those areas in which, by common consent, they vest powers
in the state for the achievement of agreed purposes. Having said that,
it is worth remembering that the Judaeo-Christian tradition has always

identified areas where freedom depends on the observation of agreed constraints: the family, the economic order, and the sociocultural order. Without these 'orders of creation' which provide a framework for human relationships 'freedom' can result in anarchy and the denial of human rights.[13]

These strategic considerations can be illustrated across the whole range of broadcasting activities, where the balance between freedom and restraint is crucial. Consider the field of news reporting which we discuss in greater detail in Chapter 4. Here, in particular, the balance between freedom and order is essential if professional standards are to be maintained. John Habgood, a former Archbishop of York, has identified the emergence of what he calls 'the culture of contempt' in news and current affairs. In the Priestland Memorial Lecture for 1995[14] he drew attention to

> the contemptuous tone of much of today's reporting. Contempt hijacks understanding, it stops communication, it is less concerned with truth than with demonstrating the author's cleverness. When the media indulge in it they usually defend themselves by saying that their aim is to reflect the nature of society, not to change it, and they would claim that they are merely expressing the anti-authoritarian flavour of modern liberal culture. The truth, I suspect, is more complex. There seems to be a kind of vicious circle whereby the media feed back into a culture tendencies, which may indeed have had their origin elsewhere, but which are magnified by constant public reiteration and which thus provide the apparent basis for more and more extreme versions of themselves. The culture of contempt, in other words, feeds on itself. And the appetite for it grows especially among those who work in the kind of corporate culture where direct criticism of authority is dangerous, where debate is stifled, and where disillusionment with those in control is allowed to fester.

Habgood continues by identifying a crisis of authority which derives from a weakening of the agreed constraints to which we have referred.

> There is an awful suspicion in some quarters that there are no universal and objective truths to be found; there is only my truth or your truth, my morality or your morality, our culture as only one among many, no better and no worse than any other. The present

crisis of authority is that authority is perceived to have no basis; in the end everything boils down to a matter of individual opinion and personal choice. How has it come about? It is obviously not unconnected with the spirit of criticism which in the past has been so fruitful in helping to shape our culture by exposing abuse and falsehood. Siren voices tell us that all we are witnessing now is simply an extension of that process, and that there is nothing to worry about. Human beings will find ways of living with the new freedom to think what they like, and do what they like and to base their lives on the belief that there is no ultimate source of truth or goodness to which they can appeal. Humanity has survived massive cultural changes in the past, and will survive in the future – so they say. That sounds fine and noble for those who already know where they stand and are used to sophisticated mental gymnastics. But would any of us actually want everybody – and I mean everybody – to pursue the policy that there is no truth or morality beyond what individuals believe?

These two quotations illustrate the delicate relationship between freedom and order. They show that the public interest cannot be equated with the interests of the government-for-the-time-being. Such a government should, of course, govern in the interests of all citizens, but it shares this responsibility with the Parliament and the judiciary. Yet the actions of government are often determined by the need to honour promises to particular interest groups made at the previous election. They tend also to be coloured by the wish to win the coming election and with this in view, to pander to interest groups which are thought to hold the key to electoral success. Thus the extent to which any government can be said to pursue the *public* interest is generally inhibited by these two considerations.

Nor is the public interest to be equated with the interest of only the present generation of the people as voters. As Walter Lippman has pointed out, 'Because of the discrepancy between the People as voters and the People as the corporate nation, the voters have no title to consider themselves the proprietors of the common wealth and to claim that their interests are identical with the public interest.'[15] This interest has to take account of the inter-generational influence of those who have gone before as well as the interests of coming genera-tions. 'This invisible, inaudible, and so largely non-existent commu-nity', Lippman goes on, 'gives rational meaning to the necessary objectives of government.' And Anthony Smith looks back with some nostalgia to

> American thinking in the first decade or so of television (which) was still suffused with notions of this organic public interest, one in which the information media played a facilitating part. Television did not exist only to gratify immediate needs, but to help the whole process of historical evolution. What we are working with today is a survival of some of these strands of thought, but in the context of a society dynamically determined to alter the terms by which public and private interests define their roles within the play of the economy. We are no longer content that the regulators can go unregulated and we have found no fresh device, no way of regulating them without the interposition of the market. The alteration is still socially driven and still in pursuit of an updated vision of the public interest.[16]

The public interest operates positively and negatively. The positive reason for asserting the public interest is that it serves to ensure for all citizens benefits which they could not achieve by individual endeavour. Thus the provision of public transport, of a universal postal services, of public education and health services and of social security has been regarded as being in the public interest. It is only in recent years that the consensus on this subject has been called into question by the advocates of private enterprise and the market economy.

The negative, or regulatory, aspect of the public interest operates when it is considered that the individual is not alone able to protect him or herself from harm which is, or may be, prevalent in their environment. Examples of this concern are the public water supply, sewerage, street cleaning, police services and environmental protection, none of which the ordinary citizen could provide on his own. Public control of misleading, inaccurate, biased and offensive material on the broadcasting services falls within the 'protective' definition of the public interest argument.

The argument in favour of government intervention to secure the public interest began to be seriously challenged only with the development of satellite and cable television in the 1980s. Both these technologies are multiplying the potential number of channels available to individual households. Moreover, disposable incomes are now such that large sections of the population can afford to exercise choice about subscribing to cable and satellite services. The potential diversity of channels lessens, it is argued, the need for the 'guarantees of fair treatment' on which the Crawford Committee insisted.

The proliferation of choice made possible by technological changes has been reinforced by a reversal of the public interest argument in political terms. 'Whereas in the past actors in a number of countries saw government intervention as the instrument of public benefit, they now tend to place their faith in a revival of market forces and the interplay of individual motivations as a sure path to collective benefit.'[17]

Governments since the 1980s have seized on this utilitarian approach as an antidote to the interventionist policies which governed political thinking from the Second World War to the end of the 1970s. There has been little effort to test these options in the context of different sectors of public policy. It is assumed that the application of market forces to broadcasting has the same effect as their application to housing or employment.

Broadcast regulators, the broadcasters themselves, and to an increasing extent the ordinary viewers, are now asking to what extent the public interest will continue to operate in the new conditions. What considerations remain; or, indeed, what new considerations arise, in the pluralistic context of transmission by cable and satellite and the development of digital means of frequency compression? Is there a future for the public interest in broadcasting, or does the public interest fade away when *broad*casting gives way to *narrow*casting. Which gives each citizen the potential to adjust the communications system to his or her individual interest? Given such multiplicity the dilution of, for example, contradictory political messages on different channels could render the present complicated arrangements for political balance redundant.

Aspects of the public interest

In the light of the preceding paragraphs one is tempted to abandon the concept of the public interest,

(a) because it is no longer necessary in the light of the deregulation of broadcasting and the multiplication of channels; and
(b) because the administration of the public interest will become increasingly ineffective as the nexus is broken between the responsibility of governments and their power to implement measures arising from their responsibility.

Before abandoning the public interest it is, however, useful to identify the areas of broadcasting in which the public interest operates at present, and to consider what might be gained or lost by abandoning the principle.

Universal access

The right of citizens to receive, on equal terms, radio and television signals wherever they live (with a few *de minimis* exceptions) has been a principle of public broadcasting from the beginning. The cost per household of providing a good quality radio and television signal varies by a factor of up to 100 between urban centres and outlying areas, particularly in the mountains. The difference is met by the application of the exchequer equalisation principle. Substantial expense has been incurred by the broadcasting authorities over the years in providing terrestrial transmitters, and by the Ministry of Posts and Telecommunications in linking transmitters with each other and with production centres. It is not yet certain how the privatisation of the ITV transmission system and the proposed privatisation of the BBC transmission system will affect universal access in future.

The relative ubiquity of satellite signals means that those with the means to install a receiving dish and the necessary ancillary equipment can receive them. The fading of signals towards the edge of the reception area, however, puts an additional burden to install a larger dish on those living in outlying areas. Cable also involves both access and the means to afford it. Thus both these modes of transmission involve price differentials for viewers.

The question arises whether public funds should be used to reduce or eliminate these differentials in situations where:

(a) differential access arises from economic causes, for example between the few who can afford the extra cost of taking cable and satellite, and the many who cannot; or
(b) differential arises from geographical causes, for example between those who live in an urban environment with access to cable and those in a rural environment dependent on signals transmitted over the air or by satellite.

The maintenance of public service broadcasting

Any proposal for the maintenance of public service broadcasting needs to identify the purposes which public broadcasting services are expected to serve. But first we need to know what these services are.

Under the previous government the then Secretary of State for the National Heritage, Mr Stephen Dorrell, defined the present system as 'delivering public service broadcasting by three methods: BBC, ITV and Channel 4'.[18] There is no reason to believe that Mr Dorrell's successor does not subscribe to this definition. At present these public services still attract the major proportion of the viewership of television, as Table 1.1 shows.

These figures show that in 1999 the terrestrial channels retained 62.8 per cent of the average daily hours of television viewing compared with 68.7 per cent in 1993. The share of the BBC2 and Channel 4/S4C has remained steady during the same period at 13.6 or 13.7 per cent. The gainers during this period have been cable and satellite services which in 1999 took up 37.2 per cent (from 31.3 per cent). The decline of the combined BBC1 and ITV audiences from 55 to 45.2 per cent is so far by no means disastrous. There is every indication that they will retain into the medium term between 40 and 50 per cent of the audience. They do so because they provide an across-the-board service of entertainment, information and education, and by refusing to be pushed out of the entertainment area. In this they are unlike, for example, the Australian Broadcasting Corporation, which has effectively been marginalised at between 10 and 15 per cent of the audience. ABC has reconciled itself to providing the difficult and expensive programming such as news, current affairs, documentaries, serious drama, leaving the commercial stations to sell advertising on the back of high-rating light entertainment. The impact of Channel 5 has been felt by BBC1 and ITV in the first instance.

If the BBC is to continue as at present, the licence fee revenue has to be assured. Allowing the Corporation to compete in the market for spot advertising is no solution. Indeed, there is a case for limiting the amount of self-advertising and cross-promotion that at present breaks up the BBC television schedules. It effectively removes for the viewer the distinction between ITV and the BBC programmes in that the spaces taken up by advertising on ITV are filled by BBC advertising on the Corporation's channels. In this way no channels are really free from the distraction of advertising or promotion. This aping of commercial television by the BBC should be discouraged. BBC2 is demonstrating that excellent work can be done with two-minute slots before the beginning of *Newsnight*.

Given the loyalty of audiences to the public broadcasting services, there are strong arguments in the public interest for maintaining them. Indeed, there is little evidence that the dilution of the public service obligations of ITV under the 1990 Broadcasting Act have been appreciated by its audience. As Table 1.1 shows, it has suffered the largest decline in audience of any public service channel in the period 1993–99. Although the assertion by the managing director of BBC News and Current Affairs that the BBC is 'the only provider of serious wide-ranging current affairs in the UK'[19] may be too triumphalist, the burden is on the ITV companies to prove the BBC wrong.

Quality

It is evidently in the public interest that everything possible should be done to promote high quality in programming for radio and television. But the concept of quality in broadcasting is by no means unambiguous. In most other spheres quality tends to be identified with high cost, whether it be clothes, food or houses. Quality also tends to be identified, particularly in the cultural industries, with something that is highbrow, elitist, accessible only to people of superior intelligence or sensibility. A third tendency is to identify quality with seriousness, high moral intent and an element of didacticism. In broadcasting at its best producers have tried to transcend these shallow forms of classification. The BBC's report *People and Programmes* has found a better definition of quality:

> There is another way of looking at quality, namely as an absolute measure of excellence which transcends both individual consumer satisfaction and professional judgements of merit. [People] return again and again to the idea of the 'classic' programme, a term which for them is just as applicable to the classics of popular entertainment like *Dad's Army* or *Fawlty Towers* as it is to *Civilisation*, or *The Ascent of Man*. Audiences would be pleased to find classic programmes on any channel, but they *expect* them from the BBC. Our research therefore suggests that viewers and listeners analyse and discuss programme quality in sophisticated ways. We also discovered that their judgements tend to correlate very closely with the judgements of programme makers and their peers. We asked programme makers to place various sets of programme in order of quality, we then compared the programme makers' lists with quality rankings we derived from audience research. The match between producers' verdict and the public was usually close.[20]

Having discarded the simplistic identification of quality with serious, expensive and upmarket programmes the BBC, however, promptly falls into the trap which it has just avoided:

The BBC has a simple choice. It can either make for an uncompromising commitment to quality and move up-market, in which case it will risk losing audiences, becoming progressively more marginalised and so jeopardising its funding. Or it can compete head to head with commercial television and radio by moving down-market and so risk undermining the case for its own existence.[21]

Similarly the Corporation puts itself in an impossible position by claiming: 'the BBC will never allow a desire for competitiveness to deflect it from its core responsibilities as a Public Service broadcaster. Everywhere we must strive to offer audiences the widest possible editorial range, even though the consequences may be a less competitive schedule.'[22] Alas, we all know colleagues in the BBC who tell us that the Corporation has perforce to transmit certain programmes in order to remain competitive. An example is BBC2's absurd, but hilarious, attempt to outdo Channel 4 when it devoted a whole evening to pornography.

We have quoted from *People and Programmes* because in matters of quality the Corporation regards itself as leading the way and holding the fort. ITV has never made that sort of claim. Indeed Mr Michael Green of Carlton Communications is quoted in the margin of *People and Programmes* as saying, 'there always will be a large volume of programmes that fall short of creative excellence, which the critics roast, but which the audience enjoy as part of the immensely wide mix of their viewing week'.[23]

The tortuousness of the argument so far illustrates the close relationship between quality and structure. Unless a broadcaster has a structure which puts quality at the top of his or her desiderata, short-term exigencies such as cash shortages, the need to maximise the audience and straightforward laziness lead to a decline in quality. The Department of Culture, Media and Sport fights shy of using the term 'quality', presumably for these reasons. It is easier to define 'plurality' or 'diversity' than it is to define 'quality'. But quality is affected by ownership. In the Green Paper on media ownership the word is used only once: 'programme requirements are focussed on securing quality objectives and on ensuring the accurate and impartial reporting of views and opinions rather than on securing plurality'.[24]

The Green Paper does not seem to realise that 'the accurate and impartial reporting of views and opinions' is a qualitative measure. And if this type of reporting depends on diversity of ownership, then quality broadcasting is unlikely to be assured if media concentration is permitted or even encouraged. To that extent Charles Curran was right to call his book about broadcasting philosophy and practice *A Seamless Robe*.[25] He wanted to underline the fact that quality of broadcasting depends on structure and economics, as well as on adequate resources and the genius of a particular producer.

Choice and diversity

Even if all quantitative requirements were to be satisfied by the new technological and entrepreneurial developments, will the requirements of choice and diversity of programming be met? There is a legitimate public interest in ensuring reasonable choice and diversity for the wide range of viewer interests. For example, how central to the broadcasting output are news and current affairs? It is generally regarded as being in the public interest that there should be an adequate supply of up-to-date, truthful, politically balanced news supported by programmes about current affairs. Again, is education both of an intensive and extensive kind, a sine qua non of broadcasting output in an age when individualised recordings in sound or vision are widely available? What about programmes for the whole range of minority interests pursued by viewers and listeners?

There is a tendency for low-cost channels to do without news or sports programmes. Moreover, the trend towards thematic channels changes the nature of the discussion. The viewer makes his or her choice, and if that means that particular programme strands move out of his/her range of experience so be it. At present most people in this country have a choice of five terrestrially transmitted television services. These services are moderately well assorted so that in switching from one channel to another viewer can often exercise a real element of choice. Certainly the choice is more accessible than the 200 satellite channels on offer. Among these there are programmes originating in half a dozen or more different countries; there are a number of news channels; similar quiz shows in different languages and, just occasionally, a brilliant programme of high quality. But, without a subscription smart card, choice among the satellite channels is woefully restricted and the viewer is likely to revert to one of the terrestrial channels in this country. Those who argue that digitalisation, cable and satellite will provide the ordinary viewer in the UK with a much enlarged choice, need to demonstrate the attraction of these additional services.

The main reason why the evidence at present is so meagre derives from the economics of multichannel television. One of the few immutable statistics in this field concerns the audience. There is only 100 per cent of it. If the total audience declines and is carved into ever

smaller slices by the blandishments of an ever-widening range of programmes, the resources available for any one programme are bound to
decline. Whereas money alone does not create choice, the choice is
likely to be wider if broadcasters have at least some money to devise
original programmes or to buy good programmes, instead of scraping
the barrel of Hollywood third features. It seems evident that the provision of even a limited range of choices requires adequate resources for
each of the channels providing such choice. The effective enlargement
of choice requires a regulatory framework which encourages broadcasters to develop and maintain diversity.

Cross-media ownership

The Government's Green Paper of May 1995 is producer- rather than
consumer-led. Paragraph 3 of the summary says:

> the Government has decided that there is a need to liberalise the
> existing ownership regulations both within and across different
> media sectors. The decision to do so derives from the Government's
> wish to introduce greater flexibility in ownership, to reflect the
> needs and aspirations of the industry, against a background of accel-
> erating technological change, including the introduction of digital
> broadcasting.[26]

The pressure to relax the ownership regulations certainly did not come
from the viewers, listeners and newspaper readers. Of the 65 organisations listed in Annex 1 of the paper as responding to the consultation
exercise conducted by the Department of National Heritage, only four
or five can be said in any way to represent the interests of consumers.
But, of course, the users of the media are traditionally badly organised.
Where the press is concerned, they can vote with their purses. With
radio and television that is more difficult as yet, although an element
of consumer choice is becoming evident in the satellite and cable connection statistics. The Green Paper tries to meet the pressures from the
industry while continuing to have some regard at least to 'preserving
the diversity of the broadcast and press media in the UK'.[27] It is
arguable that Parliament represents the ordinary citizen who is at the
receiving end of the mass media, and that the imbalance between the
producer and the consumer interests will be redressed when the Green
Paper is debated there. The arguments for diversity and the prevention
of concentration of ownership and control should not go unheeded
due to a lack of effective consumer representation.

Of the many things that could be said about cross-media ownership two in particular are relevant to the maintenance of the public interest in broadcasting:

(a) The argument that you have to be big in order to operate in international markets is not supported by the evidence. British companies, if they were good enough, have always been able to sell their programmes overseas. They have done this for a generation. One only has to cast one's mind back to the success of Associated Television in the 1960s and 1970s in breaking into the American market. It is not easy. British programme makers lose out, not so much in terms of quality as in terms of format. ATV had to develop what came to be called a mid-Atlantic idiom, not to say a mid-Atlantic accent, in order to succeed. So what was good for exports was not necessarily good for the British viewers. In the public system broadcasters are licensed first and foremost to provide material of interest to British viewers. An unsupported argument is being fostered by some of the larger companies to the effect that they have to compete in the world market to survive. This is no part of their contract with the ITC and should not be allowed to become common currency. The government Green Paper asks 'How important is it for companies to be large for them to succeed in the international market place?' This question is inappropriate, given that the ITV companies are operating under public contract, as yet in an oligopolistic market. This presents major commercial advantages as well as some minor disadvantages. It certainly modifies the operation of the market in the interest of the contractor. The government cannot have it both ways.

(b) The second comment concerns the prevention of local media monopolies. Local monopolies are, curiously enough, even more likely to occur than national monopolies, partly because the latter are politically more vulnerable. At the local level there is the practical reason that many towns can afford one newspaper and one radio station (more rarely one television station), and unless firm action is taken they may all end up under the control of a single entrepreneur. This can have nefarious effects on local democracy and freedom of expression. The avoidance of local monopolies should therefore be given as much attention as the avoidance of monopolies on the national scene.

2

Needs Must When Innovation Drives

Broadcasting arrives: radio

Broadcasting generally is essentially driven by supply. This means that the people who invented radio had the task of persuading potential listeners to take up the technical facilities which were supplied by the Marconi Company from 1897. The first broadcast of music and speech was made by an American, R. Fessenden, in 1906. There were no 'triode' valves in use until about 1912. In December 1916 the American Radio and Research Corporation was broadcasting radio concerts two or three times a week. A ban imposed on 'amateur' radio in Britain on the outbreak of war in 1914 was not lifted until 1919. The first well-known American broadcasting station KDKA, Pittsburgh, went on the air with regular broadcasts in 1920. During the same year regular concerts began to be broadcast in Europe from The Hague. Also in 1920 the Marconi Company began to broadcast from Chelmsford. Later in the year the Post Office withdrew permission for these broadcasts to be made. On 14 February 1922 the first regular authorised broadcast service in Britain was started from Writtle near Chelmsford. It was organised by the experimental section of the designs department of the Marconi Company. Their London station 2LO began its broadcasts later in the same year on 11 May. In the meantime talks between the radio manufacturers and the Post Office had started on 18 May with a view to forming a broadcasting syndicate. The BBC, which was at the time the British Broadcasting Company, was born in the course of these talks. Its first programmes were broadcast on 14 November 1922, although the company was not formally registered until 15 December 1922 and did not receive its licence from the Post Office until 18 January 1923.

Having provided the technology of wireless communication, the stimulation of user demand was uppermost in the minds of most businessmen in this sector. They concentrated on its private use as a means of point-to-point communication, and saw it as an adaptable and profitable substitute for communication by cable. The limit of their vision was not the radio station with large numbers of scattered listeners, but a network of radio communication links across deserts and oceans which dispensed with the use of copper wires, gutta-percha coverings and iron sheathings. They thought in terms of telegraphy without connecting wires. When the manufacturers of broadband radio transmitters began in the early 1920s they had no idea whether their signals would be used.

The seven ages of television

The launch of television in 1936 marks the beginning of the first age of television identified by Martin Jackson who compiled Figure 2.1 on the seven ages of television. Until television was stopped on the outbreak of war, signals were available only in London and the number of receivers had increased from 400 in November 1936 to 5000. Although transmissions were resumed in June 1946 the second age of television did not occur until 1952, when the prospect of seeing the coronation gave a great boost to the sale of television receivers. Some 500 000 receivers were sold, and it was estimated that more than half the population saw the ceremony transmitted from Westminster Abbey.

The arrival of the first commercial television service in Europe in 1955 launched the third age of television. But the impact of the commercial channel did not become significant until the early 1960s. The launch of BBC2 in 1964 began the break-up of unitary television. The unifying experience which had been so important a feature of radio during the war, and had been transferred to television, reached its apogee with the coronation of Queen Elizabeth II in 1953. The introduction of choice, though limited, represented by the opening of ITV and underlined by the arrival of BBC2, destroyed once and for all the 'unifying experience' argument against diversification.

Similarly uncertainties about consumer take-up accompanied the move in 1967 towards higher television line definition from 405 to 625 lines. This and colour introduced the fifth age of television. In the event it was the demand for colour television which helped to boost the sale of 625-line receivers. But even so dual systems had to be maintained for a quarter-century in order not to deprive the owners of 405-line receivers of their programmes.

Satellite television

The first satellite signals became available with Sky channel in 1984 and launched the sixth age of television. At present the take-up of satellite technology is similarly sluggish. After a decade of satellite signals the five terrestrial channels still attract about 85 per cent of viewers, while more than 50 satellite channels attracted between them only about 15 per cent of the audience. Even in satellite homes the five terrestrial channels attract 64 per cent of the audience, whereas the ASTRA satellite channels and an unspecified number of other non-terrestrial channels,[1] attract 36 per cent.

24

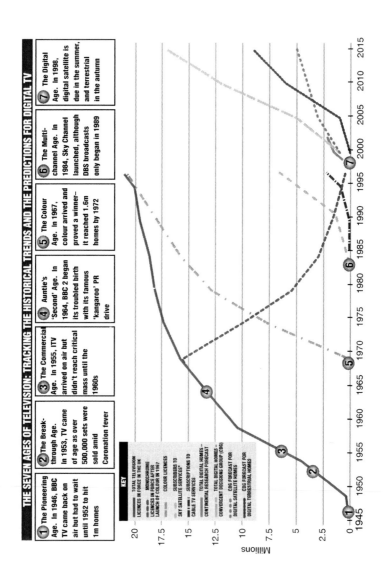

Figure 2.1   The seven ages of television.
Source: Martin Jackson, 'Digital: a Warning from History', *Broadcast*, 09/01/98, pp. 18 and 19. Official subscriber figures from BSkyB only start in 1991. Prior to that, the figures are for Sky Channel and are based on historical data published by the BFI. Other sources: BBC/Cable Communications Association/CDG/Continental Research

Cable services

The history of cable is fairly chequered. The sheer gap between investment in the necessary infrastructure and the time when one can expect some form of return has discouraged most British entrepreneurs from taking up the original cable franchises. So a substantial delay occurred between the time when cable became technically feasible and the time when it actually took off. When the Thatcher government decided to allow American entrepreneurs to enter the cable field things began to happen. By October 1997 58 cable services had become available to 10 million homes, of which 3 million were connected to broadband cable television (32.4 per cent). This figure covers a surprisingly wide range of take-up from 14 per cent in York and Harrogate to 60 per cent in Mid Glamorgan. The variation is not easily explicable either in terms of a north/south divide or on socio-economic grounds. It may reflect differences in the marketing of cable services.[2]

An interesting change occurred between the top ten cable channels between 1996 and 1997, as Table 2.1 shows. By 1997 BSkyB channel, Sky 1 and Sky News had disappeared from the top ten altogether. Sky 1's potential audience had declined from 1.96 million homes to 1.90 million, and Sky News from 1.87 million to 1.53 million. The

Table 2.1   Top ten channels on cable

1997		*Potential homes*	1996		*Potential homes*
1	UK Gold	2 329.295	1	Sky 1	1 956 739
2	Channel Guide	2 266 419	2	Sky News	1 866 574
3	QVC	2 184 962	3	UK Gold	1 845 625
4	Live TV	2 135 317	4	Eurosport	1 802 850
5	VH1	2 121 007	5	Channel Guide	1 801 018
6	Eurosport	2 119 687	6	Discovery	1 792 440
7	UK Living	2 099 191	7	UK Living	1 780 682
8	Discovery	2 047 372	8	TCC	1 794 220
9	TNT	2 024 589	9	TNT	1 764 129
10	Bravo	2 007 724	10	Parliamentary Channel	1 753 867
Total homes connected to cable TV		2 454 931	Total homes connected to cable TV		1 965 911

Source: ITC.
Figures are the total number of cabled homes receiving the various channels available from satellite or otherwise.

decline of Sky News is attributed to the decision in November 1997 of General Cable and Comcast to drop the service from their 'bundle' of transmitted channels. The fact that the UK Gold channel was at the head of the 1997 list, followed by Channel Guide and QVC, the shopping channel, suggests that cable subscribers look for channels with fairly precisely defined content.

Cable services at present appear to provide just under 60 different programmes. Sky 1 and Sky News headed the list in 1996, being available in just under 2 million and 1.86 million homes respectively. At the lower end of cable subscriptions the Adult channel and HVC are taken in 48 000 and 43 000 homes respectively. Of course many of the satellite channels transmitted by cable also have substantial audiences either on cable or by direct-to-home satellite transmission on the European mainland. Those channels carried on the ASTRA satellites are also received by British viewers using individual satellite dishes. Unfortunately the ITC collects no statistics on the direct-to-home audience.

The clear message which these cable figures send is that the era of restricted air space has come to an end. There is no single viewing pattern any longer. The other message is that only one-third of homes to which cable services are available, take them up. Two-thirds of the population are content to do without cable. In this respect the take-up of cable is not unlike the take-up of direct-to-home satellite services. In October 1999, 14.4 per cent of the television audience watched channels other than the five terrestrial channels. The great majority of viewers still hold to BBC1 and ITV (with 28.9 and 31.3 per cent of the audience respectively in October 1999) or to BBC2 (9.1 per cent), Channel 4 (10.6 per cent) or Channel 5 (6.0 per cent). The reason for the low level of take-up of both cable and satellite services appears to be that there is not, in the event, a significant difference between the programmes transmitted by these two new technologies and the programmes available on the traditional terrestrial channels.

But it is evident that television viewers are essentially conservative. They know what they like, and like what they know. This makes the more unreflective forecasts of those prophets who foresee the convergence of television and the Internet in the course of the next few years less than wholly credible. This convergence has become, in the view of *The Spectator*,

a modern myth, appearing to free its users from the shackles of geography, allowing instant communication from country to country. It encourages freedom of thought, being almost impervious to censorship. Its very existence poses a threat to repressive regimes everywhere. It is also proclaimed to be the new commercial frontier, where Britain must compete successfully if our economy is to thrive. Last, but by no means least, it is hailed as the cornerstone of a truly modern educational system.[3]

The Internet

It is a seductive scenario. However, the justification remains as yet to be produced. 'We regard on-line as the third broadcast medium' the BBC announced recently.[4] Microsoft's Internet Explorer is a piece of software that enables people to surf the Internet. It is said to be trying to achieve the global dominance already enjoyed by Microsoft's Windows software.[5] It is claimed that at present more personal computers with Internet capability are being sold than television receivers. The possibility of convergence of personal computers and television certainly exists. Broadcasters can transmit their programmes over the Internet. The BBC is already offering live feeds of some of its radio output from the World Service. The BBC's 24-hour rolling television news service will provide a much more comprehensive online news service. But the idea of convergence remains an area overshadowed by more questions than answers. The issues involved are complex. The biggest issue of all is whether the promoters can develop a sufficiently consumer-oriented service that ordinary viewers will be willing to pay for.

A significant proportion of Internet software is owned by Microsoft who bought WebTV in April 1997. Its rival is another American company Netscape, which claims to have 62 per cent of the corporate market, compared with Microsoft's 36 per cent.[6] Given only two Internet providers, the policy issue is likely to be the control of the Internet. It appears evident that no single delivery system will reach all households. Television broadcasters will therefore seek to distribute their services, particularly in the field of news, by as many delivery systems as they can afford. WebTV was expected to become part of one or more of the digital TV platforms. Both companies are developing their sales strategies. WebTV hope to persuade viewers that they can provide more information and facilitate interactive services such as banking. Net channel also hopes to persuade ordinary viewers that they can enhance their television experience. It seems that they would like to be seen as an additional channel with interactivity. Once connected, viewers get access to a home page that offers a variety of channels featuring entertainment, lifestyle, news, sport, shopping as well as the Internet. Since other providers are aiming at similar users, the competition will be intense.

By the time this book is published digital television may have become part of the third major innovation which television viewers have experienced since the arrival of television itself in the 1930s. The arrival of colour television in the 1960s proved to be an innovation which gained virtually universal acceptance during the 1970s. The arrival of satellite television in the 1980s has, as indicated above, so far secured only a minority audience.

Digital television

The promise of digital terrestrial television development constitutes the seventh age of television. It arises from the technological innovation which allows signals to be compressed, enabling ten times as many channels to be transmitted as can at present be accommodated on the present five terrestrial frequencies with national or near-national coverage. A compression ratio of 10 : 1 should be possible, even while existing analogue services continue to be broadcast. This will allow for between 40 and 50 separate terrestrial services to be accommodated. This of course is distinct from the digital use of satellite transmission, which will make available at least 200 separate channels by means of the compression of the present satellite frequencies. And, of course, cable operators are already offering a selection from the terrestrial and satellite services as well as cable-specific channels over their fibre-optic networks. In addition the telephone companies are offering broadcast services over telephone wires. For the ordinary householders this range of delivery systems will be confusing. Mercifully no single delivery system is likely to reach all households. And in order to receive digital services, most of which are likely to be subscription channels, householders require a decoder on their television receivers which will have to be bought or hired (now given away) and which will include the accounting system for the subscription channels on offer. By 2001 the world set-top box market is thought by some to be worth £2.7 billion to chip manufacturers. Digital television is expected to be the principal sector of growth.[7] Much depends on the design of the decoder. It started with a simple decoder, which did not support interactive services such as home shopping or banking. This will be provided for on a more sophisticated Mark II model after a year or two.

In the spring of 1998 the promoters of digital television became distinctly less upbeat in their prognosis than before. It is true that the plans for digital terrestrial television had already been put in question by one or two brave television executives. In the autumn of 1996 David Elstein, by that time chief executive of Channel 5, described digital terrestrial television as 'a dead end technology and a complete waste of time and money'. He said, 'digital terrestrial television is a dead-end technology with limited capacity and high costs. In the age of digital satellite to be followed by digital cable and even telephone it is a complete waste of time and money.' Since then BSkyB which had promised to launch its digital terrestrial service in the autumn of 1998 discovered that its plans to be the first television company in the digital market, would cost it dear. The company's brokers BZW reduced their forecast for profits in 1999 from £400 million to £320 million. And already in January 1998 a similarly downbeat circular from JP Morgan put BSkyB shares down to 385p in the course of a continuing slide from their high of 669p in the previous year. Commentators began to say that 'digital is the cure for which there is no known disease'. The fact is that television viewers have yet to learn what, if anything, to do with an additional 40 or so television channels, particularly when the cost of digital programmes is raised by some uncomfortable figures.

As for set-top technology, BSkyB accepted early on that digital decoders would have to be subsidised if the system were to stand any chance of becoming a best-seller in the retail trade. In 1997 BSkyB unveiled its master plan for the interactive set-top box to be produced with British Telecom under the name of British Interactive Broadcasting. But the vexing combination of a telecommunications operator and a TV company made the proposed alliance a target of the competition watchdogs at the European Commission. By the beginning of 1998 these had not yet given the go-ahead to this alliance. In the circumstances BSkyB hoped that the football World Cup in June 1998 might act as an incentive for householders to equip themselves with the new hardware. If BSkyB were to launch a successful digital terrestrial service there remained a lingering question on how effectively it would be able to hold on to its existing market. The brokers did not think that satellite subscriptions would produce much growth. The subscription packages are at the lower end of the price range. At approaching £30 per month it seemed at the beginning of 1998 that BSkyB might finally have to face the arrival of consumer resistance. In February 1998 Carlton Television-led British Digital Broadcasting (BDB) announced that it had chosen to launch its digital terrestrial television service with a decoder box manufactured by SECA instead of one from

Murdoch's company MDS. At this point BSkyB claimed that the decoder would not be compatible with its own digital satellite decoder. Taking the view that in order to protect the consumer there should only be one decoder box available, BSkyB claimed that it would take legal steps to force BDB to adopt a compatible system. ONdigital claims that there is interoperability between the two systems but this, of course, depends on whether MDS will allow SECA access to its technology, so that it can make a box that is usable by both systems. There is a suspicion that Mr Murdoch is anxious to become the digital gatekeeper in the UK, as elsewhere.

It would, of course, be possible to require that BSkyB should comply with competition rules and share its box technology. The government might be reluctant to do this in order not to test too severely Mr Murdoch's relations with New Labour. The third force which is in a dilemma over this is Granada Television which is a partner of Carlton in BDB but also has a shareholding in BSkyB.

In the face of so much uncertainty the predictions for digital terrestrial television (DTT) are bound to be suspect. One firm estimates it to be worth around £5 billion by the year 2005.[8] Another suggests that by 2002 some 1.1 million UK homes will have DTT.[9] Another third puts the figure at a more conservative 606 000.[10] The comparative revenue forecasts for some European countries for 2005 are given in Table 2.2. It is not surprising that there are those who think that there will be no interest (other than the public interest) in maintaining terrestrial free-to-air television. As has been the case before during the two generations of television development, those who have always wanted to commercialise television are likely to remain antagonistic to free-to-air, unencrypted broadcasting. This then does become a matter of the

Table 2.2   European digital television revenue forecasts, 2005 ($ million)

	Basic services	Premium services	Pay-per-view Films	Soccer	Total
France	1 374	1 031	738	286	3 429
Germany	5 811	4 345	2 623	5 021	17 800
Italy	629	705	395	773	2 503
Spain	599	749	562	799	2 710
UK	2 880	1 663	1 212	2 505	8 240
International	1 588	1 943	1 477	n/a	5 008
Total	12 861	10 436	7 007	9 384	39 690

Source: Baskerville Communications Corporation.

public interest. The classical arguments in favour of providing, at low cost to the viewer, a public service of television for all citizens, irrespective of their pockets, do not need to be rehearsed here. A recent market research study by Pace asked 1200 adults about their attitude to digital television. Pace has reason for wanting digital television to work; it makes set-top decoder boxes. Hence it might be supposed its conclusions would favour the new technology. In practice the research suggests the chances for digital television are not good. Only 36 per cent of those questioned had heard of digital television or could explain what it is. The survey did not go into detail about the new capital outlays required of viewers to put themselves in the way of digital signals. Even without this disincentive only 21 per cent thought that 'more choice of programmes' might be a reason for buying digital television; 35 per cent did not think increased choice was of any value. Of the respondents, 57 per cent rated interactivity as a useful added value; 64 per cent of those questioned could find no value in it at all. Another 65 per cent of people saw no value at all in the ability to make impulse purchases or pay-per-view programmes. Only 8 per cent of those asked cited impulse buying as a reason for buying the service.

Thirty per cent of respondents thought that improved picture and sound quality might be worth having and a further 46 per cent thought this enhancement would be of 'some value'. It is questionable whether the responses on picture and sound quality are reliable. On the whole the British public has never had to worry much about quality in its television signal in contrast to American experience where picture quality tends to be inferior. So not too much weight should be attached to these opinions.

At the height of the television boom two channels have recently gone bankrupt: the Weather channel and the Country Music channel. There are likely to be further failures as some of the lucrative must-carry agreements, which prescribe what channels cable and satellite companies have to carry as part of their agreements, come to an end. At this stage the guaranteed pence-per-subscriber deals which have kept a number of channels afloat are likely to be abandoned.[11] Two developments, flat-screen technology and the realisation of an electronic programme guide, are likely to be significant in determining the medium-term success of digital initiatives.

Flat-screen technology

The development of flat-screen technology which produces picture sizes of up to 40 inches (102 centimetres) diagonally but is no more than a few inches thick is evidently slower than expected. The early models of such receivers are priced at $8000, almost three times the price of big screen television receivers. The Japanese electronic manufacturers have been promising this development for some years. They forecast that by 1998 the liquid crystal display units would overtake the cathode ray tube (CRT) used in conventional television receivers. The motive power behind this development is the convergence between television and the computer market. The conventional CRT monitor used by desktop computers is getting too big for the desk. New computer programs, particularly Microsoft's Windows 95, cram lots of graphical detail on to the screen; already 17-inch computer monitors have replaced the old 14-inch version as standard. An increasing number of users are buying 21-inch models which cost more than $900, are the size of a small packing crate and weigh a ton. At these dimensions and prices space-saving flat-screen alternatives begin to look highly attractive.

Given that worldwide 70 million desktop computers are now sold every year this looks like a promising development, particularly in the light of the long-awaited convergence of television and the personal computers. The chief problem with PC monitors as TV sets is that they are too small for the picture to be seen from across the room. If only the CRT receiver could be replaced by a flat panel display, the problem of size would be resolved. So that is why the Japanese electronic industry is putting its efforts behind a product which will achieve this. But here again we come up against consumer conservatism and the reluctance to change capital equipment until it is thoroughly worn out. It seems therefore that liquid crystal display units will for some years yet lag behind the sale of CRTs.[12]

The electronic programme guide (EPG)

The inability of viewers to use the *embarras de richesse* of 200 or more channels has so far rendered the multichannel universe largely nugatory. Nobody can remember more than a few channel numbers. It is, moreover, impossible to find out what the many channels available offer in the way of programmes. Hence the urgent need for a new piece of software which will enable viewers to make a choice, and return to the programme providers the revenue which they seek. Hence BSkyB, for one, has spent around £10 million since 1995 in order to develop an electronic version of the traditional programme journals.

These electronic programme guides will, according to Nick James, BSkyB's EPG manager, 'allow people to make better choices over what they really want to watch. . . . People are baffled by 200 channels and this guide helps them to put them into some kind of order.'[13] The EPG's functions include a 'personal planner' which

> allows users to organise their viewing via a log of their favourite shows, plus a 'search and scan' feature that gives viewers access to listings information on programmes on all channels while watching the show. The EPG's core functions . . . are accessed via on-screen icons that identify four key features: *TVGuide* channel offers listings and other programme information; *Box Office* which offers access to pay-per-view programming; *Services* with options including electronic Sky Mail and parental control; and *Interactive*, the gateway to British Interactive Broadcasting's information and transactional services.[14]

BSkyB claim that their consumer testing showed that viewers were able to learn 70 per cent of the skills needed to use the EPG in 15 minutes. Since the viability of the whole system depends on the accuracy of this result, one can only hope that the tests were carefully designed and the results assessed in not too optimistic a fashion. EPG is claimed to become a market leader in terms of sophistication, ahead of the systems that have emerged in the United States. The available evidence there is that most viewers rely on the sketchy programme guides that are published in the daily pages, and that the use of electronic guidance is confined to the minority of viewers who are skilled in the use of computerised information systems.

The Independent Television Commission (ITC) has stipulated that all broadcasters should be given 'fair, reasonable and non-discriminatory access to an EPG'. BSkyB claim that their system does this at present, and that it will continue to do so. Time will tell. Given the highly competitive situations in which broadcasters will find themselves, it is difficult to be confident that the BSkyB system will not, *in extremis*, find it hard to resist the temptation to give BSkyB programmes more prominence. Nor has the compatibility problem been resolved. It is by no means established that the set-top box of BDB will be compatible with that produced by BSkyB. Since this company ceased to be a shareholder of BDB only in July 1997 the abandonment of a non-competitive approach to EPG is fairly recent. Similarly the adoption of a single programme guide by other transmission systems is by no means settled. So the potential use of these innovations is left in the dark. It is by no means certain, moreover, that it will be the consumers whose interest will be paramount in the event.

Conclusion

The outlook is distinctly uncertain. J Walter Thompson, the advertising agency, has been one of the few organisations which has been willing to put its head above the parapet. The result is shown in Table 2.3 which compares actual figures for 1995 with forecasts for the year 2000.

Table 2.3 essentially reflects the large areas of uncertainty. It breaks down into three groups of technical options. The first consists of the existing analogue terrestrial programmes. They provide universal access; indeed they are the only ones which do so. All other options involve outlays additional to the standard licence fee, even the video recorder which was available to three-quarters of households in 1995 and which is expected to rise to 85 per cent by 2000. The VCR is effectively an additional channel for those households which have no more than the five existing free-to-air channels. Its use seems to be confined largely to the showing of films which are not available, or are available only at inconvenient times, on the terrestrial networks. It is likely that the use of VCRs will decline as and when video-on-demand becomes available. J Walter Thompson estimate that one household in five will have video-on-demand or near demand facilities by the millennium. (The difference between these two devices is that the first responds directly to consumer choice, whereas the second supplies the required film at a predetermined interval.) Once the necessary hardware becomes available, probably mainly in cabled areas, the demand for either of these options might well expand fairly fast. A film at the end

Table 2.3   Take-up of information technology equipment in the UK, 1995 (actual) and 2000 (estimated)[15]

% households with:	1995	2000
Television	99	99
Video cassette recorder (VCR)	78	85
Personal computer (PC)	18	40
PC/modem/online subscribers	2	26
Games/CD-console/PC CD-Rom+	24	40
Digital terrestrial TV (set-top box)	0	19
Any satellite/cable (including set-top box)	22	36
Video-on-demand ADSL telephone link	0	21
Any digital or analogue multimedia	22	40

Source: J Walter Thompson/Graphic News.

of the day is bound to be attractive to the majority of households, particularly if the cost matches the cost of hiring a video cassette. In view of the essentially leisure-oriented demand in the evenings it is likely that the demand for games, etc. is also likely to accelerate. Personal computers, multimedia events, satellite and cable access will also enlarge the freedom of choice of the next generation.

This leaves the third group of options which are more professionally oriented and whose expansion depends on the growing tendency to work at home and whose use may well be intensive, but by a relatively small number of households.

On the general question of expanding the choices becoming available as a result of technological innovation, the growth of demand is less certain. The existing use of terrestrial TV is not necessarily a guide to future levels of demand. It is arguable that information and entertainment fatigue may occur so that the law of diminishing returns may apply.

3
The Accountants Drive out the Guardians

The title of this chapter ascribes more violence to the encounter between the accountants and the guardians than the facts warrant. In practice the accountants walked in, and the guardians conceded defeat before any guns had been fired. Indeed, in the case of the BBC, the accountants were invited in because the guardians thought they could not manage a competitive situation. The climate of the BBC in the Thatcher years matched the defeatist climate of the Chamberlain government in the years before the Second World War. The government's conviction that everyone has his price effectively came to dominate public policy across the board. The motto was privatisation at any price and in any sector.

The gurus of the media sector were advertising and public relations people to a man (no woman comes to mind). No doubt they shared, even if they had not inspired, the then Prime Minister's view of the role of government. But it was not a disadvantage that their general view happened to carry with it clear and specific advantages for the economics of the mass communications sector. For this reason complaints from the advertising industry about the restrictive approach of what was then still the Independent Broadcasting Authority, and suggestions about ways of relaxing the Authority's hold on the control of advertising, on the safeguards for the autonomy of television companies, and in favour of the injection of some cut-throat competition into the broadcasting industry, fell on ready and willing ears.

The early history of broadcasting has been rehearsed in Chapter 1. Underlying these early developments was a social philosophy which was moderately utilitarian, and did not take a particularly 'high' view of human nature. It did not ascribe any particular virtue to the individuals who make up society. But it did at least recognise that there is such a thing as society, for whose collective well-being governments do have some responsibility. And since it is the job of governments to govern, governments cannot escape responsibility for aspects of life where collective activities and institutions impinge on the individual. The public corporations referred to in the first chapter were designed to implement what were seen at the time as public interest objectives, which could best be pursued without (literally) the tangled web of party politics.

Hence, a public interest having been defined and seen not to be susceptible of being met by the normal operation of demand and supply, the case for a public interest organisation was regarded as made. This held good for practical purposes (health, security, defence and financial stability as, for that matter, the pit props for coal mining in wartime).

As Dorothy Emmet taught her undergraduates: 'Reference to wider and vaguer goals like "democratic values" is perhaps better described as the "common good", reserving "public interest" for this more restricted use as a "shut up" word, invoked as a reason for a decision which foreclosed further discussion in that context.'[1] It may well be that Lord Reith would have agreed with Professor Emmet that 'the common good' was a more accurate description of what he wanted the British Broadcasting Corporation to pursue than 'the public interest', tinged as that has come to be, when used by politicians, with a decision by government which would not necessarily survive if exposed to full public scrutiny. After all, the public interest as defined by government was not necessarily what Reithian BBC orthodoxy would claim to be pursuing. From the General Strike in 1926 to the present day, BBC managers, particularly of news and current affairs, have insisted that they are not governmental mouthpieces; rather they give voice to what they consider to be the common good. This independence of governments is what, both at home and in the World Service, has given the BBC the reputation for objectivity. Generally this reputation has been well deserved, even though its exploitation by BBC advertising on the occasion of its seventy-fifth anniversary has been cynical to say the least.

It is in the field of the primacy of the viewer interest in the mass media that a real culture clash between Britain and the USA exists. Britain began with guardians responsible for a medium of education, information and entertainment; the Americans launched an entertainment medium, watched over by accountants and manufacturers. At present, as we have seen, US accountants, aided and abetted by their British counterparts, are intent on realising their established conviction: that what happens in the USA is reproduced in the UK ten or so years later.

Percipient observers of the American scene have, however, noticed an element of reverse influence. Not the media industry which is impervious (as yet) to such influences; but the American consumer of television has begun tentatively to fight back. There are several initiatives which aim to place the intelligent and articulate viewer at the centre of their concerns. Whether that will grow into a significant movement capable of taking on the National Association of Broadcasters and the other industry trade associations remains to be seen.

For the present the media seem to have it largely their own way. Since politicians depend on exposure on television for their election success, the media organisations have disproportionate influence on Capitol Hill. And since accountants have always been the media bosses it is they who exercise the influence. The standardised media exposure in the UK, provided gratis by the broadcasters as part of their public service responsibilities, is, by comparison, a great blessing. It prevents media auctions, it ensures equal (or proportionate) exposure and it prevents political airtime from becoming a function of the length of purse. When Americans marvel at the British system and wonder whether it could be replicated across the Atlantic, the answer is an unequivocal 'yes'. There are technical problems, but these exist to be overcome.

One of the apparently major obstacles is the First Amendment of the American constitution which, as is well known, guarantees freedom of speech. The present system by which ability to pay determines the exposure of politicians on television, is thought to conform more closely to the Amendment than any rationing of airtime by other means. The logic of this escapes the independent observer.

The effective absence of guardians, other than the Federal Communications Commission (FCC) whose brief is largely technical and judicial, has in recent years given rise to citizen and consumer initiatives to introduce value-determined controls on television. These developments will be discussed in Chapter 9.

Returning to Britain, it is the concern for the common good that generations of 'guardians', at the BBC and later at the Independent Television Authority (ITA), have regarded as their proper stance. There was some uncertainty about this in the early days of independent television. Sir Robert Fraser, the first director-general of the ITA, was inclined to take the view that the Authority and its programme contractors should be one large happy family. George Wedell took the view at the time, as secretary of the Authority that, if Parliament had intended that to be the case, it would have written it into the 1954 Television Act. The intention of the legislators, in fact, was quite different: the ITA, as a public guardian of independent television, had a distinctive role to secure the public good by employing commercial television contractors to provide high-quality and diverse television programmes. The contractors would make such profits as they could from the sale of advertising between these programmes and in 'natural breaks' within the programmes.

It is this role of the public 'guardians' that is now in danger of final demise as a result of both technological innovation and political Laodiceanism.[2] It has been the theme of recent broadcasting legislation that neither governments, nor their agencies, should be too hard on television entrepreneurs. The government appointees to the ITA, and to a lesser extent the BBC, progressively shifted from the 'guardian' profile to the 'accountant' profile. The apex of 'guardian' influence in the ITA could be said to have been reached under the chairmanship of Lady Plowden and when Sir Brian Young was director-general, between 1975 and 1980. (They were jointly dubbed 'the schoolteachers', since they were both professionally concerned with education.) But then schoolteachers are 'guardians' of a kind. So they were by no means miscast. They recognised that the Authority's chief concern must be with the quality of the output, i.e. the programmes which ITV was able to provide for the ordinary viewer. Their successors, Lord Thomson of Monifieth and John Whitney, had a similar view of the role of the Authority, and fought hard to maintain it during the Thatcher years.

Now, as Ray Fitzwalter, formerly of Granada and now a successful independent producer, has pointed out, what has been renamed the Independent Television Commission 'is dominated by just two men, and two money-men at that. The chairman, Sir Robin Biggam, and the chief executive, Peter Rogers (who was promoted from his post of finance director) are neither of them famous for focusing on how the best programmes get on the screen.'[3] As evidence, Fitzwalter cites two ITC decisions:

> The writing was on the wall when last year the remaining digital licences were on offer. The ITC chose to give them to ITV companies that already had assured places and that promised to deliver only more of the same. They declined a vigorous consortium that offered much that was new. . . . The same hands can be detected in the almost surreptitious relaxation of Channel 5's licence commitments . . . in which original programming is cut and repeats (are) increased.[4]

The nature of this fundamental change has not spared the BBC, even though the licence fee continues to provide it with a secure income. During the Thatcher years the BBC governors came to feel less secure about the future of the licence fee and tried to pre-empt any government criticism by making the Corporation more efficient. That, of course, is an obligation on all those in charge of activities funded by the taxpayer. So there was an element of premature deathbed repentance in the BBC's conversion to the advice of Messrs Arthur Anderson and other management consultants. These, at great expense, gave the sort of advice that they know how to give to commercial enterprises of all kinds. The organisational changes, such as producer choice, they have proposed, and which have largely been implemented by the Corporation, seem to have been largely irrelevant to the role of a major creative organisation in the nation's cultural life.

The BBC unions – pre-eminent among them BECTU – have a vested interest in maintaining the maximum number of jobs for their members. Nonetheless, their recent attack on the proposed privatisation of the BBC's Resources Directorate also addresses wider issues. They argue that 'if the Resources Directorate (of the BBC) becomes a wholly-owned subsidiary of the Corporation, it spells the break-up of the BBC and the beginning of the end of public service broadcasting in this country'.[5] It is one of the ironies of history that the BBC has, over the years, been resolutely opposed to all proposals for giving autonomy to any of its diverse activities. For example, proposals to give independence to radio services, to hive off local radio, or to make BBC2 an autonomous unit, have been stoutly resisted on a variety of grounds. The doctrine of a 'seamless robe' was taken up by Charles Curran, a former director-general, in a book of that title.[6] The underlying argument has been that the BBC could not yield up its role as 'the main instrument of broadcasting in the United Kingdom' without losing its entitlement to the whole of the licence fee.

A similar argument has been deployed over the years in support of the BBC's claim to omnicompetence in broadcasting. The Corporation has maintained that 'anything any other broadcasters can do, we can do better'. In consequence ventures by independent television into regional broadcasting in the 1950s and 1960s were strenuously, though only in part successfully, duplicated by the BBC. The advent of local radio stations under the auspices of the Independent Broadcasting Authority saw the creation by the BBC of local radio stations. These have done well even though they have been woefully underfunded.

Now, at the behest of the accountants, the BBC, having in the past invested in real estate, has found itself vastly oversupplied with production resources, many of which are underused if not wholly redundant. Hence the idea of giving producers a budget and encouraging them to go into the market place for the most economically priced production resources. This in turn required an entirely new (in itself justified) accounting system. Money that might possibly be saved by hiring outside plant, equipment and human resources has, as likely as not, been spent on the new array of accountants and managers needed to calculate whether it would in fact be cheaper to go outside than to use existing resources. Hence 'John Birt's producer choice internal market' is, in the view of the unions, 'entirely to blame for the situation in which the Resources Directorate finds itself'. Under the internal market every department must break even or make a profit. But huge Corporation overheads have been piled on, while at the same time production departments have been allowed to make financial service agreements with individual parts of the Resources Directorate, and to hire crews from outside, a state of affairs which no commercial organisation would ever countenance.[7] Thus the unions are convinced that the long-term aims of the Corporation's management is to privatise its Resources Directorate. Having gone so far along the road of tearing up 'the seamless robe' it may well be that privatisation is the logical consequence in accounting terms.

At this point BECTU sees another potential danger: discrimination in resource allocation between different types of programme. 'The proposals underline John Birt's continuing obsession with news at the expense of the rest of television.'[8] Having ten years ago argued that there was no place (on the BBC staff) for caterers, cleaners and security guards, now camera persons, sound recordists, engineers and others who help to make television programmes, may well be declared peripheral to the BBC's requirements unless they are concerned with making news programmes. It has to be remembered, of course, that most writers, actors, musicians and other creative workers, have customarily been freelance contributors.

These concerns of the unions illustrate fears that occur also in other sectors of industry. They derive from the proper concern of accountants with resource utilisation. Does the BBC – does any other production organisation – have a large proportion of specialists spending idle time waiting for their skills to be called upon? And, if it does, can it get better value for the money spent on those specialists by sacking permanent staff and hiring temporary or contract staff to take their places? The answer to this crucial question depends on wage rates, the overheads attributed to the staff concerned by their employers (if any), non-cash considerations such as waiting time, travel time and the management costs incurred in finding temporary and contract specialists when they are needed. The assumption of large organisations tends to be that the answer is favourable to such proceedings in all (or even the majority of) cases. Only rarely are the actual and complete accounting results available.

The hubristic but nonetheless significant argument addressed by the unions concerns the quality of the work done by BBC staff. 'If the BBC loses control of the quality of programme production the ripples will spread throughout British broadcasting.'[9] The high quality of BBC programmes has, traditionally, been a challenge to the BBC's competitors. Falling ratings on ITV and the persistently poor take-up of satellite and cable television are thought to be the direct result of failure to maintain comparable standards. Poorer quality of BBC programmes will lower the traditional benchmark, and could well lead to a closing of the gap between BBC audiences and the rest.

Other variables, of course, come into play, such as standards of direction, the allocation of production credits and the professional commitment of the production staff themselves. There are plenty of examples of high-quality programmes being made by less well-cushioned staff than those at the BBC. But the argument about standard-setting should not be entirely discounted for that reason. What is evident to all but the least sophisticated observer is that the BBC Board of Management, few of whom had much experience of cost accounting, allowed themselves to be over-impressed by their hired management consultants when the cost-cutting exercise began in the 1980s. They, the board, and indeed the governors, failed to take into account two factors:

(a) the categorical distinction between a public service broadcasting organisation and a private sector enterprise providing more easily defined goods or services; and
(b) the cumulative and long-term effects of adapting a neo-classical economic model to the operations of the BBC.

As Richard Collins has pointed out, 'Broadcasting doesn't fit the standard paradigms of neo-classical economics – it's a failed market.'[10] And he goes on to argue that 'market failure in broadcasting has positive social consequences and making broadcasting fit the Procrustean bed of the neo-classical paradigm . . . causes social loss'.[11] This well-meaning attempt to excuse the particular character of free-to-air broadcasting is doomed to failure since it predicates that a neo-classical market requires a socio-economic model appropriate to an analysis of broadcasting.

As we saw earlier in this chapter, we are dealing, in the case of public service broadcasting (in which it is still the practice to include the British model of independent television) with a corporation operating in the public interest (as, *pace* Dorothy Emmet, operating for the common good). Never having been designed to operate in the market sector of the economy, public broadcasting is not properly described as a market failure. And it is, of course, not alone in the category of non-market enterprises operating for the common good. Other cultural activities, such as large parts of the theatre, opera and musical enterprises, as well as the public health, education and welfare systems (not to mention the legendary pit props) have not, traditionally, been market operations. It is, alas, indicative of the continuing and nefarious legacy of the Thatcher years that issues of broadcasting tend to be described in monetary terms by reference to a market in which traditionally they have had no part. We return below to the attempts of Thatcherite economists to use the market analogy as normative. At this point we content ourselves with a categorical rejection of this way of describing the structure of broadcasting as the only legitimate one.

This position, of course, in no way absolves the non-market sector from the careful, responsible and accountable use of resources. The fact that such use has not always been evident in enterprises existing for the common good in no way invalidates the validity of operating the non-market sector. All taxpayers contribute to the cost of the sectors, and in many cases the absence of hypothecation increases the difficulty of insisting on public accountability. In the case of broadcasting in the UK that has not been the case, since the licence fees received by the BBC are clearly identifiable as money paid for the right to receive broadcast programmes, both in sound and vision, even though there may no longer be a specific allocation for sound radio. In the case of ITV the indirect character of the link between advertising revenue and the provision of programmes reduces the element of accountability. But it exists nonetheless. One of the main economic arguments for the development of pay television or, *a fortiori*, pay-per-view television is that it strengthens the direct nexus between the broadcasters and their 'customers'.

The intellectual and political failure of the BBC to resist the Thatcherite attempts to typecast the Corporation into a market-dominated cost–benefit analysis is at the origin of its present malaise. Having once conceded the application to its operations of simplistic neo-classical economics, the BBC is now, ten years later, caught up in the spider's web of management consultants' arguments. It may well find it difficult to disentangle itself from the seemingly logical sequence of cause and effect. One can but hope that the difficulty will not cause a terminal defeat of the guardians by the accountants. The most serious obstacle to the survival of the guardians is that they appear to have lost confidence in the legitimacy of their guardianship. To our knowledge no governor of the BBC has ever resigned on a matter of principle.

The descent of the public debate about values into relativism has deprived the guardians of their independent foothold. They have largely resigned themselves to shrugging their shoulders about the values of the civilisation which they are appointed to reflect, of which we are all members, and from which we all benefit. The concept of the common good referred to by Dorothy Emmet was taken up by the late Cardinal Basil Hume in a speech in Oregon, USA. Referring to the values which, in his view, should inform those responsible for the media, he claimed they tended to hold a neutral 'no value' position. The attempt to hold such a position ignored that

> there is a common good of society, a set of conditions which pro-motes the well-being, and thus the moral good, of each citizen. There are fundamental moral values on which all societies depend, such as respect for truth, for justice, the need for compassion, for care of the environment, and above all respect for the sacredness of human life.[12]

We deal in Chapter 10 with the views of the late Sir Karl Popper from a humanist rather than a Christian position on the role of the guardians of a civilised society in regard to broadcasting. It is evident that we are dealing here with a concern which is shared by people of widely divergent philosophical and religious views. The question we have to ask ourselves is: why, given such a high degree of convergence among civilised people about the values which should inform our broadcasting services, do these values in many instances not prevail?

The Royal Television Society's (RTS) answer, used in advertising its 1997 convention *Beyond 2000: Out of Control?* was that the new controllers of broadcasting were those 'with the prime positions in the global market place, Michael Eisner, Bill Gates, Rupert Murdoch'.[13] No longer was control vested in those who used to be responsible for broadcasting in the UK: the BBC governors, the members of the ITC and the government department responsible for broadcasting. Significantly, control in the past was attributed by the RTS to bodies two of which are no longer responsible: the ITC and the Department for Culture, Media and Sport. And the new controllers are all American: Mr Eisner of Disney, Mr Gates of Microsoft and Mr Murdoch of the News Corporation (admittedly an American citizen of recent naturalisation). According to the RTS we now have controllers who are certainly accountants. In addition they are interested in British broadcasting only as a segment of the global media market, and in their business as part of the American mass media sector. Is this an inevitable development? Most people seem to think so. Even British media entrepreneurs, even the managers, try to convince politicians that broadcasters in this country have to go global or perish. This is demonstrable nonsense. There is a viewership of nearly 60 million: more than adequate to sustain a healthy television industry. British broadcasting has a not undistinguished history. The broadcasters claim that it is the best in the world. There is no need to be as chauvinistic as that in order for the broadcasters to hold their heads high. Essentially the unique achievements of British broadcasting have been:

(a)   the concept of public service broadcasting, independent of government but at the service of the whole community (the BBC);
(b)   the concept of broadcasting paid for by advertising under the control of a public authority accountable to the citizens (independent television);
(c)   the concept of a minority interest channel financed from advertising revenue (Channel 4);
(d)   the concept of the broadcaster as a professional with a recognised commitment to agreed standards;
(e)   the concept of a devolved broadcasting system providing 15 different communities up and down the land with television services under local control and responsive to local needs and interests.[14]

The last-mentioned of these achievements was particularly significant, given the centripetal pressures applied to the cultural life of the country and the metropolitan emphasis of the BBC. The strong regional emphasis in the policy of independent television had caused the building up of centres of local creative endeavour in 11 provincial cities and towns where ITV regional companies were based: Aberdeen, Belfast, Bristol, Cardiff, Carlisle, Dover, Glasgow, Newcastle, Norwich, Plymouth and Southampton.[15] These centres were in addition to those substantial production centres in Manchester, Birmingham and Leeds established by Granada and ABC, Associated Television and ABC (later to be reorganised as Central Television in Birmingham, and Yorkshire Television in Leeds).

The decision of the ITA to create a network with strong local roots, providing employment opportunities for broadcasters in their cities, has constituted a significant contribution to economic development. As the Authority explained to the Pilkington Committee in 1961,

> in 1954–55 (i.e. eight years after the post-war resumption of the BBC television service) the Corporation had produced 254 hours of television in all its regions. In 1960 the five-year old Independent Television was already producing at the rate of 3750 hours a year outside London, and the BBC in that year – whether or not under the stimulus of competition – some 1220. It pointed out that every programme company was contractually bound to produce a prescribed number of hours in its own studios.[16]

Even this substantial expansion in the regions did not satisfy all those giving evidence to the Pilkington Committee. The Welsh and Scottish Nationalists pressed for more, 'in Wales a separate Welsh language television service', and in Scotland the Scottish National Party asked for 'a full-blown Scottish Broadcasting Corporation'.[17] It is noteworthy from the perspective of 1999, that the structure adopted by the ITA was well ahead of its time in recognising the growing concern in Scotland and Wales for a means of expressing the cultural autonomy of these national regions.

But the concern for regional devolution in England was manifested also in the evidence given to the Pilkington Committee in other ways. The Radio and Television Safeguards Committee of the trade unions concerned with broadcasting recommended a strengthening of the representative character of the regional councils and committees of the broadcasting organisations, without any specific reference to ITV. The Liberal Party Broadcasting Committee demanded substantially more regional output. And the Parliamentary Committee of the Cooperative Union recommended that ITV programme contracts should be awarded to popular and democratic organisations with strong roots in local life.[18]

The Cooperative Party had supported an unsuccessful application for the East of England contract. The ITA did not know what to do with applications from local community groups. They were willing to credit businessmen with the ability to hire broadcasters as necessary; they were less willing to credit local interest groups with similar competence. In this way Palatine Television, a competitor to Granada which 'based its appeal mainly on its almost exclusive regional origins and character', did not succeed in convincing the ITA. Palatine Television argued that Granada 'projected no more than an outdated folk image

of the County Palatine [of Lancashire]. They, by virtue of their membership and associations, could do fuller justice to the rich and varied
industrial, agricultural and cultural life of the area.'[19] Moreover
Palatine Television, whose chairman was Mr Charles Carter, Vice
Chancellor of Lancaster University, and whose directors included
George Wedell, former secretary of the Authority and by then Professor
of Adult Education in the University of Manchester, intended to vest
the financial operations of the company in a non-profit-distributing
foundation. This would have secured substantial financial benefits for
the region. But the ITA felt 'it would be taking too great a gamble in
preferring them to the proven all-round competence of Granada'.[20]

It is understandable, but unfortunate, that those responsible for the
development of independent television did not take the time and
trouble to explore the options arising from the monopoly franchises
which they had in their gift. In much the same way as the creation of
the national lottery 30 years later created resources for social and cultural infrastructure in regions largely starved of them for many years,
the independent television franchises could have been used, under
carefully controlled conditions, to reinforce the sociocultural capital
of the regions of the UK.

It is therefore the more regrettable that the autonomies of the
regional independent television companies are, in the latter half of the
1990s, being destroyed at the behest of the major ITV contractors.
There is no doubt that the decision to devolve the organisation of
independent television of 15 regional companies was not the most economic way of structuring independent television. It would have been
much cheaper to run ITV from London as a single channel. But that
would have wasted the unique opportunity to encourage sociocultural
growth at the regional and local levels. A full analysis of the benefit
derived from the devolution of the system remains to be undertaken.

In the meantime governments have yielded to the pressure of the
major ITV contractors to allow them to maximise their already considerable profits regardless of the damage done to the communities in
which they operate. At the end of 1999 the number of ITV contracts
has effectively shrunk to three. At the time of writing two of the three,
'Carlton Communications and United News and Media are expected to
announce a £7 billion merger, creating the UK's largest media empire
ranging from national newspapers and television to the Internet.'[21]

The two companies already own Carlton Television in London,
Central Television in the Midlands, West Country Television in Devon
and Cornwall, Meridian in the south of England, Anglia in East Anglia

and Harlech Television in Wales and the west of England. These six would account for 33 per cent of ITV advertising revenue, whereas the legal limit of the proportion which can be owned by any one company is 25 per cent. In addition Carlton owns 50 per cent of ONdigital and Lord Hollick the *Daily Express* Group of Newspapers. Both Hollick and Green are examples of the accountants who have taken over the ITV franchises. Their interests are, as are those of Granada's Mr Gerry Robinson, in the consolidation of ITV into a single contract. As Mr Robinson explained to the Press, 'There are a large number of regulatory issues to be addressed. But if the rules were to be redrawn so that consolidation were possible, we would obviously want to be at the forefront.'[22]

There are evident conflicts here with the rules laid down by the Office of Fair Trading. The tactics of the media accountants are to argue the need to achieve economies of scale, particularly in relation to the United States. The interests of viewers living in the coverage areas of the contracts are considered little, if at all. As described in Chapter 2, technological developments, many of which are yet to be realised, are causing governments to abandon the vision with which their broadcasting systems were launched. The tendency is to abandon ship well before, if ever, the torpedo might strike.

The mistakes of Conservative administrations appear to be being adopted by 'New' Labour. They in turn are yielding to media moguls, advertising agents and Friedmanite economists. As a result it is not only the family silver that is being sold, but also the crown jewels represented by the British genius for sustaining our cultural heritage. There is no doubt that media policy will change, in response to the new technology and to changing sociocultural conditions. But there was and continues to be a need to identify what we want our basic television services to be, and to create the conditions for them to fulfil our objectives. Other services will exist, originating within the UK and outside. Those making a living from this sector can confidently expect a more than adequate return to sustain the sector; those financed from the licence fee should have no problem as long as their expectations are reasonable. Those for whom the returns are not sufficient should apply their investment to a different sector. It is, after all, the viewers whose interests matter. If control of television could be returned to the guardians who have the interests of viewers at heart, there would be hope for our heritage. But that requires of the government a cool head and a steady nerve. Even then the sheer multiplicity of outlets may render such a recovery unlikely.

Part II
The Content

4
That's All We Have Time for: News and Current Affairs

An important place in the schedules

News, and to a lesser extent current affairs, has traditionally held a place of high esteem in the hierarchy of programme genres of broadcasting. And the television news inherited the reputation of the radio news made during the Second World War, when the nation gathered round their radio receivers for the 9 p.m. news every evening. It has ever since been assumed that, whatever else viewers are prepared to give up, they will want a regular news service. This news service must be serious, it must be well researched, it must be reliable, and it must arrange its items in order of importance in order to guide the viewer in the assessment of the day's events. That is why, when the BBC monopoly was broken and independent television was established in the middle 1950s, there was doubt about providing any news at all on the commercial channel. There was a serious view, as Sir David Nicholas recalled in 1995, 'that it should carry no news at all and that, if it did, it should be provided by the BBC'.[1] The ITA insisted however on the creation of a news service, but stipulated that it should be separate from the programme contractors. So the contractors were legally committed to take the news services provided by ITN, a separate organisation. In order to ensure that ITN was adequately funded all the programme contractors were contractually committed to contribute.

The political impartiality of news services has always been one of the articles of faith of British broadcasting, even if governments in office have from time to time found it difficult to credit such impartiality. Because the news service has to assert its independence, and because much of it is provided by correspondents who are young and liable to be critical of the established order, governments have tended to conduct an armed truce with the broadcasters, which has occasionally flared up into an open warfare. But governments are in a relatively weak position. They need a reliable news service to provide evidence of their activities. They cannot very well require the subservience of the news services to their political purposes. Nor can they expect the news services to be uniformly supportive of their actions. In the event ITN created a new phenomenon in British journalism: the journalist-presenter, later to be called a newscaster. ITN developed a new way of doing things, the definitive news picture would be there, controversial issues would be tackled head-on and in a balanced way, and would be explained to the viewer in a form that they could easily understand.

The longer a government is in power, the less it is likely to feel fairly treated by the broadcasters. When Mr Rupert Murdoch started to establish himself in broadcasting in the UK in the mid-1980s, he knew very well that the then Prime Minister, Mrs Thatcher, was disenchanted with both the BBC and ITN and felt that they did not give her administration the credit it deserved. Hence he proposed to Mrs Thatcher in the first instance the establishment by BSkyB of a 24-hour news channel, which would, so he claimed, give a fairer and more sympathetic account of the management of the country's affairs by the Conservative administration. Such a news service was of course, a loss leader. Mr Murdoch knew very well that 'opinion is cheap but facts are expensive'. But, providing as it did, a point of entry into British broadcasting for the News Corporation, he thought it cheap at the price.

Sky News is merely the first of several round-the-clock news services which now offer their versions of the day's events to television viewers both in this country and abroad. The multiplication of these services has created a whole new area of study and comparison between the different broadcasters. Since, dating from the war years, the BBC occupied the prime position at 9 p.m., ITN established itself in 1955 with a rival bulletin for its main evening audience at 10 p.m. At the time of writing the independent television contractors have been allowed to move this bulletin to 6.30 p.m. on the grounds that they need a clear two hours after the ending of the family viewing period[2] at 9 p.m. for the main evening film. Politicians in particular do not like the shifting of the main ITN bulletin because they believe that this will rob them of peak-hour exposure. The drop in viewing figures of the ITN 11 p.m. bulletin suggests that they are quite right. It is likely that the present arrangement is not the last we shall hear of the ITV news coverage.

A useful bulletin is also put out by Channel 4 at 7 p.m. This bulletin has three-quarters of an hour to do its job. Therefore they can afford to be more discursive than either BBC1 or ITV whose allocation is limited to the inside of a half-hour. Until the move of ITN news to 11 p.m. the last television bulletin of the day was *Newsnight* on BBC2 at 10.30 p.m. This late placing has the advantage of being able to report votes in the House of Commons which tend to take place at 10 p.m., it also has the customary advantages of a last speaker in a debate in that it is able to inject into its bulletin the last word both as regards the importance of stories and as regards the outcome. Also, having 45 minutes at its disposal it can afford to take a slightly softer news story and explore it at length.

The dispersion of the audience

This relatively neat and complementary pattern of television news bulletins over the four terrestrial channels is currently under challenge from a range of additional information sources that are opening up on cable, on satellite and as a result of the terrestrial digital developments. It is, moreover, challenged by the growth of 24-hour news services. Sky News already provides a news bulletin every hour on the hour together with background material on the half-hour. The high cost of hard news has recently led the News Corporation to reduce the length of the hourly bulletin to a quarter-hour, after which some cheaper sports news is inserted until the half-hour. The tendency to develop thematic channels has been taken up by the BBC for its own 24-hour news service which is provided on a digital channel. Since these news services round the clock have a great deal of space to fill they have a tendency to subdivide their news services so as to differentiate between national news and world news as well as business news, news from the world of the arts, and sport, etc.

The devotion to news has, however, been undergoing a massive change in the last ten years. Television news is no longer the focal point of the day's or the evening's broadcasting. There has been a vast expansion of news bulletins. There are news channels on all platforms, news is available on the Internet, and the provision of news every hour on the hour has become a staple of terrestrial services. As a result news slots are no longer impregnable, and audiences are no longer rock solid.

In 1987 ITN's early bulletin was watched by an average of 8.9 million viewers. By 1997 this figure had slumped to 4.7 million. Over the same period audiences for BBC's 6 p.m. news slid from 7.0 million to 6.4 million; for the 9 p.m. news from 7.5 million to 5.6 million; and ITN from 7.5 million to 6.0 million. Only *Channel 4 News* held its audience of 700 000. *Newsnight* on BBC2 fell from 1.3 million to 1.1 million viewers.[3] The situation has not improved since then.

How did this decline in terrestrial audiences come about? Tony Hall, the former BBC News chief executive, confirms the hypercompetition to which we have referred. The news supply increased eightfold between 1986 when there was an average of 30 hours of news material on television, and 1997 when a total of 243 hours a week was available in multichannel homes. In addition the Internet offers an alternative to the mainstream broadcasts. Desktop services are set to multiply and both the BBC and ITN have invested heavily in their news websites.

This scale of competition creates a self-defeating vicious circle: because there is more and more on offer, none of the options can attract audiences large enough to justify substantial investment in news services. News therefore becomes dependent 'event' television, a programme which, according to Emily Bell of the *Observer* will cause the audience to break their viewing habits for an evening, hang up their remote controls and all migrate to the same place at the same time. Tiffany's untimely departure from *Eastenders* was one such event for the BBC1. *Who wants to be a millionaire?* is genuinely successful Event Television in that, at the coffee machine the morning after, it is a hub of general conversation. . . .[4]

The bias against understanding[5]

All these developments combine to attack traditional news values. They tend to turn the serious treatment of news into something that has come to be called 'infotainment'. Here the boundary between fact and fiction becomes blurred. The definition of what is news and what is gossip is often unclear. The emphasis is increasingly on the retention of the audience rather than on the effort to help the audience to understand what is going on in the world. When the standards of professional journalism are weakened the objectives of the news services are affected.

This was recognised already in the 1970s by John Birt and Peter Jay, both at that time working for London Weekend Television, who claimed to be developing production techniques for dealing with complicated issues.

> The journalistic tool almost always chosen for dealing with issues, especially abstract issues, was the studio discussion . . . these discussions are generally set up to examine disagreements rather than areas of agreement, and they place an unnaturally high premium on the resourcefulness under pressure of the participants. . . . But even when that small proportion of issue journalism, which does not rely solely on studio discussion is successful, it faces a further obstacle. It runs the risk of being boring![6]

The Birt–Jay analysis attracted attention not because it was original, but because it drew attention to the need for more thorough identification of issues to be explained by broadcast news because these news services have to assist the understanding of the viewers, who are the actors in the modern decision-making process. In the event the resources, both of time and personnel, needed to carry out this 'mission to explain' were shown to be incompatible with the 'breathlessness' of television news. Progressively the time needed to achieve this mission ceased to be available. So the Birt–Jay mission failed except in regard to the ITN News on Channel 4. It is, nonetheless, worth recalling that attempt, almost 30 years ago, to establish a baseline of agreement about the ways in which news broadcasts should be conducted.

The point of news reporting

There are two objectives to news services. The first is to provide news of general interest to the audience as a whole. It is assumed that the average viewer is interested to see and hear what is going on in Northern Ireland or what petrol prices will be tomorrow. In the event the experience of broadcasters is that people are interested mainly in what affects their lives directly: petrol prices do that; Northern Ireland does not. That is why, in the battle for audiences, consumer news has come to replace less personal information, whether at the national or international level.

According to Tony Hall already referred to as the former head of the BBC's News and Current Affairs (NCA), his output in the near future needs to develop in three areas: news gathering and analysis (its core preoccupation); continuous TV news; and interactive and online services, which will become possible with the digitisation of the news process. The problem with this type of scenario is that it covers the means but not the end. All that can be said about the oversupply of 'news' is that it needs news junkies to make use of it. No one asks whether it is the role of the BBC to indulge news junkies. The obsession with the omnicompetence of BBC news and current affairs leads Tony Hall to assert '. . . we need the licence fee and we need it for many, many years to come . . .'.[7] He does not explain why this is so.

This self-defining tendency has been an occupational hazard of broadcasters since the beginning. In the course of working to produce good programmes broadcasters begin to think that what they are doing is the only thing worth doing. In a time when populism is promoted not only by the broadcasters but by the politicians, it is incumbent on the former not to fall for their own half-truths. If broadcasters are going to complain about the rise of demagogues, commercial persuaders, ratings merchants, etc., they must at least make an effort themselves to keep a sense of proportion. The importance of maintaining this sense of proportion has been borne in on a growing number of broadcasters. John Humphrys, one of the presenters of Radio 4's *Today* programme, in a recent book defends, among others, his colleague Kate Adie who was criticised for being too cold and clinical in her reporting of the Dunblane massacre. '. . . She did a reporter's job . . . we didn't need to be told what those poor people were feeling. We could work it out for ourselves.'[8] From a similar perspective of a war reporter with 30 years' experience Martin Bell writes:

> . . . Our way of reporting the wars has changed fundamentally. . . . When I started out as a war reporter in the mid-sixties I worked in accordance with a long and honourable BBC tradition of distance and detachment. I thought of it then as necessary objectivity . . . I am no longer sure about the notion of objectivity which seems to me now to be something of an illusion. . . . In place of the dispassionate practices of the past I now believe in what I call the journalism of attachment. By this I mean a journalism that cares as well as knows . . . that will not stand neutrally between good and evil, right and wrong, the victim and the oppressor . . . we exercise a certain influence, and we have to know that. . . .[9]

Another veteran foreign correspondent, Michael Nicholson of ITN, recently attacked the decision 'to kill off *News at Ten* and replace it with news bulletins that are full of showbiz packaging, gizmos and things. . . . They didn't do it for reasons of quality, but simply because they wanted to attract more viewers in that time slot – which they have not done.'[10]

These examples converge in that they affirm the need for the reporter to feel the emotions experienced by the ordinary citizen in order to do his or her job effectively. Yet, to feel the same emotions as the rest of humanity does not necessarily mean expressing them. Different circumstances require different responses.

Constraints of space and time

By the same token different stories require different treatment in respect of time, particularly in respect of the time allocated to interviews. There has grown up a tendency similar to the National Health Service, where seven and a half minutes on average is allowed for a consultation with the general practitioner. The average has become the norm, and much money is wasted on interviews which are too short to allow a proper diagnosis followed by an informed prescription of treatment. By analogy an inadequate allocation of time to a news item is worse than omitting the item altogether.

In the broadcast news services the viewers are told 'this is all we have time for', irrespective of the state of a discussion which is cut off by the phrase. Again, it is time- and money-wasting to begin an interview which the interviewer has no intention to bring to an informed conclusion. The production rules imply (a) that the witness interviewed is trained to limit his or her response to a carefully designed and prepared minimal statement; (b) that the subject matter being discussed can be compressed into $2\frac{1}{2}$ minutes; and (c) that the viewers are unwilling to stay with a story any longer. Who knows? And who decides? In a news bulletin one may have ten stories to make up 25 minutes or multiples of $2\frac{1}{2}$ minutes to make up fewer items. It is essential to build sufficient flexibility into the system to achieve optimal comprehension on the part of the audience. It is likely that many of the interviews cut short so as to stay within the time limit do not allow the viewer to apprehend the point of the exercise, and are thus a waste of time and money. 'The mission to explain' of which Mr Birt and Mr Jay were in the early 1980s such ardent promoters, appears in the 1990s to have fallen victim to an untested assumption by the broadcast controllers about the attention span of the audience.

The declining audiences for the news and current affairs programmes have been worrying the broadcasters. The BBC has been doing some work on this and has concluded that there are three key questions for journalists:

(a)   What is significant?
(b)   What do audiences want to know?
(c)   How should we best tell them?[11]

This list is largely useless. Obviously (a) is what news selection is all about. Unless the answer on significance is right more often than not, news ceases to be news. The question about significance is largely unrelated to the question about what the audiences want to know. They may want to know that things are getting better without their having to do anything about it. A windfall from a building society is news worth reading; the bottom falling out of the stock market is also worth knowing about, even though the audience may not want to hear about it! As Tony Hall writes in the same article, 'But more than anything people say "tell us why it matters". Far from wanting a diet of trivia, they want to know about significant events and decisions.'[12]

Current affairs

In the course of an attempt to recast their 'serious' contribution to independent television, Granada in 1998 conducted an inquiry into current affairs programmes in the USA. Their aim was to find out how to reconstruct *World in Action*, the ITV flagship current affairs programme. They proceeded from the assumption that 'young viewers, in particular, regard current affairs programmes as solemn and boring. But we will change that perception. For as long as our journalism is solid, we can be as cheeky and entertaining as we like.'[13] Granada concluded: 'the American approach to current affairs can be adopted here to a great degree. That means that we should focus more on human emotion and drama, develop our story-telling skills, be less sniffy about seeking the journalistic angles on populist stories.'[14] These conclusions reflect the immature chasing after unproven chimeras. They make no attempt to analyse the difference between American and British audiences. Nor do they take into account the distractions inherent in the commercial considerations which dominate American current affairs output. The researchers

> believe that the successor to *World in Action* should nearly always be multi-item, and they list five types of item, which might appear each week. This would allow an average of ten minutes for each:
>
> (a)   an original investigation;
> (b)   the hidden angle on a major running news story;
> (c)   an irreverent approach to a current controversy;
> (d)   a news-related report;
> (e)   a news-related biography or human interest feature.[15]

There is no recognition of the fact that the allocation of time for each category is unlikely to be sufficient to achieve an element of understanding. The whole approach is geared to keep the audience on the edge of their seats, rather than using their brains to understand what may be complex issues. The best objective the researchers can set the producers is to say that each segment should be post-produced 'almost to the standard of commercials'.

The fear that current affairs programmes will go to the wall unless they can attract vast audiences, and that this can be achieved only by treating the material like an advertisement, destroys the traditional relationship of trust between producer and the audience. Instead of accepting the viewer as a fellow human being to whose intelligence and interest it is legitimate to appeal, the producers are advised to treat the audience, at this moment as at other times, as fickle customers who have to be manipulated, presumably against their better judgement, to attend to programme material which they would rather avoid.

The recommendations of the *World in Action* report appear to have been largely accepted by the team responsible for the planning of *World in Action*'s successor, *Tonight*, which was launched on 8 April 1999. In effect *Tonight* has taken over the format of CBS's *60 Minutes* in the hope that this will enable it to survive in what is seen as 'the last chance saloon for primetime current affairs on ITV'.[16] The ITV network controller of news and current affairs, Steven Anderson, has followed the American pattern. He wants to 'reconnect' viewers with current affairs on a large scale. And he recognises that to do so takes time and consistency. As such he has 26 programmes planned for 1999 and 44 for 2000. That is better than ITV's rival on BBC1, where Alex Salmon, the channel controller, can guarantee no more than a ten-week run to his current affairs producers at any one time.

It remains to be seen whether the American formula will work. It has Trevor McDonald from ITV as presenter: it will have up to five stories in the hour; and investigative journalism will rub shoulders with news-making interviews and items that relate to people's lives.

But for all that, the brief is to provide an audience of 8 million so as to keep current affairs in prime time, regardless of the content. This amounts to a total reversal of what British television, in the BBC as in the independent sector, has used as its working hypothesis in the past. It destroys whatever relationship of trust and reciprocity has been built up with the viewers over the years. However smart and elegant the result, the exchange has been emptied of the human relationship which lies at the core of communication. As such the exercise becomes valueless, and the production team is bound to ask whether all the blood, sweat and tears are worthwhile if the required audience size does not, by the end of the year 2000, materialise.

The problem of accuracy

News and current affairs had always relied on accuracy to maintain their reputation, that is, until the need to sustain an audience became the key objective. A few years ago the notion of narrative, culled from the definition of literary forms, came into fashion. As part of the effort to make news more acceptable to the viewer on the Clapham omnibus, television directors appear to have discovered around the year 1995 that storytelling is more persuasive than giving the facts. Speaking at the Edinburgh International Television Festival in 1997, Robert Phillis, at that time deputy director-general of the BBC, maintained that 'People want to be caught up in a narrative.'[17] Brenda Maddox, at that time media correspondent of *The Times*, criticised the people who took up Phillis's suggestion. 'Narration in non-fiction programmes takes television producers deep into the moral maze. How tempted are they to bend the truth to fit the story? And how tempted are ordinary mortals to play up for television?' Lady Maddox went overboard in claiming that

> All narrative . . . is a lie. Imposing a beginning, middle and end on the chaos and cruelty of events that have no beginning, middle or end, is always a distortion of reality. . . . Every essay tries to mislead by assembling arguments in such a way as to emphasize one point and obscure others. And news stories are called *stories* for good reason. If they are not made interesting, no one will read or listen.[18]

This could well be, but the role of the reporter is to represent his or her materials in a manner that is as truthful as possible. This is part of the professional skill of the journalist. That is why the consumer, via the editor, pays a professional fee for the journalist's skill and experience. It is one of the problems currently facing news reporting, that the commitment to accuracy falls victim to the wish to tell a good story. If there is no professional restraint the journalist is unable to maintain his standard.

Echoes of a golden age

When George Wedell published his book *Broadcasting and Public Policy* 30 years ago,[19] he was asked to do a television interview with Mr Bernard Braden, a Canadian who at that time was, with his wife Barbara, host to popular chat shows on Associated Television. Mr Braden was at that time persuading a number of people to commit themselves on his show to views about matters in the public domain. He intended to put these tapes away for some years, then to resurrect them, to face the original contributors with their views at the time, and to see what had happened to these views in the intervening years.

The following interview was taped and stored. Before it could be used Bernard Braden died and the second half of the enterprise has never been realised. But it is interesting to compare the doctrines and opinions of 1968 with those of a generation later.

Bernard Braden   Reverting to what you said about the responsibility of the professional broadcaster, it has always seemed to me that, whenever a body is set up to represent the public on a matter such as broadcasting, the one aspect of it they most rarely touch on is show business, on the grounds that it's a mad business anyway, and nobody who's sensible is involved in it. And yet this aspect of it is where the profits come from. Who is to decide what is good for the public? At what point do you say this is detrimental to the public in terms of entertainment? You can make such a judgement in terms of educational broadcasting, you can do it in terms of documentaries and current affairs. But once you get into the field of entertainment, who is to make the decisions there?

Professor Wedell   When you come to judge what happens when a person puts his or her feet up in front of the television for an evening's relaxation, it is a more difficult judgement to make, because the criteria are largely personal. I enjoy situation comedy more than a variety show, where you get one act after another. If I wanted that I would go to a circus. Again, I enjoy satire more than slapstick, but this also is a matter of my own predilection. I would have thought that the best you can hope for when the broadcasters show sixty hours of light entertainment a week is that most of this material will be inoffensive, even though lightweight. Of course, we hope for some geniuses who will make a few brilliant programmes. This is the stuff that show people will actually be remembered for.

Bernard Braden   One of the things that I noticed when I first came to this country roughly twenty years ago and formed a very strong feeling about, which I have not lost, is that much of what I heard on the Third Radio programme, could with a little skill and presentation quite easily have been acceptable on the Home Service (now Radio 4); and much of what I heard on the Home Service could, with a little skill be pop popd into Light programme material.

Professor Wedell   As, indeed, much of it now has been.

Bernard Braden   Yes, but what concerns me here, and I find it specific to this country, is that there seems to be a group of people who, when they have something to say in whatever form, choose to do it on television or radio, maintaining that there is a section of the public who cannot possibly be expected to understand it. They refuse to modify their vocabulary to let ordinary people understand it. I believe that many more people could understand it if a few concessions would be made to plain words and presentation that is clear and concise. Would you think there's anything in this?

Professor Wedell   I think there's an awful lot in this. It's part of the social history and the social tragedy of this country that we have until recently been two nations. This is only now coming to an end. If you were to ask me where was the watershed, I would place it at the 1944 Education Act which introduced secondary education for all. It has taken the best part of a generation for the majority of people to receive a decent education and for their horizons to be opened not only intellectually, but aesthetically in terms of judgement, criticism and this kind of thing. I think we are now moving into the age of what I call the educated society, when we have for the first time throughout the country a population who share a common intellectual and cultural equipment. This means that most people can be talked to more intelligently than most of the show business people allow. I think this is perhaps a criticism of the show biz people who still assumed that ordinary people cannot be talked to intelligently. So it may be a justified criticism of some of the early tycoons of commercial television. They came from the Music Hall tradition, from the show biz end of things, and their criteria in assessing what the public would take were those which went out at the end of the Second World War. There are now a hundred and one situations when broadcasters inadvertently stretch the audience beyond what they think they can take, and find that in the event, they take it extremely well. We noticed this a little while ago when I was involved in adult education programmes. We produced a programme on strategic studies, which I thought important. We spend a lot of money on defending this country. The programme was designed to enable people to judge why this is, what are the alternatives, and whether we need to keep the H bomb. We produced a programme called *Struggle for Peace*. This was put out on a Sunday morning in the adult education ghetto and had audiences of about a hundred thousand if we were lucky. A year later it was transmitted in a current affairs slot on Monday evenings at half past seven to audiences between 1.7 million and 2.5 million, which are quite respectable for that time of the evening. It was exactly the same programme, and it had very good reviews again. Obviously people understood it perfectly well. If it had never gone out at that time, many people would never have had a chance of seeing it. We underestimate our audience all the time.

Bernard Braden   I remember, going back at least ten years, Peter Black[20] publishing something to the effect that if Bronowski[21] were put on at eight-thirty on Sunday night, and the Palladium variety show at eleven-thirty on Thursday night Bronowski might get higher figures than the Palladium.

Professor Wedell   But many commercial broadcasters are thinking of the advertising and don't want to risk a loss. So they're not going to put Bronowski on at eight-thirty on a Sunday night and the Palladium at eleven-thirty on a Thursday night.

Bernard Braden's analysis at the end of the 1960s now seems light years away. We now have two generations of universal secondary education under our belt. The proportion of the age group going on to higher education has grown from $7\frac{1}{2}$ to 30 per cent, a fourfold increase in the last 30 years. And yet, the broadcasters treat the viewers much like their parents, according to a template which was imposed on the broadcasting system when the monopoly was first breached. The means of manipulating them have become more sophisticated and more ruthless; the ends towards which these means are deployed are more populist than ever: 'pile them high and sell them cheap'. Only now there is a deliberate dumbing down. Then the audience's intelligence may have been underestimated; now it has to be brought down to the lowest common multiple of what the advertisers will accept.

News and the parliamentary process

The coverage of Parliament by television news and current affairs should have been much enhanced when Parliament decided to televise parliamentary proceedings in 1989. These proceedings were studied in a report published by the Hansard Society (for parliamentary government) in May 1999.[22] This report was preceded in July 1998 by a Chatham House Briefing Paper on media coverage of Parliament in the UK, France and Germany.[23] The main conclusions of the Hansard Society inquiry were:[24]

(a) Coverage of parliamentary news stories has declined significantly in the ten years since cameras entered the Commons (from an average of 3.4 per cent of news bulletins to under 1 per cent).
(b) Criminals are now given 6 times more airtime in bulletins than Parliament with celebrities being given 11 times more airtime.
(c) Concentration on the sound bites and staged rows of *Question Time* reinforces negative perceptions of politicians, and a misunderstanding of how Parliament works.

(d) TV increasingly treats Parliament as a 'scenic backdrop' for coverage of ministers and shadow ministers, marginalising back-benchers.

(e) Millbank and College Green have become rival forums to the Commons chamber; publicity-seeking MPs see TV interviews as worth more than catching the Speaker's eye.

(f) There is now less parliamentary coverage on terrestrial channels, and fewer people watch parliamentary programmes, than ten years ago.

(g) Broadcasters resent the restrictions on what they can film in the Commons, arguing that TV coverage of other events such as football has changed enormously since 1989, while parliamentary coverage remains dull and overregulated, forcing the output to focus on confrontation.

Having ten years ago been a matter of fierce controversy, the televising of Parliament is now a matter of course, albeit under rules which are widely recognised as out of date and inimical to the participation of ordinary citizens in the democratic process. A decade after its introduction MPs are worried that not enough people are watching the parliamentary channel. Some 71 per cent of 16-year-olds admitted that they 'seldom or never' watch television coverage of Parliament. The broadcasters, for their part, have noticed 'the paltry ratings for parliament and are cutting back coverage'.[25] The fact seems to be that *BBC Parliament*, like *C-Span* in the United States, appeals mainly to a tiny minority of political obsessives. But then the digital channel providing gavel-to-gavel coverage of parliamentary proceedings has limited reach and tiny audiences.

The BBC has, from the beginning in 1927, been bound by its charter to 'broadcast an impartial account day by day, prepared by professional reporters, of the proceedings of Parliament'.[26] In practice it has been left to news editors to determine what should be transmitted on any scale. In 1993 Jack Straw, the Labour MP and at the time of writing Home Secretary, published a report which argued that press coverage of Parliament had been substantially reduced in recent years. Up to about 1988 parliamentary debates had received between 400 and 800 lines of newspaper coverage daily. By 1992 coverage had declined to fewer than 100 lines. In 1991 Simon Jenkins, then editor of *The Times*, decided to end the practice of carrying extracts from speeches. He claimed he could not find anyone, 'apart from Members of Parliament who read the page'.[27]

The reasons for the decline in coverage appear to be twofold. 'Parliamentary broadcasting as presently conceived kills the drama, the chase, the revealing slot that tells the tale. The head and shoulders coverage of parliament may represent a public service of record, but it is no longer an easy fit with the evolving hold of television news and current affairs.'[28] This is the reason that John Snow of Channel 4 gives for the decline. 'Yet if I try to capture (the excitement of the Palace of Westminster) on camera or, worse, try to transmit it, I risk having my present Commons pass removed, being banned from the precincts or, almost literally sent to the Tower.'[29]

Because the television services find it boring to take programmes on the terms laid down by Parliament, governments try to inject an element of drama into their news instead of observing their own rule, that announcements should be made first in the House of Commons. 'For the past decade, under both parties, the government has been getting its act together – bouncing *Today* or the lunchtime news into a pre-emptive release of information MPs once thought (it) was their prerogative to hear first.'[30]

So the decline is caused by the vicious spiral caused by attempts to inject drama into politics, where it only rarely belongs. It was T. E. Utley, the brilliant blind *Spectator* journalist of the 1950s, who postulated that 'politics ought to be dull' because in a well-run country the government would not need to take dramatic action. The progressive failure of newspaper proprietors, radio and television news controllers to live with this truth has destroyed the professional competence of journalists to identify what is news and what is not. This failure of judgement is due as much to the changes in the time allowed for news as to the changes in news values. 'That's all we have time for' has become the dominant consideration in the scheduling of news, and politicians, ex officio, have been affected.

> Although MPs generally made more appearances on television news in 1996 than in 1986 – for example 64 as against 52 on Channel 4 news – the average length of each appearance (or sound bite) was much shorter:

News bulletin	1996	1986
Nine o'clock News (BBC)	13.3 secs	19.5 secs
News at Ten (ITV)	13.1 secs	17.1 secs
Channel 4 News	27.3 secs	58.2 secs[31]

These changes may be small in themselves, but the accumulated evidence suggests that competitive pressures, actual and imagined, militate against the responsibility of broadcasters for open and accountable political reporting.

5
Sport: Does the Tail Wag the Dog?

A remarkable symbiotic relationship has grown up between sport and broadcasting. This has accelerated with the coming of a more competitive market-oriented business for the latter, and the arrival of digital, cable and satellite modes of distribution. In this way more sports programmes can be distributed without reducing the availability of other programme genres.

Sport and money

Given that advertising revenues have become more dominant influences it might be thought that financial and economic considerations would be paramount not only to commercial broadcasters but to the BBC also. Indeed such a powerful symbol did monetary returns become in the 1990s, that it is believable that every choice of programme, timing, duration, etc. must hang on the audience attracted, which will in its turn determine resources allocated, and thus potential earnings from advertising and sales. Each genre was held to make some contribution to the total, however slight or long term.

Broadcasters must therefore be diligent in assessing the benefits of sports coverage, and undoubtedly those from the sports themselves are concerned about what advantage accrues to them. The prevalent obsession with the magic of money is fostered by outside business influences as well as from curiosity among the public at large. Tabloid press coverage, for one, gives considerable prominence to financial transactions between broadcasting and sport, spurred undoubtedly by envy of these newspapers as much as the desire to expose. Industry publications and the broadsheet papers are equally alert to the significance of what by comparison with earlier times, seem to be the astronomical sums which are now exchanged.

Reports of eager competition to obtain broadcast rights, allegations of intrigue and deception between bidders, wild guesses of sums of money which were or could be offered, hints of consequent benefits in earnings for players or shareholders all fan public attention.

Football as the national sport, or at least the favourite of many, is central to the excitement engendered. Certainly sport is a significant component in broadcast television schedules throughout the year, and as one reasonably distinct genre can be identified as composing just over 8 per cent of BBC television output, about 5 per cent of ITV and 10 per cent of Channel 4.[1] These are modest proportions of available airtime and comparable to the distribution of sports pages in the daily press, which interestingly come at the end of the newspapers. So is it the nature, tone and presentation of sports coverage rather than the quantity, which give it importance? If, however, there are sums disproportionate in revenues or expenditure to volume of coverage of sports then there may be a perception of the tail wagging the dog. The National Heritage Select Committee of the House of Commons tried assiduously to obtain financial details of current sports broadcasting. It appeared that £201 million was spent by the four major UK providers, including Sky, in 1994, about 5 per cent of their total revenues, although the pattern for individual channels would have differed.[2] Overall then their expenditure was not wildly at variance with provision. Indeed it looks to have been a profitable enterprise, roughly proportional to their activities overall, and despite their complaints to the Select Committee at how expensive sports coverage had become.

Competition for rights and ratings

It is true that competitive bidding pushed up such costs rather faster than for other genres but they hardly constituted a burden when taken in context. What is not known of course, is how much time, effort and stress were caused for broadcasters as the implications of a market economy for broadcasting became manifest. It was no excuse to say that the product quality was poorer as competition within sports was also enhanced, and more jobs had been created in the television industry with the growth in sports transmissions.

So there appears to have been some exaggeration of a reported crisis for television, particularly when national income was rising. Probably like other entrepreneurs the media moguls can never admit the certainty of success. An element of anxiety adds a frisson to the world of business.

Nevertheless generalisation has its risks too and some lacunae remain in the information picture. Companies are naturally wary of revealing what advertisers actually pay. Informed guesses and indirect calculations may enable some of the financial benefits to be discovered as later pages will show. Yet the complexities of interlocking relationships of pricing, secondary rights, repeats and extracts, and the divergence of published advertising rates from prices paid, make a full picture impossible to portray. How can one value the ambience of publicity, audience enthusiasm and loyalty, which the spotlight of attention casts over the coverage itself, the outcome of matches, the controversy and hype?

Diversity in sport

Sport, although a specific genre, is composed of a large number of different games, with divergent followings, dissimilar settings, timing, durations and history. The unfamiliar rapid and abrupt changes, which have accompanied the market economy of broadcasting, have undoubtedly contributed as much to the present concerns as the central place which sport evidently occupies in the national psyche.

Curiously the broadcast coverage of sport took many years before it gained its present importance. Its trajectory in radio and television has differed, reflecting the technological characteristics of these media. For example, in the first decade of radio in the 1920s coverage comprised about 0.5 per cent of wireless transmission time. It increased very little before the Second World War and until a second national channel became available in 1945, the Light Programme.[3]

Unsurprisingly, football was the major component but circumstances limited the nature of the broadcasts. The restricted spectrum was one constricting factor. Available time slots were carefully rationed but also the cost, equipment bulk and weight and inconvenience of outside broadcasts limited their use.

In effect sports coverage consisted largely of *post hoc* reports, results rather than games in play. The measured reading of football match outcomes on Saturday evenings was a major turning point of the week for many households. Listeners took down the scores to compare with their copies of football pool coupons, posted earlier in the week, by which they made lottery forecasts to win what were then previously unimaginable monetary prizes, despite the enormous odds against predicting a substantial number of correct scores. So, although direct sports coverage was minuscule, there was considerable sociological significance in uniting families around their crystal or valve radios, holding probably a majority of the nation in suspense as correct forecasts might accumulate, but could also enhance geographical knowledge of the location of minor teams scattered over the country, build loyalties to successful league teams, and stimulate followings for skilled players.

Television football by contrast engaged the viewer more in the match itself because of the visual element. Radio commentators for a sports match likely to be covered in the limited number of outside broadcasts certainly could generate tension and excitement in crucial contests. But they could never match the detail contained in graphic portrayal, nor compensate for the moderate sophistication of listeners who, in the early days of broadcasting, might never be able to attend matches of the leading clubs as spectators, because of travel distances and costs.

The small screen certainly brought new vistas. It does not really lend itself to the panorama of war games, hardly even to an entire football pitch, whereas for indoor games it has the advantage, especially snooker which is almost ideally suited with its close-ups. Chess too, despite its slow pace overall, can through large display boards engage many more viewers than participants with the bonus of competitive stimuli and the personal rivalries of chess champions. With multiple mini cameras for each player's hand is it possible that one day even card games could engender the tension and excitement of established competitive sports?

Television greatly enhanced the action movement, and the immediacy of its coverage allowed the excitement in the living room to emulate that of the crowds on the stadium terraces. Audiences for television sports broadcasts were however much smaller than the numbers actually present at games until the late 1950s, when mass set ownership facilitated home viewing. For example in the 1948–49 season 41 million persons attended football league matches, its greatest ever achievement. This was more than a million each Saturday, when television set ownership was but 300 000.[4]

Obviously, given the limited first-hand experience of the visual medium and thus modest expectations, broadcasters were able to meet the basic requirements and interests of the citizens of the time. Thereafter the growth of outside broadcasting in both radio and television enabled greater satisfaction to be given for the exceptional events like the annual football cup final and crucial rankings of the tiered football leagues towards the end of the season. Interestingly, sports coverage of competitive league matches can maintain or even raise viewing figures as uncertainty about top and bottom rankings increases towards the end of the season, whereas audiences are likely to fall towards the end of entertainment series as impact wanes.

Football provides a crucial test of public interest as the sport with the greatest national following and the foremost, apart from athletics, in promoting international competition and standing. But even from the early days, the BBC, as the monopoly provider, faced certain dilemmas. The mass audience gathered to hear the broadcast football results, while enhancing interest in the games, was primarily so that the listeners, and in time viewers, could assess their chances in the football pools. The broadcasters could therefore be argued to be encouraging an unhealthy interest in gambling rather than a wholesome love of exercise in the open air. This was certainly an obnoxious thought to John Reith.

A recurrent issue, both for the future of broadcasting and the study of leisure, was whether sport, and football in particular, were competitors of, or complementary to, broadcasting. In some ways today the question has been outmoded or blurred. With the rise of the transistor radio and digital broadcasting, the audience can listen, or even view alternative matches elsewhere (with hand-held portable receivers), while spectators at sports events or at home can switch between sports and other broadcasts with their 'zapper'. In effect the audience, with the aid of the new technology, is trying to do two things at once.

Broadcasters have for many years now abandoned final responsibility for encouraging balance between uses of time or increasing dependence on particular kinds of activity or inactivity. In the commercial sector their task is to varying degrees to maximise audiences. Provided their costs are covered and profits earned, the resolution of possible conflicts about the use of time and activity is the responsibility of the audience alone, tempered only by the constraints of competition and prevailing notions of value.

Public service providers now seem to make diversity and choice their priorities but with their wider remit must also confront ethical considerations and obligations, if politicians and regulators support them, which takes one back to the central issue of what broadcasting is for. Is it to be normally a carrier of whatever is available or might be desired, devoid of moral consideration, or is there a variety of other duties, for example to stimulate, challenge, lead or warn its consumers rather than merely satisfy only the briefest attention span or punctuate audience passivity with peaks of excitement from competitive sports? Surely power confers some responsibility in every industry whether it be agriculture, manufacture or entertainment.

At different times in historical experience there will be different needs and priorities. For example, in the post-war period there was a universal demand to promote recovery; in a time of stress or disorder comes a requirement to provide soothing balm, or in a time of discovery and instability to inspire. Such phases in society at large also arise within life spheres such as sport, since most people have some interest in a game or exercise, even if only as spectacle. It will be no service to sport if broadcast coverage destroys its essence. But life is about more than sport, even although it may be a career for some or an all-consuming passion for others. Coverage of it will have to take its place as a part of the scheme of things. Equally important, sport is itself not a single activity but an umbrella term for a vast range of activities.

So a partial answer to the problem of positioning in current schedules is that, while football may be dominant in sports coverage, it is only one of about 50 sporting activities receiving some attention at this time in broadcasting. Not all take place outdoors and most are allocated small fragments of time, such as brief reports in an afternoon magazine schedule, but adherents of even the esoteric can be active or influential, or perhaps despite their paucity, important to advertisers because of their potential purchasing power. Some like snooker achieve considerable coverage during selected competitions. With the advent of cable and digital transmissions small audiences can be economic, especially locally or regionally, even to specific districts which was inconceivable in earlier days.

New technology and new sports

Technological change has also facilitated exposure to new and unusual sports. Nurtured by broadcasting, i.e. being seen, or open to sponsorship because with a modest base they are inexpensive to advertisers and benefit more than proportionally from any earnings. They can now reach audiences possibly satiated by existing coverage of major sports. Some more readily succeed than others. Ice-skating or skiing, once the preserve of winter tourists and the affluent, can now be enjoyed by the millions, at least on the screen. By contrast, bungee-jumping has limitations in its objectives and thus its emotional and competitive potential. Sky-diving remains expensive and hardly for the faint-hearted, even when viewing from the comfort of the sofa. Australian football, or pools betting on it, extends the season for viewers and gamblers through the British summer. Football itself has however become a year-round activity because international competitions with more nations participating require many more fixtures to complete their cycle. World Cup games seem deliberately contrived so that the northern hemisphere nations can participate in and see events in a previously quiet period. Is the dating of such events influenced by commercial broadcasters faced with seasonally smaller audiences in summer?

The process by which sport and media seem increasingly to be regarded as complementary, once less problematic for commercial broadcasters, also now becomes important for the BBC. Competition for audiences, if not for resources, forces it to take account of the strategies of independent broadcasters. It must allocate additional time to more popular sports and so reduce coverage for the minor. It is compelled to enter competitive bidding for the key events or series in the sports calendar. Illustrative of the sea change is that in 1946 the BBC paid £225 in total to cover by radio the Wimbledon tennis championships, and in 1955 £5000. But in 1994 it spent £3 million on television coverage. At the international level such escalation is equally dramatic. In 1984 the cost to the European Broadcasting Union (EBU) for the broadcast rights to the Los Angeles Olympics was £13 million. In 1996 the payment for the Atlanta Olympics was over £150 million.[5] Even sharing the cost, this competitive bidding has created an almost insupportable burden for the BBC as for other European public service broadcasters. It is not only the cost. The purchase of exclusive rights by competitors means the removal of some events or series from the screens of BBC viewers.

Cooperative arrangements or bids with commercial broadcasters in the exceptional circumstances of, say, the four-year Olympic cycle, or as in time of war, may seem a reasonable compromise, since in principle they do not differ from the shared payments of the EBU on previous occasions. They also fit the commercial autonomy of broadcasters in the market economy, manifested in burgeoning co-production. But they could be the slippery slope for public services, if other conditions, such as secondary rights, lessening competition, are part of any agreement, such that joint provision becomes an accepted feature of television broadcasting.

Independent producers, to whom actual filming, etc. may be farmed out, can work for any broadcaster. Nowadays too, personnel move freely between public and commercial broadcasting organisations. Programme and series names can be transferred because of their market value. Complex programme guides also confuse the viewer. The audience, it is alleged, in homes equipped with digital television, are already less channel oriented than previously. What now are the parameters of competition and collaboration?

To show extracts from competitors' newscasts is understandable; but if the end game is joint programming, that is quite another matter. The ramifications of broadcast sport are considerable.

Despite these constraints broadcasters have notably increased total sports coverage since the advent of near universal television ownership, and as they have on radio. The latter is more probably due to the availability of extra channels since local radio has found that football coverage especially has fostered local audience loyalty and provides moderately cheap source materials. In the case of the BBC Radio 4 it fills about 7 per cent of transmission time, rising to a quarter of the total on Radio 5 Live.[6] But the transformation on television has been noteworthy. As was pointed out earlier, from a very marginal exposure, sport had already risen to one-tenth of transmission time by the early 1990s on BBC1, and 13 per cent on BBC2 where indoor sports have secured a remarkable niche. On the commercial terrestrial channels levels have hovered around 8 per cent recently.[7] We may now have reached a plateau in broadcast coverage. There are still some seasonal variations and of course peaks with World Cup football and the Olympics, with lesser heights for cricket and rugby, and the rarer but spectacular feats for individual boxing matches. The relative calm of current contractual arrangements after the abrupt changes and frenetic debate of the early 1990s still leaves some issues unresolved.

The increased hours of sports broadcasting over the last decade or two may not be the gift they are so readily assumed to be. By skilful bundling of channels Sky Television is able to generate a greater income from its viewers than might be achieved by the selection of single channels, or programmes under pay-per-view systems. Although numerous sports get occasional coverage, in practice it has meant that there is a greater concentration on the major sports and within that on top-ranking teams, especially in football. Some losses are keenly felt as when ITV, despite being able to offer substantially greater potential audiences than Sky, lost coverage of certain major football games to Sky after the 1994 bids debacle for the next cycle of key league matches. The changed range and balance of programming may also lead to overexposure of particular events or sports. Some viewers find three weeks of Olympic athletics excessive, and apparently many housewives complain when the World Football Cup series is in full flow. But broadcasters must use such occasions to recoup, or maximise the benefit of, the substantial rights payments they make. Such perturbations do affect viewer satisfaction and loyalty, and so have importance in the market when consumer sovereignty is said to be paramount. One response is the pursuit of novel presentations. Much thought goes into the generation of new or less familiar forms: Italian football (rather than German or French), new tiers of (European) competition, or the esoteric motocross, dog-sledding and sumo. Mudwrestling and wellie-throwing have not proved draws. Who knows when arm-wrestling will arrive? The invention of such contrived games as *It's a Knockout* took the idea to an extreme, but was at least lighthearted and an entertainment rather than a serious competition.

Expanding sports coverage

There may still be some detailed elaborations which are possible, but the main aspects of exercise, competition, team or individual performance, or alternative environments have probably been realised. Three-dimensional presentation may be a future achievement but it is difficult to see changes and additions having more than a marginal effect on the size of audiences. Whether some participative engagement with selection by viewers of alternative camera positions at a match will attract more attention is problematic. One promised development is to be able to view all the tennis courts at Wimbledon using alternative digital channels. It could enlarge the experience for the aficionado but seems unlikely to increase total viewership. Like the record button on the home audio-recorder, which is much used on first acquisition by the owner for self-recording, the use of multiple camera positions for competitive sports presentation may not fulfil its assumed promise. For example, who wants to miss the action on centre court, or where the ball is at crucial moments in a football match? Split-screens are one solution but hardly an attractive permanent feature. For many viewers part of the attraction of games coverage, especially when competitive, is the simplification of the contest, focusing on specific incidents such as the goal, the catch, the immediate action, indicating that complex rules and processes of a game are an encumbrance, although manna to the expert fan.

By responding to the preferences of the audience, which might give greater prominence to particular sports, the reduced autonomy of broadcasters in this new era is exposed. But indirectly this is probably more an indication of deference towards advertisers and sponsoring companies, alert to ratings potentials, rather than to the viewer alone. In the meantime sports bodies, concerned to maximise income through sponsorship and television exposure, are ready to adjust schedules and formats to their advantage.

Subordinating sport to the schedules

The example of costs for American Olympic coverage quoted earlier appeared to show that the US broadcasters were on to a bonanza as a result of what they could charge overseas broadcasters for relays and extracts. But the former were themselves in thrall to sports and city facilities. Providers are only willing to house international events if they can also earn a surplus from them. In turn advertisers and sponsors of programmes strike hard bargains or impose conditions more suited to them. Matches and Olympic events are now allegedly timed not purely for optimum body operating temperatures, such as avoiding the heat of the day, but so that they coincide with peak hour-viewing times in the world's largest television advertising market, i.e. eastern USA. Even more ominous is the tailoring of sports to maximise elements of action, conflict, tension or curiosity so as to attract and hold audiences. To start with, the duration of events may be modified by revised rules or editing of coverage to fit predetermined programme slots, or what are considered to be acceptable attention spans. In the case of equestrian showjumping the established conventions of points and penalties awarded, and graded tasks have changed over recent decades to accelerate previously more dignified routines and magnify perceived risk and challenges. Added to this have been pressures on competitors to dress and equip themselves to show more acceptable images of decorum and appearance, rather than the original informal, even cowboy spontaneity, of rural equestrian events. While everyone involved might prefer an idealised image, the pressure to conform to the new comes largely from the paymasters.

In cricket, monetary inducements alone were insufficient to ensure conformity with the prescribed niche of a traditional but less universal sport than football. Much thought has gone into restructuring the game and competitors so as to build audiences and so fit the procrustean bed of schedules. For example, one-day events have been developed to complement the conventional leisurely five-day Test matches; and more aggressive populist styles have replaced gentlemanly restraint in an attempt to meet the expectations of more plebeian and multicultural viewers as well as spectators of the games. Channel 4 has gained critical approval for its coverage, possibly by clever selectivity in its modest budget, so demonstrating there need not be a single path to excellence.

Another major annual sports sequence intensively broadcast is the Wimbledon tennis tournament. Here rules of the game were less mutable. Instead television coverage focused on ancillary features such as the behaviour and idiosyncrasies of the players, even the dress and underwear of nubile female competitors. One fears for the likely prurient interest if other sports dominated by or attracting women were thought to have marketing potential for audiences, such as netball, women's football or wrestling. Precedents already exist with ballroom dancing and ice-skating where the ladies' dresses appear more appropriate for sensual display than the outdoor life in a temperate climate.

The last example demonstrates very well the expansion of sports broadcasting, which may compete with or overlap other genres such as light entertainment. While there are always difficulties in defining genre boundaries in a world of changing lifestyles and markets, any statistical analysis or policy prescription which depends on unambiguous categories and continuity of measurement is greatly hampered. Of course it is to the advantage of the marketing entrepreneurs to have either fewer or indistinct boundaries, which might possibly restrain them.

A major difficulty in evaluating the power situation in televised sports is that each sport is in a different situation due to tradition, complexity, financing and degree of competitiveness, so that a uniform treatment seems unreasonable.

Although full details of advertising revenues from sports coverage are unpublished, in aggregate it must certainly remain a minor funding resource. Nevertheless the monies derived in the 1990s have probably been the fastest growing source of income for commercial broadcasters, given for example the charges now accepted by viewers to receive selected games and the evidence that, while maximum audiences for light entertainment have tended to diminish, key sports events now have the highest ratings. But total revenues or average prices do not show the dynamics of the situation in their entirety. More important is that marginal pricing will always attract interest by demonstrating new cost levels, especially in an oligopolistic market and in a time of change when the institutions try to hide behind a veil of commercial secrecy. So key price settlements resulting from the 1993–94 football coverage bids and the surrounding furore had a significance for concern and comment beyond the immediate figures and events, since an escalation to new levels of expense was revealed with major long-term and probably irreversible consequences for all sports.

The advertisers are under continuous pressure to increase profits since growth is the prerequisite of business success. If existing sports coverage cannot be further rationalised and made more profit-productive, then the striving to invent new forms or to encroach on other broadcasting genres seems inevitable.

Sport, leisure and entertainment

The pressure on sports providers and advertisers to diversify their product indicates how enmeshed in the market process they and the broadcasters have become. The symbiotic relationship has led to constrained interdependence as well as hoped-for mutual benefit and freedom.

In addition to changes in content the broadcasters think technological development may give some respite. Sale or rent of videos provides a supplementary income since historic matches will have educational or sentimental value to consumers. Digital, or possible three-dimensional, transmissions seem to offer new perspectives as once did colour, and in other times sound in the cinema. They do create new opportunities for creative endeavour to exploit the added qualities, but mostly consumers find they are getting rather more of the same when the novelty has worn off. The speed of technological innovation nowadays means these phases are truncated, in turn increasing the pressure yet further.

In the larger social context the changes in sport and broadcasting confirm the overwhelming ambience of the leisure society, which subsumes more and more everyday activities. And not only actual pastimes and contests but virtual or imagined reality. Training videos, such as those available for tennis or golf, enable novices to practise and learn the finer points of style. But such facilities can be two-edged, since their widespread use, and that of recorded activities generally, increases dependence on mechanical reproduction. The Frankfurt School, even before 1939, predicted an enhanced process of canned spectating supplementing direct personal experience in mass entertainment, with dire consequences of cultural and political conformism.[8]

Even leading sports persons are not free of the treadmill. They become well known as much for their personalities and character idiosyncrasies and behaviour through so-called 'sports reporting', of which coverage of events is only part, as for their triumphs on board, field or track.

The notable expansion of television sports coverage in the 1980s greatly enhanced the earning potential of major sports and teams. Led by the Murdoch Sky conglomerate, multinational broadcasters raised their monetary bids for broadcasting rights of the Olympics but especially for football. In addition sums, which were substantial to the authorities of minor sports but practically insignificant to large companies, were offered in sponsorship in return for, usually exclusive, rights to broadcast some of their games on condition that advertisements were prominently displayed where their matches or other activities took place.

Football naturally is an important quarry for these predatory advertisers, with its large attendances at their stadia and more so for their potential television audiences. The BBC found itself quickly outpaced and even the UK independent contractors were outbid as the furore in 1993–94 and subsequent contract periods has showed. The transnational broadcasters, despite their initially small audiences due to limited household possession of satellite reception dishes or, in the UK, low cable penetration, began to advance by audience size, and once the satellite transponders were airborne the cost per household reached, with DTH (direct to household) transmission, fell dramatically. Terrestrial broadcasters by contrast had always faced the problem that the capital cost of reaching ever more homes rose steadily as more distant or less accessible locations could only be covered with yet more transmitters.

More ominously, following American and other European practice, transnational broadcasters began to try to purchase significant shareholdings in leading football clubs. They had become vulnerable to takeovers by outside interests, after a number of the more successful, like Manchester United, became publicly quoted companies, having previously been privately owned. If realised, even only indirectly, it would give broadcasters a voting or bargaining influence on the football clubs' side when they were already on the other side of the table as contracting broadcasters. The bids for dominant shareholdings in Manchester United and Newcastle by broadcasters fell by the wayside, but such potential quasi-monopolistic threats alarmed government, sports bodies and public alike. In the UK the House of Commons Select Committee on National Heritage (now Culture, Media and Sports) recommended avoiding action to prevent such market domination.[9] Nevertheless the acquisition of some foothold minority shareholdings by broadcasters has proceeded, revealing the symbiosis between sport and television.

The coverage bidding wars also caused the UK government to ring-fence key national sporting events like the Grand National and the Cup Final so that terrestrial broadcasters should have protected rights to cover them for television. With the change in the climate of political opinion, following the downfall of the Thatcher government, and also reflecting market realities, the sale of secondary rights to show extracts and highlights from major sports events to maximise earnings from television coverage, became increasingly important for broadcasters, who, forgetting past rivalries, were now prepared to show clips from their competitors.

A new financial framework

The whole edifice of sports broadcasting finance, despite some greater stability in the late 1990s, remains vulnerable. Reluctantly terrestrial broadcasters in the UK have had to come to terms with the new cost structures, but international pressures will not go away. Even the European Union and the Council of Europe, lumbering regulatory giants, may eventually get dragged into the fray. Alternative means of distribution are also having divergent impacts. Video cassette recordings of major events have only a limited market, although pirated boxing match recordings may have a brief but intense life. On the other hand closed distribution systems like WIRE TV to a million homes, or Satellite Information Services linked to licensed betting offices to show racing, reaching 3 million persons weekly, illustrate additional routes to the viewers.[10]

More important is the rise of pay-per-view charging, which the satellite and cable operators find can be highly profitable, especially as the number of cabled homes grows, since the infrastructure has already been provided in the most populous areas. A payment of £10–£20 for a key sports or boxing match from even a half million homes, with perhaps three times that number of viewers, will earn much more for the broadcaster than could be gained by spot advertising or subcontracted sponsorship for the same audience. Probably it would be at least twice as much, although the ramifications and commercial secrecy surrounding advertising rates can make this only an informed guess, especially in relation to specific broadcasts. For example, due to the large number of potentially viewable sports, providing a broad portfolio to schedule, and to compensate for the minimal audience for some of the most esoteric, rights agents in negotiation with broadcasters try to secure contracts based on a package of sports, so costings become a matter of internal company valuation. As in the book world of authors' rights and publishers, hype and disinformation are the order of the day. As yet sports and broadcasters are not burdened with the problem of remainders, i.e. unsold copies.

As will be perceived, the lack of transparency over aspects of sports broadcasting finance in a time of rapidly changing technology and patterns of viewing is an obstacle to analysis or effective intervention, compounded by the conventions of commercial secrecy and privacy.

Sports television coverage does remain a modest proportion of schedules and is likely to remain so. Digital systems are most likely to increase the number of niche channels, so the power of the moguls is more likely to decrease as the average audience per channel diminishes. It is really the capacity to deliver peak audiences which is the main issue. Production costs have fallen and could go further as portable equipment proliferates, and sports venues equip themselves with studio-level facilities at their own expense to attract broadcast coverage, such as Arsenal Football Club have at their ground. Nevertheless the question has to be faced: is sport the tail that really wags the dog? Beyond the sensationalistic treatment of players and processes typical of the tabloid press, there is a problem for national cultures and the funding of broadcasting when massive or abrupt changes take place. Sometimes it will be triggered by occasional events like the Olympics or World Cup football where escalation to a new plane of costings seems to set consequent new elevations and expectations in other sports events. Or it may be the result of transitional business links where bargaining power is suddenly changed or broadcasting rights change hands.

How much is sport worth to broadcasters? One can establish what it costs. Transmission costs are important but given and predictable. Production costs are fairly common knowledge. The BBC provides information on production costs by genre in its annual report, and details for their services were made known to the House of Commons Select Committee by the commercial broadcasters. But the number of independent producers makes it impossible to hide informed figures. There was also published evidence to the Select Committee on the sums paid for sponsorship by business firms to sports bodies in anticipation of their hoardings and banners being filmed during sports matches. The key figure is how much do advertisers pay directly for spots and programme sponsorship? For this one has to employ indirect evidence as used by Howard Nead on the profitability of a diverse selection of genres, which allowed for some peak-time transmissions and likely audience profiles.[11]

If sports programmes advertising drew the same average revenue per programme hour as ITV broadcasts generally, then at 1999 levels it would attract about £140 million per annum. Taking proportionate sums for Channel 4 and the Sky operation, and allowing for audience viewing hours, one may calculate the likely position as shown in Table 5.1. It excludes Channel 5, whose contribution would make only a modest difference.

Evidence to the Select Committee showed £250 million per year was also being paid by (non-broadcasting) companies to sports bodies in sponsorship on the assumption that they benefit from stadium and site advertising during broadcasts. Inevitably there is an approximation about the figures in Table 5.1 but they do give likely orders of magnitude. Of course the surplus is not pure profit as administration and transmission costs have to be taken into account. There are no

Table 5.1   Annual television sports coverage finance, 1999 (£ million)

	Income			Expenditure
	Sponsorship and spot advertising revenue (1)	*Subscriptions and pay-per-view revenue* (2)	*Gross* (1 + 2) (3)	*Production Purchase of rights* (4)
ITV	140	–	140	75
Channel 4	60	–	60	20
Sky	95	250	345	100
BBC	Figure will be a budgeted share of licence fee			95

Source: Estimates by B. Luckham.

published figures for them. For some minority sports where audiences are minute then for some broadcasters it could be an unprofitable activity. Are sports broadcasts then loss-leaders? No doubt companies see their expenditure as an investment in goodwill with the sports bodies, partly as sustaining audience and probably most of all as symbolic support for an image of the British as sport-loving people. Expenditure will not however be a constant as it will wax and wane over the conventional international four-year Olympic and sports tournament cycles. Viewer loyalty meantime is more fragile, given greater choice, and they may have to be coaxed back each season. But even the big broadcasters feel the strain and the 1991 World Rugby Cup with elaborate arrangements for ITV to gain coverage were only ensured by the manufacturer, Sony, sharing the costs.[12]

So is the dog wagging the tail? If one continues the metaphor, it may depend at which end of the dog you are looking. Sport is evidently important to the human psyche but the power centre depends on the particular point in time or in the process. At one moment when the sport bodies invite coverage rights bids we seem to have a seller's market. When there is a technological development, the manufacturers have an upper hand. The broadcasters battle with one another as well as with their suppliers and partners. And in the long run the regulators and lawmakers have their say.

Where one can effectively intervene, should that be desired, depends on the window offered, the lever available, the timescale and the sense of responsibility and political will to carry any action through. So both tail and dog can wag, and be agents, depending on circumstances, and from which position the scene is viewed. They are not necessarily equal in either influence or effect, but the dog can be leashed or the tail docked!

There is a general presumption that public demand for sports coverage is not yet satiated, witness the sports promoters' almost frantic attempts to create new super leagues or championships on already crowded schedules, so as to draw additional revenues. Although total sports revenues do not grow exponentially there can be short-term advantage to certain agents in the overall game. Sports clubs become more like entertainment businesses with revenues ancillary to the main chance. For example Manchester United Football Club, one of the world's most successful and profitable clubs, is now reputed to earn more from broadcast rights, its own commercial television channel, shopping facilities and other ancillary business, than from match gate receipts. By floating as public companies on the stock exchanges, such clubs can in turn experience the dizzy volatility of share prices. Other sports like rugby, tennis or cricket, once characterised by amateur participation, are keen to follow media exposure with other business activity.

The sports players themselves have not been slow to take advantage of the helter-skelter. Football players in Britain, once regarded as but semi-skilled members of the working class, may occasionally now become millionaires through match fees but increasingly through celebrity appearances or even as writers in the press. With winners come more losers too. The increase in sports injuries is also more manifest, reflecting occupational pressures. Sports physiotherapists and doctors have consequently achieved significant recognition.

At international level the tradition of host nations adding national traditional sports to the Olympic panoply has become a burden to scheduling and cost containment for the organisers, because however unusual or exotic they may be to others they do not necessarily win more viewers in other national television markets. With national identity at stake, the concern of public authorities about promotion, order and regulation of sport becomes more evident.

Sport, for many years relatively free of government intervention in contrast to industry, education, health, even perhaps the arts and religion, now finds in almost all countries, Ministers of Sport. The courts too become involved as the social and commercial impact of sport grows. Unfortunately they have less expertise in this area than some others and tend to apply criteria from other fields like economics in their judgements. For example, the potential creation of Big Cities Games Leagues or a Euro Regions championship and now a proposed World Champions Football Cup, the likely squabbles over inclusion or exclusion, could well lead to decisions about restraint of trade similar to that in which the US Supreme Court has historically played a defining function. After the European Court of Justice, perhaps even the World Trade Organisation will have a part!

Some unresolved issues

To revert to the central matter of public interest in relation to sports coverage several questions must be asked.

Has broadcasting contributed to the promotion of diversity in sport or sports coverage?

Some new sports or quasi-sports have been created. Many sports are now given broadcast coverage. The number has increased since the early days of broadcasting and total hours provided have risen. Perhaps the new forms of sport are not so creative, as the elements most likely to be emphasised in broadcasting will be action, speed, national or other rivalry, conflict, even violence, possibly brighter colour or louder noise to increase attention so that distinctions are diminished and the events more stereotyped. On the other hand it would be difficult to argue that some sports have been killed off although they may have been devalued by the mercenary characteristics now emphasised rather than amateur, voluntary, informal, honourable or fun qualities.

Have standards of performance and portrayal been enhanced?

The increasing professionalisation of sport has raised performances by some participants but this may be at least in part due to other secular changes in society rather than from broadcasting alone, for example health and fitness training. But portrayals by the media if they have emphasised the conflictual or financial elements will have detracted from certain long-standing traditional or Olympian qualities of sport. The raised performance standards revealed by the broadcasters may, however, have increased the gap between player and spectator, and could even have discouraged some from trying or persisting as players. It must be accepted on the other hand that simplifying or narrowly focusing on certain elements of a game could make it easier for the less informed to understand the rules and practices. No one, however, could deny that broadcast presentation has improved. The polished performance of specialised and experienced commentators and additional cameras, along with better lighting and improved stadium or location facilities, mean that sport can often be portrayed as comparable with the best professional theatre.

Has satisfaction with presentation increased – in learning, entertainment or interest?

It is not certain that presentation satisfaction to viewers has improved. There may be occasional greater audiences or more time spent viewing, which does at one level suggest greater attractiveness, but qualitative assessments are limited. Appreciation indices, for example used in audience research, tend to be applied rather to fictional programming. Given the greater exposure the broadcast audience may be better informed. Is more of this concerned with scores, league positions and players rather than the finer points of a game – styles, skills and strategies? On the other hand, if sports are generally perceived or presented by the media as more about entertainment and pastime, rather than as inspired competition for excellence, honourable behaviour, or education then their following and any thought and discussion which succeed them can be argued as a self-fulfilling prediction.

Have opportunities to participate in sport been enlarged?

Whether opportunities to participate in sport have been increased is difficult to assess and even more what part broadcasting may have played in promotion. Unfortunately the occupation tables in the decennial Population Census reports do not regularly include numbers of professional sports players nor are there regular published numbers of amateur sports players, so long-term trends cannot be satisfactorily identified. Degraded facilities and time at school, or the availability of informal play areas for young people, resourcing and admission charges, health and safety regulation, government policy and wider social influences are probably and certainly in aggregate more influential than broadcasting alone – although it is important as the means by which some of these other influences are themselves reported on and communicated to the consumer. On the other hand, more women are now participating in certain demanding sports such as football and boxing, although it is unlikely they will replace losses in tennis or cycling. Perhaps more significantly, have broadcasters failed to enable the other influences on sport to be effectively explained and critically examined by the public? Recent concerns about health, physical activity and happiness in Britain, especially in inner-city areas, suggest that there has been a failure to promote adequate sports participation.

Have adequate or excessive resources been applied to sports coverage, and to games themselves?

The allocation of resources to sports coverage, especially football, has been seen as problematic more by other activity and genre providers. It means their own exposure is restricted, and the rapid increase in funding for particular sports coverage in the last decade or so has not yet been assimilated or universally accepted. The willingness to accept some pay-per-view costs, for example for boxing, suggests that other consumers are not wholly disadvantaged by reallocation of resources. But sports promoters are not necessarily sportsmen or sportswomen. Is it advertisers, broadcasters themselves, equipment or stadia providers who have benefited at the cost of games players and spectators? Some sports may be losing their autonomy due to financial sponsorship. The apparent interdependence of motor car racing and tobacco advertising already illustrate this. This is an issue about the totality of lifestyles, the common good and moral values which is not limited just to broadcasting. The need to have a common policy and to share in the bidding process for coverage of sports has undoubtedly contributed to the strengthening of the ITV Network Centre and thus greater centralisation of power in the commercial television sector.[13]

Have any detrimental consequences arisen from the sports–broadcasting symbiosis: in behaviour, corruption, injury, social disharmony or malaise?

The overall balance of effects of sports broadcast coverage seems almost impossible to determine because (a) one cannot separate different media, let alone broadcasting influence and (b) complex equations and difficult judgements will be required to weigh and calculate the many aspects of life which are involved. It is evident that there are no straightforward answers to the issues raised. The evidence is limited, assumptions and values are unlikely to facilitate agreement, and outcomes and effects are difficult to establish. For example, have hooliganism or racism been stimulated by highly charged broadcast coverage? What seems probable is that external sociocultural changes are more influential than television, whose effects seem more likely to be limited and short term, but whether the necessary research is done, or can be done in time, to guide any intervention, is highly problematic.

One either has to take a determined moral stand as some partisans would or, in our view, adopt a more cautious, pragmatic stance that abrupt, substantial or runaway change is dangerous and undesirable, especially if not monitored or debated. While not advocating doctrinaire intervention, it seems preferable to have careful recording and analysis and some agreed parameters of change. For example, predetermined proportions of change in resourcing, coverage, participation and public perception might be set so that, at prescribed stages or intervals of years the issues and desirability of intervention or relaxation could be reviewed and publicly decided. Some minimal safeguards are certainly overdue. The perturbations, arising from the 1993 and 1999 bidding for football coverage, suggest that a more transparent and equitable procedure is required. The ITC might, for example, conduct or oversee the actual tender process to avoid a repetition of that fiasco.

The complex interactive web of relationships between sports agencies, advertisers, broadcasters, regulators, politicians and public demands that any intervention chosen must be selective, skilful and effective, both in cost and consequence. There are analogies with other broadcasting genres and similar problems will also arise with them. Sport, because of the evident public interest and controversy, epitomises many issues which later chapters will demonstrate.

6
The Battle for Ratings: Peak-Hour Schedules

Increased choice is usually advanced as the main purpose of technological change in broadcasting to give the audience more channels from which to select. It is therefore assumed that greater diversity of content or presentation will attract more interest and this, combined with the growth of leisure time, should enlarge audiences and total viewing.

It has already become apparent that far from bringing previously unimagined novelties to the screen, provision will be largely more of the same. Indeed rather than similar productions, it will be very much what has already been seen. Repeats, whether classics from the cinema, or even any old cheap film stock are now substantial fare.

The extension of transmission hours around the clock has revealed a dearth of new material so that schedule-filling, like shelf-filling in supermarkets, has become a major task for planners. Perhaps, not only because of limits on creativity but because too much novelty would be too demanding, or even threatening to many viewers, the extra broadcasting hours are loaded with less demanding material. Obviously reruns of news or current affairs are inconceivable and sport too has its ephemerality. Rather specific minority genres such as education, religion and children's programming are clearly not for the bulk of the audience. So programmes which seek only to amuse, to fill time or to provide background, almost like animated wallpaper, inevitably are employed to fill the void, especially, but not only, in the post-midnight hours.

Problems of definition

However, the aggregation of material into a broad entertainment category should not be seen as an undifferentiated mass. While it may be fairly easy to define certain highly specific genres such as history, science, animals, religion, children, etc., the possibilities with multi-channel digital broadcasting enable finely tuned specialities to be identified and promoted in entertainment services. For purposes of marketing and relating viewing to target audiences, advertisers desire clearer guidelines, so as to sort and attract viewers for specific products, and to be sure that the market segments do not become too fragmented and thereby unprofitable. The UK industry journal *Broadcast* provides popularity rankings for various genres, especially those for repetitive drama. One table, at the time of writing, distinguishes series from situation comedy, soap and serial. Inevitably there must be a certain arbitrariness about the inclusion of a programme in one of those categories rather than another. But maintaining the separation of such possibly esoteric items indicates how important the core nature of the categories is for hard-headed advertising accountants. It would seem it is not just detail of content which determines the definition but treatment of theme. For example, concentration on character rather than incident, how repeated are the cycles of transmission, if treatment is humorous or serious, timing and audience. There is further elaboration as to whether a series is a new one, a return from previous transmission seasons, continuous, for example every week or day, or is a repeat broadcast. Once titles are allocated audience researchers may be able to match content, form and audience type. There is thus a highly detailed, arguably rational and refined analysis possible of so-called pastime programmes.

More controversial debate and discussion, about television and its effects, usually arises with news and documentary programmes, and those involving sex and violence. There is a tendency therefore to lump the entertainment programmes together in a bin, labelled 'less important' or 'non-threatening', or as a residual category of 'all other'. But this is to make a value judgement at odds with the apparent preferences of many, perhaps most, viewers. The soap opera may be regarded by most critics and analysts as concerned with trivia, stereotyped and technically undistinguished. However, Dr Dorothy Hobson showed that the soap opera based mainly on her study of *Crossroads* and its audience, while not claiming to change or misrepresent society, played an important part in the life of many viewers. Although focusing essentially on women viewers, it offered models for appearance, dress, behaviour, furnishing, lifestyle, helped establish personal identities, indicated possible solutions to personal dilemmas and broadened horizons psychologically and socially. Many of the themes presented in programmes contained little to excite the chattering classes but ranged over matters of fundamental human interest in sensitive and helpful ways, particularly for those whose life boundaries were largely confined to home, family and friends.[1]

The growth years of network television coincided with the rapid economic development of the 1950s and 1960s, enabling a remarkable increase in living standards for the mass of the British people, with greater equalisation of wealth and opportunity, by taxation and education. Advertising revealed new products and lifestyles to extend personal horizons. Broadcast programmes themselves often presented a wider panorama of alternative values, especially from the increasingly dominant North American culture. There was demonstrated a dreamworld, which the medium brought directly into one's living-room, an early virtual reality.

Much of this was to the general good, but since there was an element of make-believe, for some it proved an empty illusion. Promoting entertainment as the paramount purpose, while ostensibly bringing families together around the set in the corner, rather than by the fireside, may also have had a certain hollowness, since life is not all fun, and so fragmented families with consequent intergenerational conflict. This process was further consolidated by new media technologies, such as transistor radios, portable television sets and later mobile phones and personal computers, which together contributed to a more privatised and isolated existence.

Television, paradoxically, by offering choice and diversity enabled individual viewers to use it in contrasting ways, and with varying effects in different households. These included, besides amusement, education, essential information, companionship, conflict over ownership and programme choice, as an obstacle to conversation at home but as a source of talk when away.

Television is not therefore a singular phenomenon. It encompasses a range of experiences, attitudes, purposes and effects, whose place in history cannot yet be fully defined. Despite its apparent overarching presence, entertainment is therefore but one aspect, but certainly an important one.

A diverse aggregate

The features of entertainment programming do not, however, remain static. Clearly fashion is of profound importance, but regulatory practices, schedules, such as breakfast, peak-time or midnight hour, as well as broader social changes, have their effect. Overall the shape of broadcast entertainment provision appears to have fluctuated markedly, although in part this perceived change must reflect some changes in definition and difficulties in establishing agreed permanent genre boundaries.

In 1960, when mass television ownership was almost achieved, the Pilkington Committee reported that light entertainment, comedy and family and child programmes comprised 29 per cent of the output for BBC and 40 per cent of independent television.[2] It may be noted that this was five years after the commercial television companies had arrived on the scene and, in order to establish themselves profitably, had provided a large-scale fare of popular material. Indeed criticism of their downmarket populist programming had been a major consideration of the government in establishing the Pilkington inquiry. Stung by the severity of the criticism heaped upon them, the ITV companies, with greater confidence in their maturation, effectively halved their provision, as did the BBC, which after early alarm felt less threatened by the competition offered.

In the late 1980s both BBC and independent companies each had two well-established national services. For their major channels, which each reached about 85–95 per cent of their potential audiences weekly, BBC1 devoted one-tenth of its output to light entertainment, excluding children's programmes, while ITV offered one-eighth.[3]

By 1997 ITV gave one-seventh of channel time to light entertainment and BBC1 one-eleventh. However, this divergence of the commercial and public channels, while hinting at a distinction in function, may be more apparent than real due to changes in definition and inclusion. Much depends on how one allocates the GMTV breakfast magazine programme transmitted on ITV. Here it is assumed to be an extension of the current affairs/discussion category. An analogous dilemma arises over the BBC category of acquired programmes, one-quarter of broadcast time, which will be very largely American film and serial material, which in terms of content will obviously overlap with the BBC light entertainment genre. On the basis proposed the comparison between the channels, combining film, serials and light entertainment, can be calculated at the end of the 1990s as BBC1 34 per cent, and ITV 35 per cent.[4]

The overall situation now is much more difficult to compare because of the multiplicity of services with the advent of satellite and cable, and niche channels operated by BBC and the ITV companies. Satellite and cable with their more extreme commercialism do have a heavy element of popular programming, especially film, sport and music, although interestingly not so much of comedy shows such as situation comedy, which are constrained by national and cultural convention, although the originated transmission, via satellite, is by definition, international.

Another aspect is that comparisons of content prevalent in the commercial market are now rather derived from terms of total monetary cost. This is only an indirect and poor substitute for material content or hours, because of the widely varying cost of production of different genres. One is therefore largely dependent on counting only numbers of programmes of various genres broadcast, such as the top-rated programmes, i.e. largest audiences in a given period, in the *Weekly Top*

Seventy of *Broadcast* magazine. Such rankings, if not demonstrating resource provision, at least give some indication of audience access and attention.

Invariably the tables demonstrate, regardless of season, that of the top ten programmes almost all are weekly serial transmissions, sometimes like the soap operas appearing three or four times weekly and almost all defined as drama. That is to say, they deal with fictional personal interactions by regular participants in familiar indoor situations of the home, or the neighbourhood, especially the pub, less frequently a shop, café or on the street. The situation consists of an almost predictable, even stereotyped, ensemble of romance, deceit, crime or accident. The story is occasionally spiced with mystery: the disappearance or sudden appearance of passing characters, magnified by tension or anticipation of likely outcomes, portraying a community insulated from the externalities of war, economic crisis or even national and international affairs, unencumbered by small children and apparently timeless. Producers define the work of soap operas as character- rather than issue-based, while critics see them as essentially conservative with social values represented, and operating in a context portrayed as stable and non-threatening, even comfortable and self-satisfying, where justice broadly, if slowly, is done. Despite the central importance of work to everyday existence job situations are played down, as are education or health. However, these environments may be portrayed in somewhat similar personal interactive series not usually described as soap operas, which are based around a specific occupation – police, firemen, doctors – and the pressures, foibles and opportunities which such action sequences permit. Cuts and framing emphasise the small scale of the portrayals for which television, with its small screen, is ideally suited. As a format they are also noteworthy for their successful transfer from radio. Three-quarters of adults watch something from them weekly. Nevertheless the audience may have little appetite for more. The keenest fans may watch them for as much as 45 hours weekly, by following each series on different channels.[5] This must certainly provide enough storylines for anyone to follow. So far the UK has not gone down the path of the Brazilian daily tele-novela.

A captive audience

Audience composition is another factor to take into account. There are some indications that the main generalist channels, BBC1 and ITV, tend to draw more on an older age group, in fact because they are more likely to be around in the daytime, and are perhaps not so interested in schools broadcasts or social action programmes on BBC2 and Channel 4. The profile may also reflect their generation, with a lower terminal education age. Such viewers are likely to bring more conservative perspectives to the fare offered.

Taking even only the top 20 or so programmes in a week, with the basic half-hour slot and estimating that viewers watch 20–30 hours per week, at least a third of their television viewing is light entertainment, including soap operas. For the enthusiast these materials will be the majority component. No other genre comes anywhere near such audience domination. With such high proportions of the watching in peak time, such programmes must be providing substantial viewer satisfaction for much of the time. Confirmation of their importance is evident from the space which popular tabloid newspapers devote to the plots within programmes, to the screen and real lives of the characters portrayed, to the relative ratings and to possible links to social values and beliefs, however tenuous.

Such series, while varying in relative profitability, are crucial as earners for their producing organisations. It is not without significance that the most popular and long-term television soap opera, *Coronation Street*, has been the prop which has enabled Granada, although as a commercial conglomerate no longer primarily a television company, alone among the independent contractors to retain its licence, from the inception of commercial television over 40 years ago. By contrast with other popular genres, such as children's programmes and sport, where the promoted sale of related products, toys, games and clothing is a major complementary business, soap opera and series television are jealously copyrighted by their owners to prevent exploitation by others.

This may be a market deliberately given up, although one can see the potential for selling garments, furnishings or equipment on the back of frequent screen exposure. There may be a dilemma here over possible competition with those who pay the broadcasters – the advertisers and their business clients. It would also raise the issue of the blurring of programme content and advertising, carefully regulated by the ITC. However, one can see that as in the commercial relationships of media generally, soap operas also generate intricate complications and that broadcasters are not wholly autonomous agents.

What is not in doubt is the existence of a highly competitive market, to which neither the BBC nor the mighty international satellite broadcasters, like Mr Rupert Murdoch, are immune. In effect the audiences for soaps and serials are an almost captive market, happy with continuity and reassurance and likely to be resistant to undue challenge. Transnational productions, though, are at some disadvantage because the soap opera particularly is culture-bound. The exception often quoted is the American series, *Dallas*, which achieved almost universal attention, even to unlikely audiences among North African nomads and Asian villagers. Others have made the transatlantic hop east but much less successfully and rather rarely the other way. What is striking is that, even within nations, soaps and serials tap regional loyalties and expression. A distinctive feature of the British products are that *Coronation Street* and *Eastenders* in particular, reflect the polarity of their Mancunian and London bases, with buildings, settings, characters and language rooted in perceived localities, despite the common human condition they reveal. Other serials try to express other qualities and stereotypes: Scottish doctors, Yorkshire veterinary surgeons in their rural setting, the Liverpool spirit. It is doubly significant that European series as yet rarely cross national boundaries. Such regionalism is a direct consequence of the decentralised British commercial television structure. It is all but impossible that *Coronation Street* for example, would have been launched by a London-based company. It will be interesting to see whether this and other examples of regional differentiation will survive the tendency towards more central planning in the independent market. Political devolution in Scotland and Wales will undoubtedly have a similar centrifugal effect. Will English local or regional television require similar stimuli or is the economic logic of concentration all powerful?

Keeping up with fashion

Resource allocation and revenue are obviously profoundly important in soaps and serials television. Entrepreneurs, while seeking the security of assured markets, are nevertheless wary of dependence on particular products. Competition in this area is not only therefore in devising new series but also in broadening their scope. For example, taste palettes may become jaded so new or recycled emphases may be tried. More humour, more scandal, pushing boundaries of sex and violence, new settings – holiday camps, cruise ships, animal hospitals, courtrooms, church vestries – there seems no end. The minutiae of everyday situations is illustrative of postmodernist deconstruction and a fragmentation of human experience and emotion.

But reform within is not enough. New genres are ever in demand. It is noticeable that fashion and apparent success are quickly copied. The game show, while an established format, has quickly become more common in the 1990s, even encroaching on to BBC2, which is not what its Reithian origin would have led one to expect. Maybe it is to be interpreted as a reflection of the market economy applied to culture, with a competitive edge applied to entertainment programmes. For example, *Blind Date*, which exposes mostly young people to the uncertainties of finding a holiday partner, is spiced by the tension of selective choice based on knowing only some of the characteristics of the other participants. *University Challenge*, with its scoring system and reference to previous achievements also promotes competitive excitement. Confessional programmes, about human frailty, and even consumer programmes, tend increasingly to pile on the agony or failure of people, products or services, to rank and set participants on scales of success or failure. The class war may be dead but new hierarchies are being erected in such programmes of human achievement and aspiration.

Blurring genre boundaries is another way to sustain adaptability. So-called 'fly-on-the-wall' documentaries were sometimes so framed and personalised, like *The Family*, a 1970s BBC series, that many new viewers might assume that they were watching a conventional soap opera, rather than, one was assured, real people in ordinary situations, although of course skilfully selected and edited. Then 'dramadocs' advanced upon the viewer, where themes, personal careers and social interactions could in effect be superimposed on the mundane process of operating a hotel in the Liverpool *Adelphi Hotel* series. Focusing again on the incidents rather than the underlying routine, it generated stories as rich or exaggerated as any conventional soap opera.

One manifestation of genre blurring has been to present advertisements as stories or entertainment in themselves. Strictly speaking the rules governing advertising should preclude such ambiguity. Quite apart from production cost, where advertisements cost much more per minute than programmes, the Nescafé Gold Blend pseudo-romance sequence was a paramount example of what the French aptly call 'Le Teasing'.

The burgeoning of the drama–light entertainment category is also demonstrated by other changes in content. There has been a long tradition of detection and crime programmes in broadcasting with an appeal originally based on the complexity of the deed, the motivation and the craft in unravelling it, as in classical detective novels. The graphic action potential of the moving image has enabled greater illustration of the perpetration of the crime to be provided and, even more, the culmination of a shoot-out or a car chase. Indeed, the latter may offer the almost balletic, if monotonous, routine of many US productions. They have so often proved very popular to UK audiences, probably envious of the American capacity to discard multiple vehicles in the process. Given the male domination of such activities, a British contribution to the genre, riding on or promoting the feminist wave, has been to provide women as model detectives in, for example *Prime Suspect*, which also allowed a romantic ingredient to be added to such unlikely fare. The difficulty then arises in deciding how much sex and violence are required to boost ratings but still keeping within regulations and conventions governing their portrayal.

While it is not uncommon to perceive previous eras as more tranquil and less liberated than one's own, it is widely accepted that television broadcasting nowadays sees more sex and violence than in the early decades, despite widespread concern and more detailed regulation. It has been a losing battle for the moral guardians, partly due to greater acceptance, if sometimes reluctantly, of more overt behaviour of this kind in modern industrial society, but also because writers and producers find the restrictions a challenge and devote much creative effort to find ways around them.

It has been calculated that a lifetime television viewer in the United States is, on average, likely to see several thousand homicides. One may speculate whether observation of the incidence of sexual intercourse is now equally excessive. There appears to be a slippery slope from 'sex in drama', to 'sex as drama' to 'drama is sex', spiced with a frisson of violence. Such developments are not without controversy, but tend, in the absence of more original ideas, to be accepted by script editors. Those who wish to limit sex on the screen have not received adequate endorsement from viewers to make restriction effective. The difficulty is that rationing sex in an otherwise romantic desert tends to be regarded as nannying parsimony, and therefore absurd. We return to this problem in the next chapter.

Less controversial, but in its way no less demeaning, are continued performances to shock or expose human weakness or fallibility. One example was the *It's a Knockout* series, in which clowning behaviour was made into a competition. In more extreme form, imported mainly from Japan, were series showing people in unpleasant or threatening situations such as cages with dangerous creatures, or eating worms. Such examples, while infrequent and shown after the family viewing time in order to protect minors, reveal the potential for cruelty in television entertainment, which is, in principle, inadmissible.

Coming from another angle, the cinema has bequeathed a notable tradition of animation to television. This art form was originally identified with Walt Disney in the USA, but has in recent years also achieved remarkable levels of quality in Eastern Europe. Today the cartoon format has become a heavy component of children's programming, where quantity seriously threatens vitality and originality, often dependent on the monstrous and bizarre at the expense of more gentle and genuinely humorous representations. Such programmes are not for peak-time adult viewing, although there are niche outlets in the United States, and occasional series like *The Simpsons*, a 1990s American cartoon series, for older UK viewers. But they have made substantial inroads into British children's programming which, even if they can be clever and attention-holding, inevitably create barriers to perceptions and experience of the real world. Technological change has unforeseeable consequences because the cost of animation has fallen. This makes such material attractive, and there is currently a fashion to combine human performance and these artificial constructions which in part bridges the reality divide such as in *Jaws* and *Jurassic Park*. The electronic manipulation of images with computer games, virtual reality and heavy promotion has cultivated a taste to which younger people will be particularly susceptible. Indeed this may well prove a serious competitive battleground for mass television, as against personal computers where both individualisation and interaction can be combined.

The light entertainment and serial drama genre is therefore both highly amorphous and very broad. While there are clearer boundaries with, say, news or educational programming, the internal sub-genres are by no means stable, and although divisions can be constructed, they are as much, if not more, titular marketing conventions or administrative and regulatory boundaries which creative minds are ever seeking to subvert, and not necessarily easily definable cultural distinctions.

If, however, it is desired to record and analyse this shifting surface or to consider suitable public interventions to raise standards or prevent use, then at least the criticisms of this area of television broadcasting must be considered.

Reversals of fortune

One can be sure that no following is permanent and the what seem to us now mammoth audiences for BBC1 or ITV which could be attained for *Morecambe and Wise* or *Sunday Night at the Palladium*, reaching towards 20 million, are possibly gone for ever. The musical variety show probably became disproportionately expensive as individual stars demanded their own promotion and sets.

Tastes too, change, and in comedy success depends heavily on the interaction between audiences and performer. Repeat of the kind of support achieved by the slapstick hilarity of Morecambe and Wise, the Two Ronnies or Benny Hill awaits the arrival of new talent, both in acting and writing. The humour of absurdity of *Monty Python's Flying Circus* or *Fawlty Towers* have also not been sustained. Situation comedy, say *The Good Life* or *Yes, Minister*, has given way to the wry humour of *One Foot in the Grave* or *The Royle Family*, while significantly American comedy series from *M*A*S*H* to *Friends* can continue a respectable cult following in the 2–3 million audience range.

Comedy often engenders nostalgia, for perceived happier days. Schedules express hope that formats may return to popularity, and the water is occasionally tested with selected repeats, to see if there is a cyclical process, whereas such attempts are much rarer with other genres. If the current pressures on funding continue, hampering programme investment, one may expect more use of revival showings in future years.

The successful distribution on video of Laurel and Hardy and Charlie Chaplin films, for example, might seem to offer hope, but these are probably exceptional and appreciated more by children, as they are closer to the clowning tradition and less dependent on dialogue. In recent years, more rapid changes in dress, language and physical environment may be increasingly important obstacles to revivals.

Loyalty to channel or genre is not highly volatile, but in the last result it is specific programmes which attract audiences rather than channel or genre, but viewer behaviour will tend to change slowly, over a period of years. International crises and disasters will disturb patterns, but only for short periods. One may expect therefore that the distribution of patronage, in the year 2000, is quite likely to be maintained over much of the ensuing decade. It would be a rash person who saw the millennium as heralding a sea change in subject choices.

Opinions about programmes are often strongly felt by members of the audience. Whether reviewers have even as much effect as those for books or films, is doubtful. While some critics may be disillusioned producers, many probably see themselves as agents of change. Given their likely educational background, they are inclined to encourage more serious and meaty programming.

Light entertainment has never lacked hostility even from the early radio days. It was the last objective of broadcasting, according to John Reith of the BBC, who despite himself starting in the private sector, placed it after information and educational programming. In those early days such programmes were coralled as occasional interludes, like Saturday visits to music halls or the holiday resort indulgence, which persisted into early BBC television. Entertainment was seen as an event, a one-off show rather than as quasi-continuous sequencing. The turning point came with independent television in 1955 when the UK broadcast contractors gratefully took American styles as well as programmes to fill their schedules. Serials were often available at lower cost than home productions. Some of this material was by common consent of poor quality, formulaic, stereotyped, and weakly scripted. Competition might have eliminated some of this over time but the criticisms from the Pilkington Committee, and also firmer shaping by the revamped Independent Broadcasting Authority, soon encouraged the independent broadcasters to challenge the BBC effectively on several fronts.

Equally damaging and sustained, however, was that the light entertainment shown on British screens failed in its potential. It lacked innovation and the capacity to sustain series, unless they guaranteed financial success through high ratings. By tending to continue successful lines, or jumping on the bandwagon of fashion, it can be argued that the viewer whose sovereignty and capability should be paramount was dulled and discouraged from being more critical, imaginative and inventive in interpreting what was shown. The quality of viewing could thus be seen as itself blinkered. For example, the convention of film that 'baddies' eventually lose may create a kind of dependence and belief that all is well in the world really, and that the drama is only make-believe, whereas an alerted and activated viewer-citizen would be more responsible and caring in his own interest, as well as of others. In other words, there can be a subliminal 'do-nothing' message.

Some would see this as a politically conservative bias, feeding deference rather than empowerment. More specifically, given that broadcasting has become an international market, television from Britain, perhaps even more from the USA, is perceived as cultural imperialism, not only for foreign audiences but of ethnic minorities in the homeland.

The broadcasters have been vocal in their own defence. From 1990 the Broadcasting Act gave even more prominence to financial considerations, and serials and light entertainment, being the big earners for commercial services, are consequently in the front line. At first, contracts for independent terrestrial broadcasters were to be awarded to the highest bidder. Subsequently, as a result of viewer protest, a quality threshold was introduced as a preliminary to the auction. But the pressure to give prominence to profitability and economy also drove the BBC, under Sir John Birt, to adopt the commercial criteria of its competitors. The companies certainly had the law on their side. They argued that it was the vacillations of politicians which created uncertainty and indecision in the industry, and made them unable to plan for anything but the most profitable output, or risk substantial new programming investment. This was certainly in line with the short-term marketing notions of the 1980s. At the same time the terrestrial broadcasters were fearful of the forthcoming transatlantic satellite invasion.

Among the commercial contractors there was confidence that they were providing viewer satisfaction with high ratings for the entertainment programmes. From the 1950s they had argued that their task was to reflect society, rather than to change or manipulate it, particularly if society itself had little sense of its own trajectory. This remains a complicated issue after half a century of research and argument. Are we to believe that the sex and violence reflect everyday life? If there were proof that programmes make the audience more fearful it would give cause for concern. But one line of defence for the broadcasters is that it has not been, and perhaps it cannot be, proved that viewing has had such effects, except perhaps on a small minority of vulnerable or unstable persons. Alternatively, if the whole process is an illusory show to which viewers give little attention, then a world of play is a true reflection of the modern leisured society. The defenders of current provision will also say that there is an elitist conspiracy against the popular programmes, with a hidden agenda to preserve their own preferred high culture fare.

The narrow path between these positions seems to depend on judgements about who is to be served and what their potential is as sentient, intelligent human beings. Such debates cannot now be confined to a single medium because although television is the major time component of many people's lives after sleep and work, it competes with radio, audio and video recordings and computers. Besides, if television is often merely an accompaniment to other activity, the moving image background to which a low level of attention is given, does it matter all that much?

If as yet we do not have the answers, it is nevertheless worthwhile identifying the key questions which would enable the debate to be taken forward.

Meeting the viewer

To what extent do television's light entertainment programmes continue to meet viewers' expectations? The most substantial piece of evidence on this issue is the fall in typical audiences for the most popular programmes over, say, the last two decades, since television ownership effectively became universal. In fact the total population continues to rise, albeit slowly, and the number of sets has grown, with multiple ownership in most homes, often in children's bedrooms, so that the potential for audience access is also enlarged. Pro rata growth in viewers, for what is the most popular genre, has not followed suit. Where have the viewers gone? One possibility is their diversion to cable and satellite services but these, despite reaching over 7 million homes – one-third of all – cannot provide the whole explanation. The paradox is that the strength of these additional vehicles is in sport, specialised or niche programmes such as for children and to a modest extent comedy serials, especially American reruns. They have made at most little impact on the major British soaps on network television, despite the moderate success of imports such as *Friends*. They seem unlikely to take over the UK entertainment audience, given that they offer few new formulas. The prospects for cable and satellite to draw the mass of the public would seem to be possible only if viewers have an overwhelming nostalgia for repeats of earlier networked situation comedy, soaps, games and interview shows. What the satellites offer are films in abundance, which significantly has now been included with drama as narrative programming, for example in ITC annual reports. Such material is differentiated by them, and by the BBC also, from light entertainment. But film, although often spoken of as a genre, is really a format, or pre-recorded image, not a category differentiated by content.

Despite the confusion caused by merged genre designation, it seems likely that fewer people now actually pursue light entertainment, or if they do, they watch for less time. In the 1990s total viewing has fallen by at least 5 per cent, and more proportionally from light entertainment.[6] At the same time use of other media has grown dramatically, utilising computers, mobile telephones, and less so but still significantly, book-reading, as well as social entertaining and visiting, eating out and driving.[7] It may be too soon to conclude that this is a permanent withdrawal from the plateau of viewing in the heyday of network television. The threats from these other activities in the early years of the new millennium will not however diminish. The terrestrial broadcast networks look likely to be more modest affairs than now, certainly if analogue transmissions end in 2006, and the capacity or need to exercise channel selection, jolts many viewers into a paradigm shift of thinking and behaviour. Television light entertainment killed the music hall and the summer show on the seaside pier. Could its own demise now be so rapid?

The strongest political argument for the introduction of independent television was the provision of choice. This is now proving a two-edged factor, as the extension of choice is enabling many viewers to opt out of all mainstream channels. The dependence on audience ratings conceals more than it reveals. It is simple to understand, and given the validity and reliability of the monitoring method used, simple to calculate, and stimulates procedures to equal or excel competitors. But how much use is made of appreciation measures and why is so little published? It is not only advertisers, with their avid concern about per thousand persons reached for given expenditures, who care about the impact of broadcasts. Beside something like the duration of applause which encouraged concert performers, surely the statisticians could produce a measure of the social composition of television audiences, the duration of attention to programmes before the zapper is operated and an appreciation rating measure at the end of a show. The design and production difficulties should be less than for the electronic programme guides, with which viewers will have to contend.

If not measured directly, several attempts have been made to gauge public satisfaction with the television output. From an academic perspective, researchers at the University of Leeds in the mid-1980s found that survey respondents 'were predominately of the view that British broadcasting in its existing public service mode should and did assert and reflect Britain as a community, society and culture'. This suggests a certain compliance by the audience with what was currently on offer but, of course, since then a market-oriented style has replaced the public service mode which was at that time more dominant.[8]

A less complimentary view indeed was advanced at the same time by MORI, the market research firm, which reported that just 46 per cent of viewers said they were very or fairly satisfied with the quality of television, compared with 45 per cent who were very or fairly dissatisfied. In their experience, the firm argues that one can normally expect about

75–80 per cent of respondents to say they are satisfied with any public service, so 45 per cent dissatisfaction is a very low figure.[9] Of course, such a study covering television as a whole is not specific to the light entertainment genre, although that is the main focus of most viewing.

To sum up, satisfaction with light entertainment seems to have cooled on network television but more precise measures are required before the extent and nature can be determined with confidence, and whether BBC and commercial provision can be fairly compared. Growing ambiguity of genres is making analysis more difficult but this may be as much a reflection of public tastes, for whom novelty of various sorts rather than content alone, may be increasingly important. Broadcasters will probably claim that these are merely minor fashions of which they are not the arbiters.

Value for money

If we cannot adequately measure viewers' expectations and taste, it is consequently no easier to assess programme impact. But one may ask whether what is on offer is commensurate with the resources devoted to it. Even if quality has diminished a little in recent years, this might be considered a price worth paying if what is transmitted comes at a much reduced cost. Certainly staff productivity has greatly increased in the 1990s despite more broadcasting hours and the arrival of Channel 5, satellite and cable services. The BBC has lost a quarter of its full-timers and typically the independent contractors have reduced staff by 40 per cent.[10] Some countervailing gains have been made by the growth of independent producers, but seems hardly likely to have fully compensated, because many employees now work part-time or on short-term contracts.

More economy has been achieved in the 1990s as a result of market competition and constraints on raising the BBC licence fee. Between 1980 and 1998 funding for both commercial television and the BBC, which also covers radio, has been fairly buoyant, despite all the regular expressions of anxiety when advertising has slackened, or the licence fee held in check. In this period the revenues for both organisations rose fivefold, about twice the long-term rate of inflation, but slowing in the 1990s with a more competitive market. Their income has therefore risen about 5 per cent faster than the gross domestic product.[11] Consumers' expenditures have therefore proportionately been diverted to the television industry, but at least in quantitative terms they are getting more for their money, and it is being sourced out of rising real incomes.

While the changes in the financial equation have not provoked substantial public opposition, there is widespread distaste over significant further imposts, particularly at proposals to increase the licence fee to facilitate the development of digital services. This may be particularly strongly felt if digitalisation means many more repeats, and may be a distinctive feature of future entertainment schedules, if the early announcements of intended programming are to be believed, although the BBC asserts otherwise.[12]

It would be unwise to take any action, or pursue inaction, which puts either of the main generalist channels, BBC1 and ITV, at risk. They do satisfy most of the audience most of the time. Despite some limitations, they offer a certain degree of variety, and yet also give some opportunity for many persons to explore new topics, when they might rarely venture on to other more specialised channels. Channel 4 and BBC2 have been strikingly successful in holding their audience share in the 1990s, despite greater competition. It is BBC1 and ITV which have been most affected by the advent of cable and satellite. If their audiences fall further, there will be the loss of advertising revenue for ITV and the difficulty of justifying its portion of the licence fee for BBC1. The prospect for both channels looks daunting. Whether the call by the Secretary of State for Culture, Media and Sport, 'urging balanced programming on public service free-to-air channels' will be sufficient to evade the likely threat remains uncertain.[13]

Impact on other media

Given that the direct impact of television on viewers is problematic, it may be easier to ask what effect there may have been on other media. Unquestionably television has ousted radio, in all industrial countries, as the main vehicle of mass communication, firstly in news but equally in entertainment, measured by time spent. But radio has not died. Indeed paradoxically it has continued to expand and diversify with local and niche services, and with considerable potential in Internet radio. Television has a disadvantage since one needs a stable setting in which to view, whereas radio can be heard almost everywhere and alongside any other activity. On its side, television can add depth and illustration through the visual portrayal. For entertainment programmes this can enhance the atmosphere and context, whereas radio depends much on the listener's imagination and insight.

However, television has greatly affected the press. Daily newspaper sales have fallen since the post-1945 heyday and many people no longer feel they can afford the time to deal with the printed word. Through recordings on tape or disk television can now be archived, with possibly greater durability than paper or other hard copy. Cecil King, who dominated the *Mirror* press group, argued in the 1950s that television had ousted newspapers from their news primacy to become daily magazines with their entertainment content.[14] Today he would find that television is usurping the entertainment function too, with chat shows, highly fragmented news programmes where limited comment links sequences of pictures, and magazine programmes (the term itself has been pirated) covering holidays, health and other domestic features. But the effect of television on print is not wholly negative.

Growing appetites and sophistication for quality graphics fed by television, along with rising income levels, have surely contributed to the increase and diversity of periodical publication. Even if many are information and education oriented, they often have an entertainment context, and not infrequently are an offspring of successful programming, especially from the BBC and commercial multimedia groups.

Advertising has become more television based, but has also recognised that to be successful, it must entertain as well as inform. While the computer and Internet revolution has not yet run its course, their relationship and dependence on the small screen are self-evident. Computer games, pornography and competitions seem likely to be major bridges in entertainment, and the possibility of interactivity with large numbers of viewers, with keypad or keyboard, is beginning to grow. The symbiosis is significant because network television has a steady revenue base, which could generate the investment required in equipment and software, whereas much Internet activity has yet to cover its operating costs, and may indeed be financed by a bubble in equity prices rather than earned income.

The potentials seem almost infinite, fantastic and not yet an illusion but must have profound implication for television, however delivered to the home. The question then becomes what is an industry, rather than what is a genre?

Technology and light entertainment

Within the entertainment field itself, major developments have occurred over the last two decades. New technologies have contributed to this. Lighter and cheaper equipment, more sensitive lenses, and electronic editing have reduced costs so that small producers no longer require the once acclaimed critical mass of the BBC and large independent contractors. Aided by the weakening of trade union influence, multi-skilling is now commonplace. The independents can bring new ideas and methods, and challenge existing conventions and standards, despite the risks this has also raised. Digitalisation has revolutionised editing, and post-production activity has become much more important. This has made easier selection and manipulation to enhance dramatic impact. What may have been naturalistic interactions can, with appropriate staging and editing, be made highly charged. For example, game shows or confessional programmes, both allowing a competitive element to outdo others, can arouse considerable emotion. In one way this is nothing new, but the greater convenience may mean more utilisation, of which the viewer may be unaware, and rarely told. Both formats have become a more common feature of schedules, emulating American practice.

Building by contrast on British traditions of documentary production, a notable introduction has been the development of docusoaps, such as the BBC *Hotel* and *Driving School* series. How much is a prepared story is again difficult to judge, but the extraordinary sequences of near disasters suggest a deliberately humorous orchestration. The commercial channels have similar offers, with perhaps a tendency towards melodrama in hospital and police settings. Obviously there are cost advantages in exploiting the serial format, without the expense of professional actors, but at the same cost as being away from the studio. The content, however, places them clearly in the entertainment genre but where are the boundaries to be drawn? In the short run the viewer may feel this is great fun with opportunity for personal identification, but there is an element of deception which in the long run can only confuse.

A serial documentary does not need, however, to be either ludicrous or highly technical to capture the attention of its targeted audience. Roger Graef's pioneering work of the fly-on-the-wall documentary, *The Family*, with a Reading family, the Wilkins, held a substantial proportion of viewers enthralled over many weeks, in a close-up, but sensitive, picture of everyday working-class life. Another of his series, *Police*, dealing with the work of the Thames Valley constabulary, also touched a nerve with that large minority who at some time have had contact with the police, whether as miscreants, victims, witnesses, jurors or lawyers, and indeed it led to reforms in police practice. No soap operas drew quite the same reaction as these series with their authentic portrayals of human situations. Television does not win on all sides and has always faced problems, as a visual medium, with the presentation of music. It is not surprising therefore that MTV, directed at a youthful audience and probably with a strong promotional function, has made inroads, with dance and graphics, which terrestrial television has not truly matched. Niche radio and music services via the Internet also advance, and together these alternatives have helped dislodge *Top of the Pops* from its earlier ratings level.

In contrast, the appetite for crime and sex programmes from the adult public is both served and stimulated by their profusion on television. Both are treated increasingly as entertainment material, smuggled in by ploys such as sex in exotic settings, such as Thailand or Hollywood, or emphasising the idiosyncrasies of personal behaviour and lives of detectives, and other members of the judicial services.

The potential of digital processes to enhance post-production manipulation demonstrates the interdependence of form and content, which new technology facilitates. It is not surprising therefore that the term 'show' is more frequently used, rather than 'programme', in the trend to become almost the all-encompassing genre of light entertainment.

Entertainment programmes and society

What effect are television, and entertainment programmes particularly, having on lifestyles, values, autonomy and activity? All are aspects of society which would seem particularly vulnerable to the influence of television, not least because of the time devoted to it, as well as its content. The question must be asked even if immediately it is seen as nigh impossible to answer comprehensively since so many other factors are simultaneously operating. Earlier it has been noted that some activities like book-reading have actually risen in recent decades, as well as book sales. Walking and gardening have also increased noticeably. But activity is often easier to measure than some of the mental processes, and the links are tenuous or possibly misleading. The weather, cyclical events like sports competitions, national disasters or accidents can also distort trends. Nor is the audience a homogeneous whole.

What can be said is that television as the all-pervasive medium of mass communication brings together many facets of human life, by revealing connections, possibilities and alternatives, which facilitate greater social changes. Annual surveys reveal that television programmes are the main topic of conversation among family and friends and usually well ahead of any other of 20 alternatives.[15]

In other words television, whether entertaining or informative or both, is more a facilitator of communication rather than a determining influence on behaviour. There seems no reason to believe that this role will change in the foreseeable future, even if the mode of delivering the signal alters. Television is powerful because of its universality, familiarity and immediacy. It is also a dense medium, with the combinations of action, sound and graphics. This results in much redundancy (duplicated or irrelevant information in a particular sequence or programme) combined with a high level of entropy (cues, data, evidence). Such complexity is often unpredictable in its effect on viewers.

If there is a general desire that there should be more informed debate and/or effective intervention in television broadcasting, then adequate tools are required to achieve this. A fundamental requirement is that more precise definition of genres is available and employed. But we need a clearer vision of what sort of society we want, and what part television should play in bringing it about. Otherwise creativity, morality and responsibility are hostages to the vagaries of the market.

7

The Exploitation of Emotion

An arena for controversy

In the last decade of the twentieth century, three factors have combined to bring certain extreme genres of television programming under greater criticism. The light-touch regulation embodied in the 1990 Broadcasting Act, originally intended to lessen financial and bureaucratic constraints, may have triggered the unintended reaction, but also the increased competition for audiences in a multichannel market, with overtones of economic recession, and a supposedly more liberal public opinion, have contributed to greater use of sex, violence and horror in mainstream television broadcasting.

The major dilemma for broadcasters, and for regulators and their political masters, centres on censorship and freedom of expression. In a democratic society a key assumption is that writers, artists, journalists, film-makers, as well as religious organisations and politicians, and now broadcasters, have a basic right to express ideas, or portray events, incidents and emotive materials freely, provided they do not harm others. The second, instrumental, problem is usually that not all recipients, viewers, readers, etc. are equally capable of coping with extreme materials. Some of them, particularly the young, the old or the mentally disturbed, may be disturbed by such materials, or deeply offended or confused, morally, intellectually or emotionally. Whether there are objective and practicable limits which distinguish these materials is a subsequent problem, which in everyday programming often overwhelms the general principles.

On the whole there has been near universal acceptance that television as a major medium of communication must be regulated, at least to a moderate degree to avoid potential risks to viewers. So there is the 9 p.m. watershed to distinguish family viewing from adult programmes. There is also the general acceptance for television of the film classification used by the British Board of Film Classification. Ultimate safeguards are in statute and common law as interpreted by the courts.

Most broadcast television, however, gives no obvious offence to the viewer. Indeed it is surprising how few persons are so provoked that they will write or telephone to the broadcasting organisations or regulatory bodies to complain. Often complaints, when they arise about a particular programme, number less than ten, and a three-figure score may be regarded as an unlikely torrent.

In relation to the millions of typical audiences such as for the most popular weekly programmes, it may appear that there is no problem worth intervention. However, any response requires time and effort which the comfort of the armchair inhibits. Sadly too many viewers may wonder whether protest or commendation is worthwhile. After all, something once transmitted is water under the bridge. Any damage done can rarely be given commensurate restitution. Even where some correction, apology or explanation results, it is impossible that all who were affected by the original can undo any harm that may have been done.

One consequence of the development of mass media is to increase the distance, physical and social, between the sender and the receiver. Although some broadcasters may be household names, few will be known or can be reached by viewers. Contrast the situation of those who fill the correspondence columns of local newspapers. If complaining they may not all receive satisfaction. Nevertheless they think it is worthwhile. Perhaps they feel a strengthening of shared identity with other readers. Television viewers, despite their numbers, seem more atomised and isolated.

On the other hand it can be inferred from the available evidence that there are many viewers who do not complain but are equally offended – the iceberg phenomenon. How broadcasters weight the complaints they receive is hardly explicit, but they feel they must acknowledge and respond to them. Dissatisfaction can accumulate and repetition of the same offence will magnify concern. Some complainants can be very persistent, and when bound together as in the National Viewers' and Listeners' Association, or Voice of the Listener and Viewer, can publicise their feelings and gain political significance and impact.

Public opinion on particular subjects can wax and wane. Account must therefore be taken of the prevailing social context. It is noteworthy that programme response can be much influenced by particular productions or external events. In the absence of consistent long-term statistical measures of opinion on offensive material or context, judgement by regulators must frequently arise from occasional selected programmes. Sometimes this takes place in an atmosphere of partisan moral panic, campaigns, or critical reporting in alternative media. The tabloid papers have a potent influence in covering such complaints, knowing that alarmist reports will often generate more attention and sales than dispassionate accounts.

The personal interest of politicians is equally crucial, as was shown by the commitment of Mrs Margaret Thatcher to the establishment of the Broadcasting Standards Council, now within the Broadcasting Standards Commission, despite the reluctance of existing regulatory bodies.[1]

Academic research or enquiries undertaken for particular commissions of inquiry can yield vital information. But they occur at long intervals or focus on narrow areas of detail, so that they are only a partial element in judging whether a situation is so serious that some intervention is necessary.

Channels, genres or programmes at fault?

The communication arts are heavily dependent upon emotional impact for their success. Without the charged atmosphere and ambience of a football crowd, pop concert, or cinema and concert hall attenders, television like radio, has to enhance its visual and auditory cues to arouse or satisfy the audience, who are probably calmly seated, or otherwise ensconced, in their own homes. One way to overcome the possible ennui is by emphasising more lively and dramatic themes, as well as exploiting sound, colour, movement, etc.

Some soap operas are so replete with sensation, accident or disaster as to be beyond the reality of most people's daily routines and direct experience. Minor family or neighbourhood fracas can be highly magnified and played out over many weeks' presentations. Some genres, like crime series, have become hallmarks of the medium, analogous to Westerns and the cinema. Sex, which is more widely familiar certainly to adults, is, not surprisingly, an area with considerable potential for home entertainment and stimulus. Horror, mystery, shame and scandal also offer opportunity to more people. Best of all, they can all be presented in combination. Inevitably, since they may easily border on the boundaries of sensitivity and moral judgement, such material, in extremes, is a potential hostage to dissent.

Of high relevance is that concerns about television entertainment programmes seem to focus on a limited range of issues, such as use of offensive language, excessive or repeated violence, active rather than hinted sexual behaviour, blasphemy, the scheduling of extreme behaviour and the absence of sufficient warning of potentially offensive material.[2] Interestingly only political bias, i.e. news and current affairs coverage, seems to arouse comparable reactions among other genres.

Where there is recurrence, the issue of offensiveness cannot be ignored. There will always be boundaries of taste but the monitoring, analysis and power to intervene must be maintained so that intensity or other undesirable trends may be contained.

On the whole the items above are elements within programmes rather than entire presentations or series. Even if it were desired to take action, simple prohibition would be unlikely to be effective, since it is particular scenes or dialogue, their use, context or degree which usually offend.

One reason that it is difficult to blot out offensive items, is that they may be perceived by the producers as necessary components of programmes for their verisimilitude or historic representation. Obviously the creative writer or director wants to provide that which is relevant to the plot. What may give cause for concern, however, is that the offensive element may be gratuitous, for its own sake, or may be used as the draw to brighten up the promotion of a programme. So what may be argued is not objection to a genre as such, but the way it is used or exploited to maximise the audience. The process can operate in different fields. While it may be most obvious in fictional materials where occasional inputs of sex or violence can add spice to a flagging tale, one finds also in advertisements, such as for cars, that sexual allure can be a major aspect of sales promotion, much exceeding the technical qualities of the product. Repetition can lead to tedium and much is probably discounted by the intelligent viewer, but the danger is compounded by intensification, and yet further extremism.

Changing tastes and provision

Much is made of apparently more tolerant public attitudes to sex since the 1960s. Monitoring and comparing opinions over time are fraught with difficulty and no single measure is likely to be adequate. The Broadcasting Standards Commission has over seven years recorded public concern, which after indication of previous decline, in 1999 reported that this has now reversed, despite an objective reduction in actual portrayals of sex, bad language and violence on screen in the previous year.[3]

The ITC in its 1999 review of independent television performance criticised the notable emphasis in recent programmes on the sex industry, and placing much adult material immediately after the 9 p.m. watershed rather than phasing it in.[4]

What has been described as the plumbing of murky depths was demonstrated in a 1999 Channel 4 scheduling, after the 9 p.m. watershed, of a documentary on bunny girls, a programme on sex with animals, a comedy show romp, a drama about prostitutes and a documentary about teenage sex.[5] This channel established to provide diversity, and to serve a variety of minority interests, appeared to have fallen victim to the jaded appetites of a majority audience.

What is called for therefore is not the application of a regulatory sledgehammer but rather the application of such controls as exist so programme contractors understand and deal with anxiety about obscenity and violence.

With extreme programmes, as in television generally, the problems of defining genres or subjects for the purpose of programme analysis or intervention are manifest. On the one hand the availability of numerous channels via satellite, cable or digital broadcasting has created the possibility or, some might say, responded to a latent demand for distinctive specialist materials in an infinite variety of niches.

On the other hand, to lessen the potential loss of many viewers to these new competing services, established broadcasters and producers have been demolishing genre boundaries so that generalist terms like 'entertainment', 'family' or 'speech' or even deliberate blurring with names like 'infotainment' or 'docusoap' indicate an attempt to try to hold an audience which has broad tastes and is willing to be led. Viewers are served with a schedule which relieves them of the dilemmas of selection or channel hopping.

This aggregate audience appears to be the 'silent' majority, not necessarily wholly uncritical or passive, but middle of the road. They are not too demanding; for them television, though important, is not the only thing in life. They will watch when they are not working, travelling, playing, eating or sleeping, or when they have little else to do.

It might be assumed that here there is a lazy quarry, an audience of sitting ducks who can be easily satisfied. But while there may be a significant number of viewers for whom television is often graphic wallpaper, merely background against which they live a life of many daily routines – cooking, eating, washing up, cleaning, doing maintenance, homework, entertaining, talking, arguing, writing, dozing, i.e. only partly or spasmodically attending, these viewers do have priorities, choices, discrimination, reservations, awareness. Their sensitivities and values should be respected.

Programme planners do have to balance a requirement to provide some measure of familiarity, reassurance and predictability against a degree of novelty, challenge or curiosity to attract new viewers or replace those lost due to demographic causes, availability or for reasons of satiety. Hence the anxiety among producers for the continued life of long-running soap operas and the frantic search for new formulas, or old formulas in new covers. The pursuit of audience share is relentless in the market economy, although in Britain we may not yet have reached the nadir of United States broadcasting where unsuccessful pilots or new series fall like autumn leaves, as the annual post-summer cycle of entertainment programmes draws on, because they fail to meet advertisers' expectations.

Always there will be a need to enliven or spice up the familiar schedules and this is most easily achieved by a sprinkling of sex or violence. But as in all programme material there is a limit to what the public want or can endure, either in quantity or depth. In the end excessive dependence on sexual themes is likely to prove self-defeating. Without novelty, it is surely boring. Even bloodletting and car chases will reach their zenith, or at least pop through cycles of exposure.

Given that there is a lively fascination with these subjects, and no doubt for a small minority an obsession, it could be argued that niche channels are ideally suited to provide such material. The possibilities of warning codes, timing devices or encryption are also possible means of restricting its availability and limit offence. In a democratic society of reasonably decent people such an argument is difficult to resist. Experience in other countries suggests that different cultures or traditions tolerate programming in subjects which are not acceptable in Britain. For example, there were in the early 1990s controversies over erotica transmitted via satellite, transmitted from Denmark and the Netherlands; late night and weekend sex films from several Central and East European television services, and in the late 1990s new pornographic films from France.

There seems little likelihood of extreme programmes, if they operate as audience bait in generalist services, being wholly shunted to niche channels, comparable to the adult sex shops. It is more probable they will develop in parallel to mainstream channels.

Most people have a clear idea of what constitutes pornography and violence in television. They will see this as portrayals of behaviour in a fictional context rather than scientific reporting, or analysis and discussion in depth as part of current affairs or educational programmes. Paradoxically, given that these are categories which are widely recognised, there are no statistics of allotted broadcasting times or audience attention. It might be thought that it is so obvious a grouping that there is no need of aid to its recognition. The truth, however, is more probably that once labelled such material would be the quarry of every individual with psychopathic tendencies, thus boosting any perceived risks and increasing the pool of potential malefactors due to its exposure. In addition, given the stereotyping of actors in character roles, they and the producers and directors may find themselves herded into a ghetto and excluded from wider dramatic features.

There may be an analogy with the red-light, although licensed, cinemas in some European countries which apparently are nowadays almost empty, despite the avid interest which is alleged to exist in this form. Video recorders now provide for private viewing of such material. As with other genres, creative workers in this field often prefer an absence of boundaries so as to maximise their freedom to innovate, cross or combine.

In consequence information on the volume of offensive programming tends to be drawn from partisan interests such as the studies by the National Viewers' and Listeners' Association or specific but limited researches by the Broadcasting Standards Commission. Such work although valuable rarely enables a long-term view of trends to be taken. The data are, for practical reasons, often limited to counts of strong language, the number of homicides, blows or crimes shown, or portrayals of sexual acts. In themselves such numbers do not define genres because such incidents might be essential inclusions in classic or near universally accepted contemporary drama, although usually isolated and rare occurrences, but which are crucial to the plot or moral, or historically accurate. One might take at random, the deaths of Nancy or Bill Sikes in Charles Dickens's *Oliver Twist*, homicides in several of Shakespeare's plays, Federico Fellini's *La Dolce Vita*, or *Satyricon* from Cretan mythology and the murder of the princes in the Tower of London.

Viewers versus broadcasters

Despite expressions of public concern, the presentation of sex and violence appear to be relatively minor problem areas for broadcasters. Prescription about them each occupies a couple of pages in the more than 200 pages of the BBC's *Producers' Guidelines*, and about the same length in the shorter ITC's *Television Programme Code*.[6]

Of course, particular cases may demand extensive consideration by senior executives in which they can draw on broad artistic or news reporting experience. The ultimate test seems to be, would a portrayal give the viewer offence? In other words, is or can the event be presented in a non-tendentious manner so that the viewer is capable of judging its appropriateness? While it is likely that regulators or executives will be alert to context, is there a moral or legal ambience which should be more explicit? If not, there is then a detached, matter of fact or coldly clinical perspective which may imply that violence and sex are pervasive, everyday and perhaps normal.

So far it seems no one has undertaken adequate research to see whether viewers feel that television on the whole presents exaggerated images of society, the extreme the norm, or accurately reflects the experience of everyday life in relation to sex and violence. Any answer would be subject to much qualification, and indeed can hardly reflect the painful experiences of those who have actually endured such incidents, and whose views must surely carry extra weight. By contrast some critics may feel, indeed, that soap operas, perhaps as counterbalance, present an anodyne picture by focusing on character rather than social issues.

Some distinction should be drawn between reporting and fiction, assuming viewers are able or willing to separate them, at a time when genre boundaries are readily broken. Finding a consistent path through this minefield is intimidating and it is not surprising that Colin Shaw found the authorities in the United States falling back on the claims of instinct as their regulatory baseline.[7] The UK regulatory guidelines, while more extensive, are still frequently expressed in general terms so that in specific instances there may be no better defence than that argued by the Americans.

One complication linking various themes is whether the portrayal of sex and violence has criminal overtones. As might be expected, the guidelines under which broadcasters operate do not permit such detail as might encourage criminal or dangerous behaviour or offend decency.

In fictional programmes is it now accepted that, on the basis that the above provisos are followed, the sex portrayed is always consensual and the violence routine and tolerable? Changing public attitudes and judicial practice in, for example, date rape and domestic violence, suggest that broadcasters should be more cautious.

Taking a forensic viewpoint, the defining characteristic might be the intent of director or player, but this is in practice impossible because of the subtle, complex or numerous alternative interpretations, comparable to the seemingly infinite variety of current book genres. In the world of film classification, the British Board of Film Classification, under pressure from politicians, public watchdogs and industry, has had gradually to increase its categories and distinctions over the years, and consequently define highly detailed measurements of possible offensive material by camera angle, extent of close-ups, duration of view, quantity of blood, degree of near realism, number of blows so as to distinguish gratuitous, excessive or incidental portrayals, and therefore relevance to the overall theme of a film.[8] Under the leadership of

Andreas Whittam Smith and Robin Duval, the increased openness of the BBFC hopes to win stronger public endorsement of its practices. At least the cinema-goer can find out more easily what are the definitions and how they are derived.

What is also evident is that the BBFC, in trying to reflect public opinion and taste rather than determine them, has sometimes found it necessary to change its judgements. In certain cases this may be to reverse an earlier adjudication, almost always it seems to loosen the constraints, or in general progressively take a more accepting stance, to what were historically seen as offensive presentations such as in relation to the *Clockwork Orange* film.

Partly this change has not only been in the BBFC's perception of public taste but due to changes in technology, i.e. the widespread access to video recordings as well no doubt to the competition from the newer media like television broadcasting itself and cable services. Understandably the Board wishes not to be regarded as ostrich-like, if other media enable the public at large readily to obtain material which the cinema is hindered in showing. Indeed some might argue that the public cinema environment to see some potentially offensive material might be less dangerous than in the hidden confines of the home.

In practice broadcasters, television regulators and the BBFC are aware and do take note of each other's conventions and rulings. No doubt the courts would also take such interaction into account. Since, however, the different vehicles do serve different markets in contrasting contexts it is not surprising that there is little unified definition of the boundaries which they observe.

If the populist notions are to be applied to the issues of taste and acceptability then unfortunately we may be faced with an unstable, even fickle, criterion. Public opinion is essentially labile and in matters of propriety, taste and decency likely to be even more so. It may change abruptly if some particularly sensational event occurs. The Moors murders in the 1960s, the killing of an infant, Jamie Bulger, in Liverpool in the 1990s, and certain paedophile cases also in that decade, or the mass deaths of spectators at a football match in Sheffield in 1989 are examples. While the specific consequences for television and media generally are difficult to elicit, it is certain that producers would have avoided immediate similar fictional portrayals in the aftermath of public revulsion. So a form of self-regulation was exercised, even if not spelt out literally. And yet this has to be seen in an era when it is thought that more liberal representations of sex, crime and violence are tolerated in television, and elsewhere. A likely factor is that matters of cost could be involved, since damages from possible civil law actions, or to re-edit film stock must inhibit rash endeavours. The imposition of financial sanctions by the regulators would certainly be effective. This is not currently operative for the BBC, which as the main public service provider, has always been assumed to be above such jeopardy. Whether in consequence a cost–benefit analysis will be applied to broadcast offence avoidance, as apparently already applied to accident-avoiding investment for rail or road, must be problematic, although the availability of analogous insurance schemes is a pointer to the future.

It has to be asked whether a general erosion of standards has occurred or whether the increasing detail of both BBC and ITV producers' guidelines and BBFC norms, is a clearer definition of what is acceptable or unacceptable in specific portrayals of behaviour, so that the artistic canvas remains the same but the causes and faults are more closely marked. Bob Woffinden has observed that crime reports in the press were a prominent element of the tabloid and popular newspapers 40 years ago but were relegated to later pages of the serious broadsheets. Now they frequently appear on the latter's first and second pages, no doubt responding to wider public interest or fear.[9]

The Broadcasting Standards Commission which has now produced the seventh annual monitoring report on public attitudes to broadcasting and programme content, concluded that there is currently evidence of a significant and long-term change. The public is now more concerned about the portrayal of sex and violence. If this were to be linked with a fall in total television viewing over the last decade, it would suggest that the dissatisfaction must be remedied. Further confirmation may be desired, but need improvement await further verdicts? Other explanations may be advanced – rising educational levels and therefore a more critical audience, the growth of alternative media, new leisure pursuits, and demographic change with an ageing more conservative audience. But even if all apply, television still has some autonomy and hopefully has not yet written off the British public as incorrigible, or its creative talent lacking. The sword of Damocles, or further regulation and sanctions, need not be awaited.

Sex and violence seem to provide more gratuitous episodes which, unless they are linked to criminal behaviour, do not automatically follow the convention that the good will eventually prevail. The situation is muddied still further in that drama-documentary uses fictional representations or at best informed reconstruction of behaviour to demonstrate the working of police, forensic and medical investigations or scientific research. These may present as strong material as the wholly fictional dramas which pervade television. The drama-documentary might even be a cloak of investigation to justify sadistic or other extreme presentations, particularly when it forms a series whose linking theme appears to be merely the violence or sex itself rather than analogies of context, situation, ethics, personality, relationships, etc.

The drama-documentary adds to the confusion, not only because of the terminology, but by indicating an intervening category where the fiction is uppermost. Viewers are bewildered when in the cycle of fashion, typical of the competitive market economy of broadcasting, at the same period, or even in the same evening, one can have wholly fictional dramas, drama-documentaries, documentary drama and pure documentaries whose titles overlap and whose classification and content are not immediately apparent, and seem differentiated only by the relative proportion of reportage and fiction.

In late 1999 a number of programmes about sex in contemporary society in all these four categories were being shown in parallel on BBC, ITV and Channels 4 and 5 under such titles as *Sex in the City* and near variants. Can a theatre of violence be far behind?

Previously the IBA, in the late 1980s, seemed to take a fairly relaxed view about the portrayal of sex on television, believing that public concern was mainly a reaction to influential pressure group opinion, although there were perhaps fewer challenges in the industry to conventional norms. Interestingly Mrs Margaret Thatcher, as Prime Minister, took a considerable interest in the campaign, and, as already indicated above, persisted with the introduction of a Broadcasting Standards Council, showing that if there is sufficient political and personal will, there is a way. By 1999 with a growing number of programmes drawing complaint, the ITC rebuked the commercial channels for several lapses of taste. The portrayal of gay sex, in particular, was to be examined more carefully.[10]

Of course one has to admit that there are still limits on what is accepted and permitted on terrestrial television and cable in Britain. This does not mean that extreme material is unavailable. Access by satellite broadcasting direct to homes from other countries with different rules where the footprint reaches across our national frontiers, via public and private channels, by the Internet or video recordings, all tend to undermine the position of our own agencies for control. The latter two routes, possibly using illicit materials, are currently of incalculable size but may be substantial. A feeling of powerlessness should not, however, lead to inaction. If there is a practical will in a democratic state to discourage undesirable or dangerous material then the law should be enforced and regulators should be alert to their responsibilities, or the law can be changed. If the universality of evil is recognised, at least its prevalence may be diminished.

Many other side issues confuse the main question. The hoary old problem of distinguishing pornography and erotica is not the least of these. The generally accepted criteria tend to be based on the intention of the producer, the degree of exploitation of the actors, and on the profitability of the enterprise. Giving weight to each of these elements can rarely be based on agreement among the parties, even when it is possible to identify them. The extent of desire to view erotica is unfathomable and no survey method is likely to get adequate answers, while anthropological or psychoanalytic studies are themselves likely to be very intrusive and expensive. In addition, viewers themselves may not be fully aware of their own predilections and would almost certainly hesitate to reveal them.

Such indirect evidence as is available suggests that violence, and strong language rather than sexual behaviour, may give more offence, qualified by matters of timing, repetition or context. In another field it appears that hits on the Internet to sites with erotic material are among the most popular. One fears there may be an unsatisfied, even an unsatisfiable, demand for such material. Broadcast television may not continue to be the major influence in moulding public taste, but for the immediate future it can provide a reservoir or containment zone which sustains, or stimulates, further appetite.

What is evident is that there is a great, perhaps infinite, range of tastes and that overall this may fluctuate. Some might argue that this is a reflection and amplification of the Swinging Sixties cultural revolution, although this can hardly be an original cause. Further it may be argued that the widening of the breach, the increased flow and availability, taking the media as a whole, is self-generating and thus unstoppable. History surely tells us otherwise, that cultural development is not a once-for-all, nor a steady state, nor an irreversible phenomenon. The 1960s might yet prove to have been an aberration, rather than a milestone. But any liberalisation in the 1990s, while possibly one outcome of the market economy, must still yet be a short-term manifestation, and thus might more readily be changed now if the matter is carefully analysed, discussed and appropriate intervention follows.

What ought to be of equal concern in any examination of programming, is not only that material which might give offence, but also the extent to which opportunities for alternatives are missed. Not infrequently sex appears in television to be merely the act of copulation.

Some observers fear media representations of sex as a 'must have' social symbol.[11] Sexual congress may in real life be brief, if repetitive, but there is more to it than that. On television the process of seduction may often be shown as briefer than intercourse itself, whereas the interest, arousal, pursuit, speech and tactile interaction offer immense scope for dramatic representation. And does it always have to be so serious on the small screen? Malcolm Muggeridge once said, in a television interview, that the comic aspects of sex were underplayed on the screen. If it is true that erotic sex is largely about older rich men and impoverished young females, or the converse, gigolos with grandes dames, then here is scope for unlimited farce, as, indeed, M. Feydeau and others have demonstrated.

Farce might be the badly needed boost to situation comedy, without giving the slightest offence, as was demonstrated in the acclaimed *Rising Damp* series, which was originated by Yorkshire Television and repeated by the BBC. Laughter and ridicule have often been employed, in community development and empowerment, to challenge bureaucracy and exploitation, for example by Alinsky in Chicago, and thus now might be used to defuse sexual threat and obscenity. The psychoanalytic perspective of Freud is also pertinent.[12] There is a real danger to artistic freedom in that if television is too sanitised then it is restricted to the level of the most anodyne soap operas.

Why are the Brechtian drama intervention to break the spell of illusion in the theatre, or the classic Greek chorus to remind the audience of underlying issues and reality, not more commonly used in television drama? Is it really assumed that the home audience is more informed, or critically aware, than that in the public auditorium?

In terms of learning potential, why are not the personal and social costs of risky behaviour in sex as well as drink, drugs or violence given greater attention, within the drama and entertainment show? There need be no heavy moralistic diatribes but the consequences of certain conduct can be equally engaging and at the same time not threatening or off-putting. No thinking person is likely to regard a regime of unlimited hedonism as satisfying. Can there be a fable without a moral?

In the end excessive dependence on sexual titillation will likely prove self-defeating. Without novelty, it is surely boring.

Crime and violence

A curious ambivalence surrounds violence in society, and ultimately in broadcast television. Partly the duality arises from historic and cultural perspectives. On the one hand the profession of soldier is seen as representing strength and order, and as honourable too, for example, the notion of the just war. Some would argue that it may incorporate dishonourable acts, so-called overkill, scorched earth, sabotage, coercion, reprisal and torture, with euphemisms about pre-emptive strikes and conditional casualties, and the development of ever more hideous weapons. Fighting is also sometimes seen as part of a macho-culture, even a necessary process for young men. Stylised violence in boxing, fencing, wrestling or jousting can lead to acceptable injury, and even be encouraged as a manly sport, or now acceptable even for women. Domestic violence was until very recently regarded as a wholly private, even legitimate action. Child punishment is still in evolution.

Knockabout farce from Charlie Chaplin to *Monty Python's Flying Circus* has also given violence a cover of legitimacy. When linked with the who dunnit theme of crime detection, violence has become a vital ingredient of numerous television series. It also encompasses a wide range of expression, making regulation complicated. At one extreme the adrenalin-raising car chase, as in the popular *Starsky and Hutch* series, was a kind of motorised ballet in which few participants ever seemed to get hurt. At the other end of the scale torture and violent interpersonal thuggery of the criminal or inter-city underworld representations, can be stomach turning. But even though real or simulated agony is prohibited in all regulator guidelines, personal perceptions of pain or injury thresholds can differ enormously.

It is significant therefore that viewer anxiety about violence looms lower than sex and strong language in surveys, such as those of the BSC. Perhaps we are better protected or broadcasters more careful. Could it be, though, that viewers think there is more make-believe here than with sex? Or is it that there is greater tolerance of violence, real or implied, than might at first be expected? Perhaps, although it is disliked or feared, most people fortunately have little direct experience of violence in everyday life. If so, television drama is grossly misleading in its societal representation. It has been claimed that an American citizen could see on television thousands of homicides in a lifetime's viewing. Presumably British observations, given the volume of US imports, would be less, but still significant. Beatings seem uncounted but are supposedly no less traumatic. The true degree of distaste is difficult to assess, especially when the means of violence differ, for example according to whether fists, knives or guns are used. Studies are rarely replicated to discern trends.

Can it be that violence on television is often seen as rough justice, as happening more to baddies than the innocent? Crude analyses generally fail to recognise this distinction. Further, it might be argued that seeing violence is valuable in learning how to defend oneself in a violent world, in which case, greater explicitness would be useful, i.e. an inoculation theory of avoidance.

Violence is more characteristic of the young than the old, so presumably the latter have already learned to control violent tendencies, and not to copy or compete in their use. The main concern over televised violence is that it will be perceived as a model by children, which they will assimilate and later use themselves. Violence for children in cartoon series has aroused concern but their patent absurdity should hardly prove a danger except to the very young and impressionable.

The regulators are rightly vehement in maintaining the watershed hour to curb violence in programmes or harsh scenes in news. The difficulty nowadays is not so much network television, per se, as the laxity of parents in permitting late viewing by their charges, enabling access to unsuitable videos or failing to watch alongside their young so as to discuss problem themes with them. The matter may then become one of criminal responsibility, but although this has sometimes been suggested as a contributory factor in juvenile crime, for example in the Jamie Bulger case, the argument has not been proven as conclusive, although the risk is recognised.

Without greater intrusion into personal privacy and parental responsibility, only either a later watershed or a long-term educational process for both adults and children is likely to make a difference. It must be admitted however that neither seems likely to offer early redress. From the USA the public resistance to strengthening gun control laws is a salutary reminder of the inertial obstacles to cultural change. On the whole televised violence is of greater concern in North America, whose output will have been sifted before acceptance in Britain. It is probably Hollywood films which prove more difficult to reject for UK television, especially if they have already been classified as broadly acceptable by the BBFC.

Distorted perceptions of danger in society can be more serious than the hazard itself, if entirely inappropriate anxiety or behaviour ensue. The risk is as likely in factual programmes as fiction. The BBC *Crimewatch* series, with very high ratings over a decade, in which viewers are invited to assist police to identify suspects but which includes dramatic reconstruction of, usually more serious, offences, has to be accompanied by reassuring announcements that most of the crimes being shown, are rather uncommon; so the risks to each individual viewer are minuscule.

Whether programmes containing violence of the purely fictional type have increased fear and anxiety among the public generally is unknown. In the USA the prevalence of the owning, carrying and especially use of guns is regarded as a national disaster by many, but a necessary insurance. Carrying knives and other weapons, disabling sprays, alarms and other house protection have all increased in Britain in the 1990s when crime, recorded or reported in surveys, appears to have fallen.[13] So perceptions, to which the media contribute, may be more important than reality.

Guidelines and codes

Bridging the gap between producers' and viewers' expectations poses immense challenges. The audience is not a homogeneous aggregate but broadcasters will have a typical or average viewer in mind whom they target. This will still possibly leave large minorities on either side whose knowledge, wishes or understanding do not enable them to gain adequate satisfaction from a programme. Whatever guidance is given, producers must make significant assumptions, as the following extracts show. For example on violence in adult drama, the BBC has said,

> Programme makers should ask whether the violent incident and detail shown is essential to the story or whether it has been included simply for its own sake. The use of violence should never be gratuitous. The degree and type of violence, and the detail which can be shown, depend upon context. Audiences may enjoy a good deal of violence in action-packed thrillers, but expect its nature and style to be as far removed from reality as the story. Serious drama demands more of the audience who may respect the challenge of a violent or distressing scene if they are convinced of its dramatic purpose. . . .[14]

Among the observations on violence in the ITC *Programme Code* are included the following.

> Conflict is of the essence of drama, and conflict often leads to violence. . . . The real world contains much violence in many forms, and when television seeks to reflect the world – in fact or in fiction – it

would be unrealistic and untrue to ignore its violent aspects. On the other hand, the portrayal of violence, whether physical, verbal or psychological, is an area of public concern. . . . There is no evidence that the portrayal of violence for good or 'legitimate' ends is likely to be less harmful to the individual, or to society, than the portrayal of violence for evil ends. . . . There is no evidence that 'sanitised' or 'conventional' violence, in which the consequences are concealed, minimised or presented in a ritualistic way, is innocuous. It may be just as dangerous to society to conceal the results of violence or to minimise them as to let people see or hear clearly the full conse-quences of violent behaviour, however gruesome: what may be better for society may be emotionally more upsetting or more offen-sive for the individual viewer.[15]

No reasonable person could take exception to these strictures, but they assume a proximity of view and familiarity of producer and viewer which is almost impossible to achieve in any form of distance commu-nication. Can it be argued that with larger and more remote enterprises the gap has diminished? In what way can this be overcome?

On violence in television, although there can be a broad continuum from acceptability to rejection, the issue is often more clear-cut because it is seen as more a measure of quantity, of how much, how often, how much is shown or implied and with what degree of effect. Nevertheless the mental and physical impact must be distinguished for analysis and to establish how long-lasting is the consequence. Some would regard damage to either persons, animals or property differently. Finally the extent of premeditation and preparation, and the recklessness, satisfac-tion, awareness or distancing by the perpetrator also feature. The latter characteristics are more problematic to judge but nevertheless such judgements are often made by viewers.

Violence generates recurrent concern, especially about abrupt intro-ductions of such elements, immediately after the 9 p.m. watershed. Bad language was more widely objected to by viewers in IBA commis-sioned research. The Authority itself was critical of gratuitous violence, but also found that viewers were not unaware that such unnecessary elaboration was being fed to them. On this basis a tightening of the regulations did not seem out of step with public opinion. Whether such admonitions have had a permanent effect is another question, since the pressure to build audiences has become more acute.

Would producers willingly set out the primary considerations of objective, reason and context for their programmes? Clearly in most programming there is no need for a note spelling out 'This is a fable.' But viewers often wish to know afterwards what is the moral of a story, or what might be learned from such an account. There is no need to put all writers and directors on trial, but many are only names to the viewer. Are the creative workers really like the proverbially inarticulate artist? Why cannot more programmes be followed, or preceded, by explanation or discussion, with phone-in enquiries. Rarely do films automatically have a duration equal to the half-hour unit of schedules. A 10- or 15-minute supplement might be very welcome. There is a common interest in having an aware and alert audience to sustain and raise standards. It is more serious that viewers should be regarded as passive clay in the area of exploitation programmes than in any run of the mill television fodder. One would have thought that to be confronted by an active, alert and articulate audience would be an interesting challenge to broadcasters. The 1999 BBC2 programme *The Viewing Room* brought producers and viewers together in some lively dialogues, but as a very short series it may have been regarded only as an experiment.

Mystery and the occult

While sex and violence may demonstrate the poles of what is objectionable there are other minor genres which also require examination. These again raise questions of the psychological effect in the field of horror, mystery and degradation. With such subjects the need for subsequent explanation may be even more important, but there may be little information in programme guides, which television reviewers are also rarely able to supply. Physical violence is not the only form of harm. Psychological damage equally might result from fear, perceptions of threat, even a failure to precede a programme by a relevant explanation or putting in context.

Many producers do take their responsibilities seriously. Private gatherings such as the 1997 ITC-supported study meeting on *Violence on Television in Britain* at Sheffield University and the BBC Governors' 1994 Seminar on *Reporting Violence and Crime* are significant illustrations of ongoing concern.[16] They often underline the need for further research and sustained care, but such events are probably unknown to the general public. Surely a programme about such deliberations, with clips from examples broadcast, could be informative and of wide interest to intelligent viewers. Does the industry prefer not to be seen as nannying or uncertain, when everyone knows that there are complex issues to be faced. Many viewers, particularly parents, care about these issues. It would be sensible for the broadcasters to take them into their confidence, and to build an alliance with viewers whose purpose would be to encourage quality in television.

Very rarely, however, do directors and producers publicly criticise colleagues for serious lapses in taste or quality. Academics are on occasion accused of closing their ranks to protect professional immunity, from criticism or breaching their own standards of self-management. It is no less serious that those in the communications media fail to expose derelictions by their peers. To some extent the Press Complaints Commission, with its preponderant newspaper membership, exercises some curbing influence in the press. The professional bodies for broadcasting such as the Royal Television Society and the British Academy of Film and Television Arts have yet to develop such adult attitudes to their work (see Chapters 10 and 11).

As yet there is nothing comparable in Britain to the American reverse Oscar awards for bad productions. Perhaps the media student organisations, or other consumer bodies, might have the temerity to do something similar in Britain, a sort of anti-BAFTA. The Campaign for Clear English has indicated a path, and is now regarded as a serious and positive action for better standards, rather than sensation seeking.

Most broadcasters, like their audiences, are probably moderate sensible people. They neither seek nor pursue extremism but are content to work within clear and reasonable guidelines. The effective regulatory authorities such as the BBC and the ITC afford them an element of protection. The alternative is to face jeopardy in the courts. Damages *post hoc* might prove considerable. Not many individual producers would risk their principles for subsequent penury, or heavy penalties for their corporate businesses.

It is said we all like a good ghost story, especially at Christmas after supper with friends and family around. For children it can be a memorable and harmless introduction to the supernatural, safely inoculated by the comfort and security of their own homes. Television with its partial suspense of reality might be a suitable vehicle for such programmes but the effects are not so predictable. Older readers may recall the 1940s *Appointment with Fear* BBC radio series where half an hour of speech and appropriate pauses could create hair-raising imagination. Was it surprising that a television revival in more recent years was much less successful? Valentine Dyall's gravelly voice in the earlier radio series may have been an important ingredient in success but paradoxically television, despite the added dimension of vision, may have its limitations in regard to imaginative stimulus, which only the most talented producers have yet overcome.

Perhaps nowadays viewers have become so accustomed to a constantly moving image that other facilities are weakened (although this assertion is somewhat speculative). But other mystery programmes have succeeded on television, most perhaps more as single presentations, because like discovering the magician's method, once revealed, repetition and serial presentation undermine the essence. Given the possible unpredictable effects, it seems important that audience testing might be a more common preliminary. In a comparable field the use of hypnotism is restricted in the theatre, and prohibited in cinema and television, where the viewers could become the subjects. Other states of consciousness can be achieved by suggestion. Viewers should feel assured that all precautions are taken in what are ostensibly entertainment programmes, that viewers themselves do not become the victims.

The mystery genre has itself become blurred in the late 1990s by the use of an apparently investigative format, rather than as a tall tale. The series, *Mysteries*, illustrates the ambiguity. It was presented by Ms Carol Vorderman, who has excellent academic qualifications and is thus likely to have considerable influence on the content of the programmes. Nonetheless some cases included are far-fetched and certainly untrue. Others have a degree of plausibility, and since the presenter wishes to be regarded as a scientist, belief in the supernatural may, quite inaccurately, be promoted. Coincidence of certain unrelated events is often a likely explanation but, if there is a failure to indicate, for example, the statistical probabilities to the viewer, the effect may be to increase confusion and ignorance. When presented as a documentary-type programme it represents a form of negative education, at odds with the ethos of television as a learning experience.

Evidently there is a variety of risks in dealing with the supernatural or bizarre. While mystery and uncertainty are to some extent valuable ingredients in storytelling, care has to be taken in distinguishing fact from fiction. Whether it concerns fables for children or sophisticated tales of espionage and the currently inexplicable, care has to be taken not to add to fears or irrational responses by viewers. In general such programmes encourage an anti-scientific or superstitious attitude which is hardly appropriate to an age of technological progress. The repeated showing of accounts of the so-called Roswell incident, the alleged landing of beings from outer space in Texas in 1947, and of the Bermuda Triangle, an area of sea where ships and aircraft have coincidentally disappeared or had their navigation affected, should not be promoted by responsible public authorities. They have repeatedly led to planes and ships being redirected by credulous travellers.

There is a fine tradition of tall tales from the Greek myths, via the tales of Baron Munchausen to Jonathan Swift's *Gulliver's Travels*. But these are set in a context of time and space which do not now make them threatening. Certain tabloid newspapers offer frequent fare of mysterious disappearances, or new arrivals on the moon which are really too bizarre, except for the comic pages. Such manifestations may be more prevalent at times of stress such as war or economic upheaval. The rapid growth of certain political movements and religious millenarian cults in the United States in the 1930s slump, or in the Pacific Islands, in Central Africa in recent decades, as well as in Japan and the United States again in the 1990s, show that these perturbations are not confined to history nor to poor countries with low educational standards.

In television schedules mystery programmes can be buried in increasingly complex schedules, with titles which may confuse rather than clarify and at hours or juxtapositions which do not alert the audience to potentially risky implications.

Confession and degradation

A less obvious television format, which conceals potentially serious misunderstanding or harm, are the so-called 'confessional' programmes, when ill-doers and those they may have hurt are brought into confrontation. On the face of it such programmes might be considered a public service. After all, what could be better for all of us than to have dishonesty exposed and morality upheld? However, a more appropriate term may be 'degradation' programmes, because they also sometimes expose victims, as well as the alleged perpetrators of knavery to opprobrium. In the USA continued confrontations of this kind not infrequently have led to studio violence, sometimes abetted by producers, and in one case even subsequent murder by one victim of another. Curiously in Britain they have sometimes been transmitted at tea time, in what used to be described as the children's hour, when parents are busy preparing a meal but children watch. Even if placed on alternative channels, that is no hindrance to expert child-zappers. It is naive to regard such programmes as victimless. Even self-harming deserves pity, not derision, from incompletely informed viewers, quite apart from provoked heckling by studio audiences.

It has been revealed that we are not free of such abuses in Britain. The unfortunate case of Miss Vanessa Feltz in the 1999 BBC series, *The*

Vanessa Show, which should have ensured competent direction and adequate research support, demonstrated that such programmes with their ingredients of boast, bravado and shame, lend themselves readily to fabrication and outright deception. In this case, inadequate or undersupervised programme research, permitted misrepresentation and falsehood by the participants, leading to serious discredit and the ending of the series. If broadcasters think what they are doing is important, that it has consequences which may be good or bad but often uncertain in degree, then they should not rely on the doctrine of 'caveat emptor' (let the buyer beware). The broadcasters have their own responsibility which includes informative labelling, more caution in programme promotion and timing, and the willingness to encourage critical review and responses from ordinary viewers, as well as professional sceptics.

A major consideration in the whole field of extreme programmes must be the nature of the audience, even more than the craft and imagination of the creators. Clearly some persons are more suggestible than others. Children obviously are a prime category here, because storytelling is so compelling for them. Stories, however, do not only consist of listening to tales from nursery books but also derive from drama, reports, pictures and other observations. Teenagers are also vulnerable because of the profound and potentially disturbing challenges which surround them and contribute to foolhardy bravado and experiment, or withdrawal from the reality of the normal world. Mass media, with television, computers and virtual reality animation, are particularly attractive to them and media convergence may have powerful and unpredictable, possibly deleterious, outcomes. Are the potentially stimulating and liberating influences always more important than possible detriment? If dangerous elements can be aroused from just below the surface, the process of scapegoating those perceived to be threatening can arouse fearsome racist or other atavistic forces in society. This is only too evident at the present time, from the example of the murder of Stephen Lawrence in Lewisham, London, in 1993 to the large-scale massacres and pillage in the 1990s in Bosnia, Rwanda, Kosovo and East Timor.

Fortunately most people can take some element of uncertainty, chance and danger for granted and come through unscathed. Sadly a minority are vulnerable, particularly if they build on unfortunate earlier life experiences. One wonders how many psychopathic or paedophile incidents there have to be to bring about a more cautious approach to such matters in broadcasting. If broadcasters wish to be protected from sudden moral panics in reaction to their coverage of matters like paedophile cases, the Sheffield football ground tragedy and the Moors murders, they might be more wise to ensure a more cautious programme policy. This might mean fewer but more expensive productions. The immensely popular Bond entertainment films depend on polished and indeed highly stylised action, often very violent but almost as predictable as a Laurel and Hardy comedy, and thus paradoxically undisturbing. By comparison much television has a low production value. Clearly extremism, popularity, effect and cost must be coordinated. Adequate research support and the provision of context do not come cheaply.

Pathways to the future

Education should be part of an alternative approach to public protection from the hazards of television. By more discriminating programme selection and assertion of their interests, viewers are themselves empowered. But education is a long-term process, and unfortunately can be subverted. Desirably it should be a continuous learning adventure to which television could make a massive contribution. Can we assume on present evidence that broadcasters wish to be on the side of the good as well as the great in this adventure?

Some key questions remain.

1. *What are the public expectations of the sex and violence elements in programmes and what have been their outcomes?*
Viewers do not come before their sets with quotas of programmes to be provided except perhaps those (few) with highly specialised interests. Mainstream schedules, in order to gain reasonably sized audiences, need to offer a diversified programme, with modest proportions of repeats or familiars, so that viewers do not become satiated, nor disturbed by too much novelty, challenge or difficulty. Minority or specialised programmes can provide choice and exploration. While this may read like nostalgia for the regulated competition of the 1950s to 1980s, viewers knew where they were, there was not such predictability as to become boring, genres were more apparent so choice was facilitated, and the rivalry between public and commercial broadcasters within accepted quality parameters stimulated a critical awareness. There was less material of the extreme programmes discussed here, but occasionally more violence or sex, etc. appeared in drama programmes, which because of their infrequency generated more informed debate

about standards than is often the case nowadays, so reinforcing a critical stance and sense of empowerment among the audience, and a debate with broadcasters in which all could join. So far as is known there has never been a significant articulate demand by viewers for more sex, crime and violence. While, of course, it is often easier to defend the status quo, in fact the increase in producer-dominated awards like those of the Royal Television Society and BAFTA (which sometimes seem like mutual backslapping rather than critical evaluation) and the limited, or declining, use of audience appreciation indexes for programme evaluation and planning have changed the balance of power somewhat away from viewers towards the industry, their accountants and, ultimately, the advertisers who hold the purse strings. The audience pressure groups and standards bodies have tried to redress the balance, but along the way the fewer major commissions of inquiry no longer provide the measure of public consultation which was previously seen as requisite. The feeling of revulsion which however arises when television is alleged to have been an influence in some horrific crime, demonstrates that all is not well. The possibility of corralling extreme programmes, on to cable channels, while apparently confining them to some pool of infamy, would however be one means of regulating the dissemination of such material, with easier monitoring if that were desired.

2.   *What trends, if any, are there in presentation of such material on television?*

It is evident that reliable information is unavailable both long term and in detail. Quantitative measures of violent or sexual acts fail to do justice to context, artistic quality or effect. However, the ITC and Broadcasting Standards Commission reports indicate a measure of unease that portrayals do not coincide with public taste. Reductions in both quantity and degree do not seem likely to generate substantial public hostility. If there is a will towards greater moderation, then more monitoring and assessment should be provided so that any intervention can be effectively targeted.

3.   *Can we measure effects on individual or collective behaviour, and on society, and what are they?*

Much time and research effort have been directed at defining and measuring possible harm from extreme television programmes, as was earlier the case with films. Unfortunately, mainly due to the complexities of research, direct effects seem only to be modest despite common public perceptions otherwise. The findings are also often subject to substantial margins of error, or are applicable only to certain groups in particular circumstances, such as Noble's work on the behaviour of adolescent boys, who might from previous non-television experience already show signs of disturbance, and this predisposition may be magnified by chosen programmes, as further research has confirmed.[17] Desegregating television from other influences has also proved near impossible. To go from the individual level, to that of society as a whole, further compounds the problem. It is evident that we are on a moving platform as standards of acceptability change, and historical comparisons may seem irrelevant. But such an argument either accepts some autonomous determinism or that little is wrong, and merely emphasises apparent powerlessness. There must be room for alternative patterns of provision and oversight, which it is incumbent as a democratic society to explore, and not once-for-all, but repeatedly with each generation. A deliberate policy choice could lead to more useful monitoring enabling cause and effect to be better determined.

4. *How does provision of extreme programmes relate to other influences in society such as changes in moral values and tastes, in other media and through financial, market or organisational factors?*
Essentially this question relates to whether television merely reflects or follows other influences or has a determining influence itself. Both processes operate, but to different degrees in varied circumstances. And broadcasters do have some power and influence, from the contributions of individual writers and choices by schedulers, producers and top executives. The point is that the factors interact and with regulation now undertaken with a light hand, the autonomy of apparently impersonal market forces is enhanced. But the decisions made by those agencies are in fact made by individual financiers, advertisers and managers. Their responsibility should also be made transparent.

5. *What losses or gains would there be, if more stringent rules applied about extreme programmes for viewers, broadcasters, performers, writers, regulators or institutions?*
Any changes in practice will mean adaptation, so in the short run there will be a period of adjustment and exploration. Viewers might find that some of the more violent or bizarre material will be less readily available. For the creative personnel it will no doubt be argued that their aspirations and endeavours will be restricted but this is their vocation and it is unlikely that their freedom will be grossly restricted,

if full debate takes place in advance of what should be done. The regulators and institutions will no doubt feel they have an additional and
controversial burden, imposed by legislation. Remarkably perhaps they
survived the halcyon days of times past! Single programmes from the
Granada Television documentary series *World in Action* or the BBC *Play
of the Week* often generated much controversy. Such healthy debate
seems much rarer now. The broadcasters and schedulers may still find
the constraints onerous but there is no reason to believe that advertisers have a vested interest in violence, even if gunmakers do. So there
should be no direct financial pressures holding back change. In fact
spot advertisers often require that the products promoted should not
be placed with possibly offensive programmes.

   On balance, then, potential losses appear minimal whereas the likely
gains could be substantial. Viewers may find more predictability in the
schedules and many will avoid bruising conflicts with their children
about suitable viewing. The regulators and institutions should have
firmer consensual grounds on which to operate. The writers, performers and directors will find new challenges and perhaps run less risk of
the stereotyping and ghettoisation which previously tempted them
into so-called exploitation materials. In financing there may be less
likelihood of pressure from resourcers who have a divergent agenda
from television as a public service.

6. *If more intervention is pursued, what would be most acceptable and
    effective?*

A major problem in broadcasting reform, as in other areas of public
affairs, is that if there is too much too often, it is often less effective, as
succeeding governments like to tinker. Paradoxically the coming of the
market economy, while ostensibly replacing socio-political judgements
by impersonal, impartial forces, has generated more frequent changes,
and so-called fine tuning has become more necessary than in earlier
times. Therefore a more consistent policy following wide debate, not
perhaps guided by politicians or moral entrepreneurs and certainly not
in detail, should be pursued. A single regulating body, more independent and self-financing, could be established with long-term actions
such as an annual *post hoc* review or yearly production plan examination, rather than daily intervention. Given the interactive and multi-
faceted nature of broadcasting, there may be an example in the
National Drug Coordinator's office where all the interests can be
brought together. Longer time-series monitoring could be supple-
mented with, say, decennial major commissions of inquiry. While this

may seem to create inordinate delay and potential procrastination because of the speed of technological development and possible international marketing opportunities, perhaps this assumption could be challenged by asking in whose interest is the technological and multimedia hype promoted, and has it not often led to the introduction of new, duplicate equipment with trivial enhancements, before adequate evaluation of consumer preferences has been shown.

8
Minority Programmes: a Major Problem

Specialised programmes inevitably raise challenging questions. In economic terms they will always be vulnerable because the audiences they attract may be insufficient to earn the support of advertisers in the commercial sector. In the public service or non-profit arena they may still be insecure, because audiences have to be found to obtain public support and, even to many professionals to justify time, talent and resources devoted to them despite individual broadcasts having substantial social value.

In the later 1990s a more serious criticism has become public, particularly among media professionals but echoed by the intellectual community, and especially over factual programming. The term 'dumbing down' is used to describe a process of trivialisation of programme content, cheapening, and simplifying materials for easy digestion. Of course the pursuit of market goals, for economy and profit maximisation, has resulted in seeking the largest audience which means drawing more of the less affluent and less educated, where sheer numbers will balance out their restricted purchasing power for the advertisers.

These viewers are often less discriminating than many who would make specialised programmes their first choice. Attention is drawn elsewhere to the regulator's concerns about the recent emphasis on sex-related themes of doubtful merit, but some of the most cogent criticism has come from leading practitioners. News, current affairs and discussion programmes are frequently considered to be in the front line of risk. John Humphrys, a leading BBC newscaster and interviewer, looks back on an extended process of softening in his field in the handling of politicians and political issues.[1]

On a different tack, an overwhelming majority of television production personnel in a longitudinal survey conducted in 1994–99 by the British Film Institute (BFI), no less than 70 per cent, felt that the quality of output had fallen generally. Although comment suggested that leaner budgeting was a crucial factor, more than half of those surveyed felt ethical standards had declined.[2]

The Campaign for Quality Television, a pressure group which has links with industry professionals, academics and other concerned viewers, had earlier expressed its criticism of weakened standards, especially in the provision of documentary programmes. Such opinions relate to both the BBC and the commercial sector. They reveal the 1990s to have brought a more critical reception to television than was typical of the acquiescence of most viewers in earlier times, when regulation was more proactive and applied at the pre-production stage, than at the millennium.

Specialised programmes are also likely to arouse debate because they often tend to approach the boundaries of intellectual difficulty, aesthetic taste or moral values. They may not necessarily be trying to subvert such standards, but will certainly attract creative minds among producers who are interested in new, difficult or sensitive areas and who might wish to push back the frontiers of conventional thinking. Some programmes may also have a dangerous attraction to easily influenced minds or to adherents of the esoteric who have obsessive liking for revolutionary, violent or antisocial materials to the harm of themselves or others. For example, programmes on crime or police work have been suggested as ways in which criminals can hone their skills.

However, specialised programmes are not by any means inherently risky. Broadcasts aimed at some categories of the audience, with physical or mental handicap, can offer benefits in ways which no other medium might equal or cost. Similarly many people have been introduced to minority sports, new ideas or unfamiliar skills which they might never otherwise have experienced. So a certain element of marginality in balancing schedules, and pioneering new developments is a more fundamental feature of narrowly focused programmes.

Nevertheless if television broadcasting is an expensive medium in its claim on national resources, and therefore more appropriate for mass communication, then niche programmes each have to justify their place instead of being distributed in other ways, e.g. radio, cinema, video or by computer.

The term 'minority' itself justifies some examination. At first sight it might appear that the main question here is about programmes that can only ever appeal to select fractions of the citizenry. However, everyone is likely to be in a numerical minority on some matter. Equally important is that a variety of topics will have interest for a typical viewer. Indeed it is unimaginable that any viewer could tolerate a diet solely of a single genre, even though he or she might use television primarily to satisfy one specific interest, and the appetite will wax and wane.

Some programmes can only be a minority provision even if they were to attract most of the potential audience on specific occasions. For example, taking a broadcast camera for live television from a space link-up is inordinately expensive and unlikely to be everyday fare.

In reality therefore the issue is about specialised programming rather than minority programming per se. However, minority provision is what is commonly recognised terminology, and probably in almost all circumstances programmes will only ever be viewed by less than the majority of viewers. Nevertheless their treatment may be of interest to all viewers at some time, since it is unimaginable that anyone can never be in that situation.

Obviously some genres will only be of minority interest, but the definition does not rest on subject alone. As argued above, some programmes will not be delivered for reasons of cost and would therefore only be provided rarely, like opera, even if they were enjoyed in repeat showings. Others could attract few viewers not because of subject but by reasons of treatment or style. One can have complicated quiz and game shows, or harrowing treatment of crime, adventure or human disability which discourage the majority of viewers.

Apart from the director's style, the specialised programme can also have a distinctive format. For example, the treatment of factual programmes can be overtly didactic rather than informal or participative. Or one can have heavy dependence on talking heads rather than graphic illustrations. The use of cartoons, while a specialism in itself, tends to be uncommon in the documentary genre. Perhaps most often the minority–majority boundary is a social division of the audience, with the highly prized (for advertisers) quarry of the ABC1 middle- and upper-class high spenders as the determining factor. But today's minority programme may, tomorrow, attract a substantial audience, depending on the steady cultivation of a majority interest, or a move to a peak or near-peak time scheduling.

For convenience and because minority programming is a common descriptive convention, that term is used in the exposition but it must be remembered that it can encompass much diversity, and even on occasion reach most of the public, such as the Princess Diana interview or, with repeats, the David Attenborough *Life on Earth* and related series.

Arts programmes

Arts programmes well illustrate the definition problem because they are such a heterogeneous aggregate. Opera, because of its production and broadcasting costs, is perceived as the epitome. Only a minority of the adult population have ever had direct experience of a live performance, partly because it is in large measure a London metropolitan phenomenon. A minute fraction of citizens will ever see a particular performance, or even attend in a whole season. On the other hand, and the same applies to ballet, a single television broadcast can reach more people than may ever, in this country, have seen that portrayal live. The same has been said of our William Shakespeare, and it certainly applies to individual plays of his.

A fine production may have a profound effect on some members of the audience, particularly if the portrayal of a particular role, or performance or presentation is a highly emotional one. So Laurence Olivier, Margot Fonteyn, Rudolf Nureyev, Jacqueline du Pré, Damien Hirst or Pablo Picasso and of course many other actors and artists have become household names. Such acclaim may not have been solely for their presentation of classical roles, traditional styles or works, but because their performance in them marked a new development or arose in particular circumstances.

Music is not the easiest art form to present on the small screen but linking some exposition, with close-ups, and novel settings as with the *Viennese New Year* concerts, or the *Three Tenors*, demonstrate what can be achieved. Pop music, with its elements of music and posture, has brought an entirely new presentational format, successfully exploited by MTV. Performing arts extend beyond traditional forms. Ice skating, ballroom dancing, diverse musical genres, painting and sculpture have all benefited and been developed through television broadcasts, reaching the less mobile, the poor and the distantly located and no doubt, occasionally, even the philistine viewer who by chance has joined the aficionados.

The exciting technical potential of the moving image to focus, provide close-up, magnify, or juxtapose detail and contrast has inspired creative artistry and direction, viz. on the works and lives of musicians by Ken Russell, although familiarity can diminish the effect as the audience becomes more sophisticated. While it can be argued that video can provide similar experiences there will be something about a live performance, or even a recording of that performance, seen in a broadcast that creates a feeling, illusory though it may be, for every viewer to feel part of the scene. Surely the televising of the *Last Night of the Proms* can be almost as exciting as being at the concert itself. Even the applause at the end of such an event can have a cathartic effect for the viewer, which an edited cassette or disk might erase.

One matter of particular concern has been the rise and fall of the single play on television. The BBC's *Cathy Come Home* is often quoted as a major social document, and a highly praised performance by the actors, and even a paradigm shift in political awareness. It has been several times replayed, to renewed critical acclaim and high audience appreciation, but the format seems nowadays to have fallen victim to the drama series. The reason for this has nothing to do with artistic endeavour or potential audience attention, but rather of market forces which emphasise short-term financing and the need to recoup or cover production costs through the economics of repertory-style ensembles, with safe and previously proven successful formulas or performers. Although the single play is not the only dramatic form, the light touch of contemporary regulation has now submerged it within the serial format, characteristic of generalist services. These are team productions to which new writers may find access difficult. Perhaps browbeaten, the ITC as a regulator merely requires Channel 5, which claims to be an aspiring national channel, to produce 12 hours of original drama per year.[3]

A crucial difficulty, arising in every subject genre but particularly acute in the arts, is where are taste and style boundaries to be drawn? People's tastes overlap. The arts are not pigeon holes but interlinked and symbiotic. The programme creators influence one another and they share the broadcast technology. Highbrow and lowbrow only have meaning towards the extremes, and many people will have a moderate interest in several genres in the middle range. There is a case for more material which offers a progression between levels and across genres.

Geography, history and heritage

In contrast to the arts, history has in some ways proved more difficult to portray. If there is heavy dependence on written materials it is difficult to make poring over texts, or sitting in a library or at a computer screen, interesting enough for the dynamic appetite of the movie camera. If, however, use is made of the burgeoning growth of film archives and photographic images then history can be brought to life. The classic examples of this were the BBC's *World War I* and Granada's *World War II* series, and a further renewal of several similar offerings in 1999. Today there is film stock, at least covering the last century, of many great events, to inaugurate the new millennium. Certainly there will be no lack of source material in future. Reconstructions of earlier events such as famous trials, revolutions, political campaigns can fill the void, although care has to be taken if it results in revisions which only falsify. Current controversies over Holocaust programmes reveal what difficulties such endeavours can provoke. Nevertheless they also facilitate an understanding of the possible divergence of fact and interpretation which can enhance historical sophistication. Equally significant can be the contribution to diminish national and racial antipathies at a time of political change as in Europe in present times. Carefully made extracts can be of great value, although it can be argued that dramatised fiction is a more attractive and honest alternative for the creative television entrepreneur. In the future one may also expect oral history to be used more as a source for programmes where older citizens can be interviewed or discuss experiences relevant to viewers.

Geography has proven to have great television potential by illustrating landscape, geological processes or travel. Even holiday programmes can, or more often could, have their place here providing environmental context. Most relevantly such programmes can take the armchair viewers to locations they would never visit, or demonstrate associations previously unimagined. The use and nature of maps might, however, be given a more prominent place since many viewers may have only limited conceptions of direction, distance and space.

Some programmes in this genre also effectively exploit the time-constrained and competitive excitement when they are based around a task where a group must reach a target destination. Libraries have commented favourably on the incentive of encouraging book, guide and map use which demonstrates the importance of using various resources to achieve the goal set.

A strikingly successful minority genre on television is archaeology, almost unexpected in view of its complex subject base. It has opened access and generated awareness of the physical and social elements of this field, reinforcing the current widespread interest in identifying the roots of modern society. Skilful use of an investigative approach in several series to problems posed, engages the viewer in a process of exploration and discovery leading often to a resolution within the space of a single programme. But equally frequently producers reveal that the difficulties of handling limited, obscure and confusing evidence mean that no complete answer is possible. This is an important learning experience for viewers that scientific discovery is painstaking, frequently frustrating and often generates more questions than answers.

Sometimes by placing the programme in a context of limited opportunity such as Channel 4's *Time Team* with a three-day time schedule, viewers perceive the tension, uncertainty and excitement of working against the clock. The lively group and interdisciplinary effort of science, rather than the persistent image of the eccentric solitary boffin in his laboratory, is also well demonstrated in this type of programme.

Substantial evidence from the past decades has shown that well-constructed programmes of this kind, as well as broadcasts of drama, often lead to substantial borrowings from public libraries as well as purchases from bookshops, which gives real meaning to convergence of multimedia communication.[4]

Minorities in the media

In the present day of instant universal communication there is a constant reminder that we live in a multinational world, in which European or North Atlantic culture and power are not universally supreme. At home, however, the fact is often ignored, or perhaps sometimes deliberately avoided, that we live in a multicultural society. Every large city is now cosmopolitan and all citizens, not merely country folk, need to be reminded and reassured about this. Racism is widespread, often conscious and, even when unconscious, pernicious in its institutional, social and personal effect.

Several studies have shown the under-representation of minority ethnic persons in the media, including both television workers and in portrayals in broadcasts, where television and film have a crucial part to play, but especially in actual and perceived positions of authority. Too often where black, Asian or other minority citizens are shown, they appear with menial status, or as the errant or less capable, or successful largely in sport or entertainment. While there are minority individuals who are prominent in all these roles, they give an incomplete picture, reinforcing white majority opinions that they are a social intrusion, temporary residents and uncommitted to mainstream values.

In addition those portrayed are too often seen in problem and conflict situations, raising emotions about hostility and divergence. Such contexts polarise rather than unite the viewers. Television has a particularly heavy responsibility in helping to integrate society rather than, however unintentionally, fragmenting and undermining it. Can there not be more accounts of integration, success in education, business, achievement, intermarriage, the services or law abiding for these minorities? There is surely a remarkable contribution, which the diversity and mixing of cultures and the genepool from immigration have achieved. Why is not the even earlier Celtic, Saxon, Norse, Norman and Flemish incomers' heritage much celebrated on the small screen? Many individuals take enormous pride in such origins. Collectively they are of profound importance since they probably apply to almost everybody.

One may speculate whether Britain is yet ready for a *Roots* series, or the Sidney Poitier detective role in *The Heat of the Night* film, where the incompetence of the American Southern white constabulary was exposed. In this respect UK television lags rather far behind Hollywood. If it is argued that there is not to hand the readily available resources or material, then there is urgent need to train and prepare rather than have some social engineering quotas imposed. It is not a good argument to say that there have been some successful minority programmes with ethnic minority representation, such as *Goodness Gracious Me* or *Desmond's*, which almost implies segregated provision or tokenism. The shared heritage, the riches of diversity and contrast, of being aware what it is to be a minority, the positive recognition that we all in a sense have coloured skins, including tanned or pink, with much in common, ought also to be promoted and celebrated, in which we can jointly show respect and rejoice.

Over the years various other groups have felt under- or unfairly represented in the media, particularly television. Women have been notably outspoken on this issue, more perhaps through playing subordinate roles in drama, but equally important, being often what appears to be the token woman in discussion programmes. Some notable exceptions are performances as newscasters or weather presenters. However, front figures may conceal underlying ambiguity. One is reminded of the deprecatory term, coined in France, of 'speakerines', to describe attractive presenters reading scripts prepared by men.

Some would argue that, in the past, this merely reflected an inferior status in society. Others, advancing a more demanding feminist viewpoint, have been critical that television, being such a popular medium, had a particular obligation to show that this was changing, and indeed, should act as a catalyst. Such political claims are highly uncomfortable to broadcasters, who may have felt that television is essentially about entertainment, especially in, say, soap operas focused on character and micro-worlds. Redressing some perceived devaluation of women has been achieved in recent years by changes in the composition of the broadcasting workforce.

Other groups, also feeling disadvantaged, have brought their concerns to the surface. The elderly, and persons with physical or mental handicap, have become more articulate about their limited visibility. Numerically they are not insignificant, but their self-image and worth are an important component of their claim, particularly as they contribute, by tax, licence fee or paying for advertised foods and services, to the cost of programmes, As in other examples, some dramatic roles may be more difficult for them to play, although this can be exaggerated, but there are other contexts, discussion groups, documentary, travel or quiz programmes which can give them recognition. Indeed, it can reasonably be claimed that, in recompense for their life adversities, they should be given some preference, as already happens in employment legislation. There is always a danger that television, seeking to please or not disturb, by ignoring a reality of everyday life for numerous families, can magnify injustice.

The BBC series, *One Foot in the Grave*, demonstrated that there might be hitherto unexplored potential in programmes dealing with life beyond retirement. Exploiting such avenues can become fashionable, as the arrival of other similar programmes revealed, but if overdue, any benefit is diminished. Here the importance needs to be accepted of a long-term balanced strategy, taking more account of the depth and diversity of human experience, which cuts across all genres.

Science, medicine and health

Science programmes seem almost to embody the essence of television, where demonstrations can exploit the visual element. While natural phenomena such as storms, avalanches, tidal waves, volcanoes or cosmological events can be shown, and their effects illustrated and described, their scale really overwhelms the small screen. But most scientific endeavour is in the laboratory, with repetitive experiment, mechanical processes, or microscopic study by individuals. Sadly, because of poor standards of numeracy and limited awareness of scientific method among the public at large, the approach in broadcasts may often be thought to require a more didactic approach. Levels of presentation, knowledge and understanding are consequently more rigidly distinguished than occurs with the emotional impact of artistic portrayals and programmes.

It is not that there is a dearth of science to show. The challenge in production is to provide a sufficient range of introductory and more advanced programmes. The BBC has earned a worldwide reputation for its work in this field, including Open University productions. In contrast to some genres of informational programming it has a permanent stock of science programmes with high income-earning value. Part of the achievement is undoubtedly due to the maintenance of a centre of excellence in production at Bristol for natural history programmes. Independent television despite its immense total resources, has failed to concentrate its efforts to provide continuity and build the type of expertise which is essential in the field of science programmes. This is another illustration of the dilemma for the commercial companies of the argument for a regional production base as against centralised planning or control.

Since science is universal there is unlimited scope for international co-production. Since voice-overs are essential for explanation there is no insurmountable, or even economic, argument against more science programmes because language transfer costs are minimal. One problem with science broadcasts is that since they may be perceived as too magisterial, and formally instructional, they inhibit further exploration, or the making of further programmes on the same topic. However it is common knowledge that there is no lack of competing theories in science. Indeed in Popperian terms there is no finality in scientific explanation, each theory is only a contribution towards a desired end, and in turn likely to be itself eventually disproven.[5]

Most popular of science programmes are undoubtedly the natural history presentations. There appears an inexhaustible appreciation of African animals, of tropical fish, sharks and whales, perhaps only exceeded by an insatiable curiosity about dinosaurs, especially by the young. Obviously other species are portrayed but large animals in accessible warm climates, attractive landscapes and shallow seas are easier to film and thus cheaper to produce. The danger of overprovision demonstrates the Charybdis of fashion as one channel vies with or copies the success of others. As regards children's interest there is a new generation annually as any teacher or librarian can attest, but science is also essentially incremental and besides the need to popularise basic scientific concepts, television producers should bear in mind the possibility of more progression in programme themes, as well as an obligation to show the diversity and breadth of the natural world.

In physics, chemistry or other hard sciences the difficulties are obvious but the public has an increasing level of graphic insight, much due to television itself. Animation and visual illustration, let alone virtual reality, have become part of everyday experience. Why cannot more of such techniques be applied to science programmes?

Medicine is covered in both factual series and in fiction, for example over healthy lifestyles or in hospital settings. Here is created a large audience, even for intricate and gripping surgical demonstrations. There are clear parallels with science in general, especially to instil a better understanding of risk, incidence of disease and recovery, and personal responsibility while at the same time helping to reduce unrealistic expectations of medical intervention.

Fashion, it seems, has a significant impact on medical and health programmes. Twenty years ago one saw a tide of presentations of complicated operations like open heart surgery. In the 1980s candid coverage of hospital life was in vogue. In the 1990s much attention has been given to mental health and morbidity, no doubt provoked by advances in psychiatry and neurology, and also in alternative therapies. The latter may reflect diminished public confidence in some health professionals, whom television might have done more to defend. The challenge in medical programmes is to keep a balance between the entertainment and the factual approaches, and yet at the same time enable and encourage movement from the former to the latter.

Broadcasters could in addition consider whether positive health promotion should be part of their remit. Although maximising audiences will retain primacy, it is doubtful that creating an era of passive lounge lizards is good for a sense of well-being, either for the individual or society. As a result of many cookery programmes there is a danger of being overfed and obese as well. Physical exercise is strongly recommended by health professionals, even simple movements for those with handicap. Perhaps even more than once per day, viewers might be encouraged to stretch and move, call at the neighbours, pop to the shop or postbox. While it may seem trivial, benefits are cumulative and could be accepted as routine, just like the weather or news reports. Such promotions need merely be brief, and done in many different ways, light-heartedly rather than instructional, possibly using cartoons or popular personalities. Irregular campaigns or fashions of the sort, sometimes employed, are no substitute. Indeed going further, developing an alert and discriminating audience could also be an achievable goal, through occasional encouragement to switch off so as to discuss a programme, or prepare for other presentations.

Promoting household skills

Inevitably it seems there will be cycles in the popularity and styles of minority programming. Many creative workers in the industry who would wish to make their mark with some serious productions follow the leader, hoping they will not have the ephemerality of most entertainment broadcasts. Striking has been the rebirth in the 1990s of provision for home improvement programmes ranging from cookery, to gardens and rebuilding or redecoration. Clothing, apart from the exotica of fashion shows, interestingly, seems not to have enjoyed the same success. Surely the intellectual and manipulative skills of dressmaking and design have not become redundant?

In 1998, 14 cookery programmes were counted in one week across television in the UK. As with gardening, the genre boundary with entertainment is sometimes rather difficult to see. There is an assumption that viewers will be encouraged to try the recipes for themselves, but although many thousands of particular utensils used by Delia Smith, the most popular TV cook, were reported purchased in 1999, the expected subsequent culinary experimentation is thought to have been much less common. The technical skill in such presentations is evident but perhaps the colour, and apparent simplicity in these and many cookery programmes have a mesmerising or dulling effect. So like holiday shows they merge into fantasy, however informative, delightful and comforting they may be. Broadcasters certainly try to build on the attraction of such programmes, sometimes including elements of competition or inviting and showing lay persons trying the dishes in their own homes. Cookery books in support can also have remarkable sales, even placing Delia Smith as the leading hardback book author. As with programmes for children, interest in the promotion of merchandising may also be a powerful latent motivation.

The gardens series present more difficulty for audience replication. Presumably the concentration of gardening series on Friday evenings is in the hope that at least some of the viewers will be out pruning, trimming, planting or watering over the weekend. Home cultivation of vegetables, however, has much diminished in recent decades. Flower gardens require some space and repeated attention, which is at a premium in the constrictions and bustle of modern society, but they are clearly the more popular with their colourful displays. Nevertheless an appreciation of design, harmony and contrast, seasonality and therapeutic benefits of gardens as well as the activity itself may be greatly enhanced. Gardening has a remarkably organised, informed and active lobby, as is demonstrated by BBC Radio 4's *Gardeners' Question Time*, the sales of gardening magazines and the proportion of the population engaged in gardening. It is worth noting that for their audience size, broadcast gardening series must be good value for the money spent on production.

Religion on the screen

Religion, despite its large numerical following, has never proved a simple subject for treatment in broadcasting, either in radio or television. On the one hand there are strong confessional loyalties, but also for many their allegiance is nominal. The early days of the BBC, a national secular organisation, and headed by John Reith, a devout Presbyterian elder in a society with well-established denominational traditions operating in an increasingly non-practising population, led by governments which wished to distance themselves from possible doctrinal controversy, show the complicated situation in which religious broadcasting has developed. Here the model established by radio, focusing on transmissions of services, was adopted initially by television. Not surprisingly congregations in pews hardly provided interesting visual images, and the esoteric nature of the conduct of some services, themselves often distanced from congregations, could hardly interest most viewers.

To liven up proceedings television presentations have exploited the potential of music to arouse, by series which themselves became immovable institutions, such as *Songs of Praise*. As upholders of tradition the leadership of churches and denominations have largely acquiesced in such formats. Other alternative programme formats have been developed both by the BBC and the independent sector, where a religious perspective instead of the promotion or presentation of religious activity has been shown. A good example of this has been the regular *Everyman* series on BBC1 on Sunday evenings, in which contemporary issues are discussed and in which there may be a religious dimension, although not exclusively, or a topic specific to religious or denominational belief or practice. Inevitably at a later hour, 10.30 p.m. or thereabouts, the audience is limited in numbers and by educational and social level. One acclaimed series in 1999, *Two Thousand Years of Christianity*, fronted by Lord Bragg for ITV, which has not shrunk from doctrinal and ethical confrontations, suffered similar timings. Remarkably this has even been scheduled at 11.15 p.m., when the devout might reasonably be expected to be abed. But a more serious practical problem arises from the defined obligation by ITC regulations and BBC practice, of a minimal weekly time allocation to religion, which seems inevitably to have become an upper limit in practice. Limited room for manoeuvre therefore exists, particularly when both BBC and the independents feel they must respect the almost ministerial authority of the Central Religious Advisory Committee which, dominated by the larger faith groups, and despite seeking to work by consensus, is in fact hesitant in regard to innovation, because it has an inherent tendency to conservatism.

Beyond this dilemma is the question of what constitutes a religion and the right, if it may be called that, to be broadcast and thus heard. The New Age religions, pagans, the business-type churches originating in America, the historic non-Christian faiths, and even the Christian charismatics, have all at various times felt unfairly treated by those controlling religious broadcasting.

Those who work within the religious broadcasting field have tried to go beyond the established straitjacket. Since 1991, when the so-called Godslot at a fixed hour on Sunday was dropped, more experimentation has followed. For example, more attention has been paid to cultural contexts as well as dogmatic belief. This has not harmed audiences as much as was first feared. An important development is the move towards inter-faith dialogue which shows an acceptance of coexistence, rather than the projection of doctrinal isolation.[6] The maintenance of a centre of excellence by the BBC, following a move of the Religious Broadcasting Department to Manchester, has contributed to these explorations, and given added confidence to those involved. It contrasts with the financial difficulties besetting those who have tried to establish independent religious broadcasting, such as the more fundamentalist groups, in the UK, who have depended much on benefactors from allies in North America.

Religious adherents meanwhile often find the transmissions of services and discussions valuable complements to their own practice. For the housebound they may be their only contact with the churches, and sensitive presentation can create a sense of engagement of profound importance to them. For many the religious broadcast may have become a substitute for attendance at church and perhaps their only link with organised religion, however tenuous it may appear. For the churches there is also an ambivalence, since although there is no articulate demand for increasing the hours devoted to religious broadcasting, few within the religious bodies would wish the transmissions to become an easy and total replacement for devotional attendance.

Educational broadcasts

Much of what has been said already in this chapter might have appeared under a heading of educational broadcasting. While not strictly educational in a narrowly institutional context, the perception of education by many viewers would drive them away rather than encourage them because of their earlier schooling experiences or from fear of assessment and ranking. These features are often difficult to differentiate. A particular transmission could vary in its emphasis from beginning to end, and all programmes, of whatever genre, must have some attention-drawing feature and a feel-better factor at the end to reinforce viewing as being on balance positive.

One development, which seems to be aimed at identifying an information niche, or attracting a more exploratory interest among the viewers, is the title *History Zone* by the BBC. This has earned a peak-time slot on BBC2. One may expect more ploys of this kind on generalist channels, which would be preferable to being shunted on to a specialised digital service.

The difficulty and avoidance of overt didactic pressure are manifest in the way BBC and ITC or IBA categorised these factual and informative programmes. Changing educational theory, perceptions of the medium's function and the sheer difficulty of film classification have meant that terms like adult education, informational, documentary or factual have alternated in annual statistical reports. A problem within that is that although the aggregate differs little from one year to another, the allocation to sub-genres, such as to science, medicine, natural history or gardening for example, is uncertain so that trends and fashions are difficult to elicit. Perhaps all programmes should have a sub-code which would make evaluation easier. Do they have such codes within broadcasting organisations? Because trying to do this subsequently is, if not impossible, at least likely to be inconsistent in the assessment, by outsiders, journalists, researchers or statisticians. One has to recognise of course that a trend may only become clear in retrospect, if it was of style or approach, rather than subject or producer intent.

The differentiation of educational programmes with the arrival of the national schools curriculum for specific age levels, of academic broadcasts such as those for the Open University, and training and professional development programming for doctors and lawyers, and for the embryonic University of Industry, has been an exciting and continuing process in television broadcasting. Advanced level, highly professional teaching has become available to all, or by encryption to those with specific occupational requirement, for example the *Legal Network* TV.

Targeted audiences are by definition likely to be small, however strongly motivated. To be of high quality, production is unlikely to be cheap. It has not proved effective to set up a camera in a classroom or university lecture theatre and just relay it to all and sundry. The careful tailoring, characteristic of the UK Open University television broadcasts, has vindicated the criticised limitations of early US, Russian and Indian experience of satellite or aircraft-borne educational broadcasting.

Such programming, apart from a few select encrypted transmissions for paying-per-view highly paid professionals, can only survive by public provision. The government has recognised this by a special financial allocation to the Open University for its broadcasts, by television as well as radio. For schools transmission, given the probably lower cost per production hour and the likely longer broadcasting life for use of recorded material, the costs are borne by the BBC's general licence fee, and out of the commercial companies' surpluses for Channel 4 provision. Satellite and cable broadcasters currently have no obligation or even expectation that they should contribute to the pool of knowledge or costs. Perhaps a future European perspective, within the European Union, may stimulate greater provision. It could through competition, but also because of the need for more comparative studies, provide finance sharing costs for scientific programming or new technology, as well as the essentials of language learning.

Although made for student and scholarly audiences, the plea is sometimes advanced that educational material, made with public funds, should be available to all without the burden of copyright. Many parents are unaware of educational developments and would like to know more, and at the same time update their own subject knowledge. A difficulty here is that schools broadcasts have been shunted to the minority channels BBC2 and Channel 4. It is a recognition, in a market-oriented system, that the real television kudos is by performance and audience in the main channels, where entertainment is dominant, and little time can be allocated to minority interests. Housebound parents can watch at home in the daytime or record material, but this does not always fit well into domestic routines. The consequence is that while, say in morning hours, there are two educational channels from which to choose, there is a segregation of the serious from the entertaining. While there is economic justification, such decisions have social consequences, subtle, small but cumulative, and once tolerated are thought unchangeable. Perhaps in homework time for the pupil, when the parent can also view, and before the peak hours, is an appropriate time for some school broadcasts.

Support material is generally well promoted, primarily through educational channels but perhaps less accessible and affordable to many parents. Is there not a case for a closer relationship between schools, publishers, bookshops and broadcasters more effectively to integrate their networks? Copyright dilemmas do arise, but such is the imperative of broadcast education as an investment that public resources should be used to alleviate the problem. In any case authors are often teachers in public employment for whom dissemination in print, on disk or in cassette form ought to be an obligation, as it is already for university teachers, with proper remuneration ensured, so that the problem is not insoluble.

Programmes for children

Aside from the specifically learning goals of educational broadcasts, it is obvious that programmes for children can be a powerful force for improvement. The natural curiosity, idealism and warmth of the young respond enthusiastically to many subjects. Children from the age of four apparently view for as many hours in a week as adults, despite their shorter day. They view at all hours and with moderate seasonal variation, especially at weekends, many until late evening hours, even past the 9 p.m. watershed, as well as before leaving for school. It is reported that over half the children turn on the television immediately on returning from school. Since half of six- and seven-year-old children in the UK have their own receiver, usually in a bedroom, the young have effectively become arbiters of their personal viewing, and a numerically significant element of the television audience.[7]

Little that passes on the screen will therefore escape them, and friends can fill in the gaps for each other in conversation. By tradition and under contemporary regulation special hours have been reserved for children's television but the audience does not confine itself in this way. The supervision and restriction of viewing are inevitably, and primarily, a responsibility of parents. Regrettably many find it difficult or distasteful to be strict, so that unavoidably broadcasters do have significant moral obligations to promote appropriate children's programmes.

The BBC, from the traditions of the radio *Children's Hour* had a ready-made formula, balancing educative and entertainment material, which appropriately transferred to its television service. In its early years the independent television companies adopted a not too dissimilar format, despite the difficulties inherent in creating a national programme from the disparate regional contractors. An inherent difficulty soon faced, apart from the very limited resources of the smaller companies, was that the desirability of making all parts of a commercial service revenue earning could only be kept in check by strong regulation of programmes for children. American experience, more powerful in this field of broadcasting than perhaps any other, had demonstrated that the suggestibility of the young made them an ideal quarry for advertisers. The Disney and similar US film producers had tapped enormous markets for toys, hobby equipment and clothing, and their products have largely overwhelmed the UK child market as well.

Parents are particularly wary of this onslaught in the pre-Christmas gift-buying period. Unfortunately the items are often garments or toys with a limited life and, unlike traditional construction kits, with little learning potential. They reinforce notions of an acquisitive throwaway society with little regard for the use of resources or ecological relevance. Such is the near universal concern about such developments that the European Union has under consideration a move to ban all advertising directed at children, as is already the case in Sweden.

The seeming inevitability of market factors in a materialist culture merely reflects the circularity of economic and social influences. Television has become subordinate to external forces and so tends to lose its autonomy in the human process. The BBC is not free of these pressures, especially now that its recognised market potential is tending to displace alternative funding.

Generally children of almost any age will be watching more material designed for adults than for themselves. While it would be wrong wholly to insulate them from the realities of adult life, it must be a very curious world on which they are eavesdropping. Why for example are there no children in *Coronation Street* or other soap operas, shown before the watershed and set as they generally are in working-class areas with high birth rates? Perhaps the sanitised nature of much of the soap-opera genre is a misguided dumbing down to make them less threatening to children. But serious problems of family life and neighbourhood can be presented in a sensitive, sympathetic way suitable for all ages. There is no point in pretending to children that the micro-world has no dilemmas.

Significantly a high proportion of children's programmes are based on cartoons, an art form highly developed in North America and Japan. The Disney enterprise exploited simple humorous tales, highly attractive and universally acceptable to a younger audience. Sometimes a whole afternoon programme for them will be devoted to a succession of cartoons of non-memorable content, difficult to distinguish, and with trivial storylines, so that the young are in real danger of a monotonous and unstimulating diet. Curiously limited use is made of animation, which is equally universally understood and perhaps a fraction closer to reality than the two-dimensional cartoon. There has been a quite different emphasis in Central and Eastern Europe where animation was more emphasised. These were not necessarily politically correct formulations, appropriate to those regimes, and thus would be fully acceptable here. As with cartoons, voice-overs are necessary so language and production cost need not be burdensome. One suspects that the American offerings are purchased at knockdown prices, in effect subsidised out of its home market profits.

On this basis British children are being unfairly treated. They are being given cheap material of doubtful benefit, probably even disproportionate to the market share of children's goods and purchases, influenced by television advertising. The reservation of minimal hours for their programmes is inadequate to protect and promote their interests unless there is regulatory intervention to produce quality output, difficult though that may be. A better way may be to require that the budget resources allocated to children's programming reflect their share of viewing! At least they would then be treated equally to adults.

An alarming survey from a consortium of American and European organisations reveals serious derogation of children's television in the 1990s, throughout Europe and not least in Britain. For example, fewer hours were being provided weekly but the proportion of imported (largely United States) material has notably increased, and much of this was poor quality animation.[8]

Much however can be learned from the experience of other countries. In Spain the tradition in children's television was to have non-exploitative programmes, largely of child amateurs performing in music, dance and drama or in arts and adventure games, rather than adults talking to them, or adult voices. Unfortunately North American influence is becoming ever more pervasive in this field which must be an indictment of European and other creative workers when we live in a world of falling frontiers, especially in Europe itself. Why not use foreign languages? This need not be narrowly scholastic. Even British adults are becoming familiar with foreign language phrases in television advertisements, and children will be glad to practise and develop their awareness.

Some adults, and many mothers especially, wish to watch children's programmes to be aware of their fare and give appropriate support. Cartoons are, perhaps unwisely, often thought to be too trivial, harmless or boring to be given critical comment. But it works both ways; many children could cope with extracts from adult factual programmes and, more important, their questions will be a valuable stimulus to adult thinking and household intervention. With their curiosity and openness, children are particularly attracted to unusual and unfamiliar topics, so that geographical and archaeological contexts could be usefully employed. Children, besides an immediate interest in others of their own age, often have a passion for animals. The memories of *Zoo Time* and Johnny Morris's presentations are still remembered by many adults, but nowadays lessened with the influx of cartoon beasts, often of unattractive character and appearance.

A major challenge is to embody activity and participant viewing. Probably the most successful example has been the BBC's long-running *Blue Peter*. The series has now raised millions of pounds sterling for good causes by contributions from children, but with its diverse elements has many thousands of youngsters making articles, undertaking discovery projects or making reports on some aspect of their community or neighbourhood. Equally renowned in the earlier ITV years was *Magpie* which, again using a magazine format, offered a diverse and full session of things to see, learn and do in its transmissions. Given the more restricted formats in today's children's programming it is not surprising that there is more to be said about filling gaps and offering more variety. The young like performing, to sing, take part in quizzes, take turns in games like Scrabble or competitions, tell stories as well as listen. It is very regrettable that more features like this are not provided.

The diminution of serious drama and the single play for adults has been referred to previously. The loss in children's programmes is no less regrettable. At one time no BBC Sunday teatime schedule seemed without an episode of some classic serial. Now such a programme is promoted as a special treat. Yet these programmes reach a high proportion of, say, under tens who could view with parents. While there are strong arguments for new versions and writers to be given opportunities, there must be a considerable library of these series which would be attractive to new generations, at a cost in copyright fees much less than that of new productions, if money is an obstacle.

To the surprise of many adults, BBC's *Newsround* proved remarkably popular to the young, in which even international news could be presented, in a form digestible to 9–14-year-olds. A risk always exists of underestimating the intelligence and insight of children. Perhaps this is due as much to adults not wishing the young to know their parental limitations, rather than a claimed protection.

To sum up, children's programmes can be faulted as much for failed potential as for deliberate manipulation. This constitutes a serious underinvestment in their and society's future. More positive action is required by broadcasters. It is an inadequate defence of the status quo to say that a choice is available for children, and that it now rests on parents to select or intervene. Information is required on screen to support them, as many parents cannot be expected to be readily familiar with regulators' rulings, broadcasting conventions, the minutiae of programme titles and appropriate daily programme schedules on so many channels. Research on children's preferences, satisfactions, needs, learning and programme effects should also be given more attention. Many of the young are quite capable of telling us what they want, rather than be merely the subject of market-oriented studies or experimentation.

An interim assessment

Several key issues are still to be answered about the performance of minority and specialised television. How far have the range and diversity of such programmes been developed? For various reasons any adequate measure of change is difficult. More hours for all television are broadcast by both BBC and ITV, but there are more repeats nowadays. On ITV and Channel 4 the picture is also confused in the long term, because of the collapse of certain reported genres into one, i.e. factual programmes.

In large measure the coming of BBC2, and probably more importantly Channel 4, have ensured that in practice there are more documentary and educational programmes, the provision of unfamiliar sports, the larger evening newscast on Channel 4 and the enduring presence of a late-hour serious political affairs programme on BBC2, *Newsnight*. No less significantly, there may now be three or four serious programmes available on each of those two channels in a typical evening, serving a more demanding audience. For the BBC the complementarity of Channels 1 and 2 allows more convenient early repeats of successful programmes. The distinctive separation of funding has undoubtedly done much to preserve the alternative nature of the four main services, which is an important guarantee of more specialised offerings.

The same cannot, however, be said of local and regional programming. The unifying nature of the BBC and the shrinking number of effective independent contractors for ITV militates against growth at the periphery. Channel 5 which aims to be a national service, but without hope because of its present limited frequencies, will have difficulty in rising beyond its typical audience rating zenith of 5 per cent, without a substantial increase in its production budget, although it can on occasion, by skilful negotiation of rights, put on a spurt with an exceptional payment, for say, a specific sports match or other exclusive contract coverage.

Whether the numerous cable and satellite channels, now coming on stream, can satisfy quality and ethics, as well as they can provide quantity, is problematic. Even among those viewers who already have access to them, a large proportion of these services draw only the minutest fractions of the public, even as little as one-tenth of 1 per cent. Such near invisibility offers little prospect of resourcing strong production bases. The ill-fated *L!ve TV* channel, with several city-linked inputs, was underfunded from the start, and it descended into a series of bizarre gestures, including topless darts and the weather in Norwegian, hardly rising beyond triviality. Indeed it can almost be said that no minority is now too small to gain television exposure.

A serious test of whether much niche and cable viability will be reached is whether many viewers will have the time and persistence to search even through their electronic programme guides to dig out the occasional nugget, in what must appropriately be called narrowcasting.

There must also be continued uncertainty, over the next decade at least, whether the telecommunications system will be able to cope, without heavy investment, in providing telephone cable connections, especially at the local level, for all the proposed cable services, with an expected exponential increase in computer Internet usage, for interactive television and video on demand. Despite the promise of technological development, a shortage of bandwidth capacity may replace the earlier spectrum limitations for network television. And it will have to be paid for by somebody.

The arrival of numerous small independent producers in the 1990s has added to the pool of potential materials and ideas, but there have been substantial personnel losses in the main providers, so the resource base may have improved little. The 1990s have seen no newly established centres of excellence, and the BBC devolution of some production to Birmingham and Manchester is largely a shift of location for possible cost savings.

A pointer to the probable squeezing of budgets for minority programming on the BBC (the only broadcaster with sufficient comparable published figures) is that over the eight years, 1990–91 to 1998–99, costs per hour of various genres rose for sports by 103 per cent, for entertainment by 53 per cent and news by 56 per cent. These were all greater than the costing of factual (documentary) 48 per cent and arts/music 15 per cent (both meaning a relative decline in their share of funding). For children, schools and continuing education with cost increases on paper of only 14, 12 and 4 per cent respectively (it meant absolute reductions).[9] Changes in shares of broadcast hours are insufficient to argue that greater productivity has wholly compensated for the disparity.

A special early feature of British commercial television was that it should have regional roots so as to provide a wide distribution of resource, talent and personnel, and particularly to reflect regional cultural distinctions. The latter has never been a simple task, as broadcasting has a unifying national effect. Nevertheless with moderate budgets, worthy efforts to present local news and to develop series of regional programmes such as soap operas, situation comedy and environmental specialisms of geography, industry, buildings and history have brought significant success, even on occasion gaining some nationwide audiences. An adequate assessment of the potential for local, city-wide or community television still remains to be undertaken.

Yet a desire to concentrate facilities to compete more effectively with the BBC, and to resist takeovers from overseas media investors has meant in the 1990s the growth of three, perhaps in the future two, main producer contracting groups. Although the regionalisation may have been more effective than devolution at the BBC, it has left the ITV control less effective in regard to medium-term programme planning. This had to be overcome for news, where ITN is the national producer, and sport where resources had to be concentrated for the major sports coverage contract bids.

The difficulties are now partly compounded by the plethora of small independent producers, who must lobby for custom, but they undoubtedly leave network television weaker in relation to shortages for minority and specialised programming.

Another perspective on recent trends is seen in the ITC 1999 performance review of independent television, which concluded in relation to minority programming that the companies could still be commended for the diversity of local programming. In relation to drama documentary the ITC wrote that there continued to be successive years where the work deserved the highest praise, but was critical that the increased provision of fictional elements in docusoaps did not match the standards of full documentaries in the earlier tradition.[10]

The effects of structural changes in broadcasting, which are still in process, are having widespread, and as yet unforeseen, consequences. Major network television is increasingly about entertainment. The so-called dumbing down is more a threat to the factual programming. With the advent of digital broadcasting with numerous channels, does this mean that specialist materials will find their final resting place increasingly by cable or satellite distribution? It may be tempting to do this, if such niches are easily identifiable and can be found via electronic programme guides. But if they fragment the viewing public, and especially divide them into the information rich and the information poor, the social consequences although unintended may be undesirable for political discourse and civil society. Few would want broadcasters to be enlightened despots, but equally they ought not to make the world worse than it is. If this happens, it may be too late to wait until it occurs. Like Pandora's box, such a development may not be easily reversible.

What effects has minority programming had for the viewing public on participation in other domestic or leisure pursuits? Unfortunately no adequate long-term systematic comparison of television viewing and activity behaviour has been made. Do the powers that be assume there is no effect or would they prefer not to find out? Nevertheless some data from the annual *General Household Survey*, taken from 1977, do provoke interesting conjecture. At three-yearly intervals attention is given specifically to leisure pursuits. Adult participation in gardening, in a four-week period before questioning, was 42 per cent in 1977, and rose steadily to 48 per cent in 1996, but for needlework and knitting it has fallen from 29 to 22 per cent, most of whom were women. Book-reading interestingly rose from 54 to 65 per cent.[11] Church attendance, by contrast, is widely reported to have fallen over this period for practically all denominations. Other relevant activities have not been quite so systematically investigated or over the same years, such as involvement in artistic and hobby pursuits, or going to theatres and museums. But visiting a cinema or historic buildings has gone up from 7 and 8 per cent respectively over four weeks in 1977. By 1996 cinema attendances were 36 per cent of adults (over a three-week period), and for historic buildings 24 per cent (over three months).

This is slim evidence and it is likely that other sociocultural factors such as educational experience, income and opportunity will also have had their impact, but certainly programmes like *Antiques Roadshow* would hardly have discouraged visits. More directly relevant to the impact of television viewing, because of the time demands, going to leisure study classes has tripled from 2 to 6 per cent, and social visiting and entertaining of friends and relatives has increased from 91 to 96 per cent over a four-week period in the years 1983–96.[12]

Equally important, however, is whether viewer satisfactions have changed about minority programming, or are changing in view of the prospective increases in channels. Here it is difficult to define viewer satisfaction or expectations as a single aggregate, or to measure opportunity and other economic costs, partly because earlier basic data are no longer available, or realistically whether hypothetical questions have much value in perceptions and behaviour, any more than one can ask readers about the book market, if they are powerless to do much about it.

Finally it would be of immense interest to compare changes in knowledge or sensitivities which have occurred over the television decades. Much research remains to be done here too. On some aspects it is likely that responses will fluctuate, like political loyalties, and again could be as much the result of other external factors as of television viewing itself. There is alarming evidence that, despite elaborate arrangements for televising Parliament, a case of niche broadcasting if ever there was one, the coverage has actually declined since cameras were allowed into the House of Commons in 1989. It means that viewers are hardly likely nowadays to be better informed of what their parliamentary representatives are doing.

Despite the concerns over minority programming expressed here, it is important to recognise the strong foundation, which past performances by both BBC and commercial contractors have created. The many awards gained in international competition gives strong confirmation that quality productions may, despite their recognition, only attract modest audiences. Inevitably, since network television has a higher production value than regional programmes, less of the latter will be made than light entertainment, which earns high ratings and advertising revenue. But on the other hand minority programmes may have a much longer shelf life as a library resource, possibly measured in decades for their potential educative use, rather than the ephemerality of many of the entertainment genre.

It was significant that the break-up of Thames Television, after it lost its bid in the 1991 award of broadcasting contracts to Carlton Television, found that one of its most valuable assets was the substantial library of earlier programmes. It is to be hoped that this library was not dissipated, since the regulator had no power to determine such matters.

What does the experience of minority programming tell about the effectiveness of the regulators? It is easier to speak of the independent sector here than the BBC, since the ITC decisions are more transparent.

'Regulation with a light touch', as envisaged in the 1990 Broadcasting Act, no doubt had an inhibiting effect in the first years of the new regime. But at the end of the 1990s the ITC has taken stronger action over infringements, with serious warnings, fines and even, in the case of Med-TV, a withdrawal of the licence. But these actions are negative sanctions, which alone may do little to improve quality levels. Undoubtedly this owes more to the amounts allocated to production, and in a highly competitive market, where short-term considerations have become uppermost, appear to be highly vulnerable.

A complete absence of regulation is unthinkable, after having proved unacceptable over the auction of television broadcasting contracts in the 1990s, and the quick reimposition of a programme quality threshold. Considering possible achievement, including some credibility in the export record, how much is the output in quality or volume due more to regulation or a market system? An objective proof is difficult because the turning point with the 1990 Broadcasting Act seems to have been motivated more by a political will than economic factors. Like research into quantum theory, the process of observation and intervention itself makes recording and analysis impossible.

The regulated market in the UK during the period 1955–90 has been followed by a decade of the market economy. It inherited a significant legacy of professional thinking from the previous era so despite the new management style, for example under Sir John Birt at the BBC, the overall effect on programme quality may yet prove less damaging than once feared.

Part III
The Future

9

Shoring up the Stable Door: the Limits of Regulation

How did regulation come about?

The attempts by governments to regulate television have become more frantic with the growth of multichannel systems. One would have expected them to decline as the profusion of outlets renders the argument from scarcity of frequencies redundant.

But, as has recently been pointed out,

> there are twice as many bodies and regulators looking after television in the UK than there are free-to-air television channels. We have the Department of Culture, the Department of Technology and Industry, the Office of Fair Trading, the Independent Television Commission, the Office of the Regulator of Telecommunications and the Broadcasting Standards Commission. And, if that weren't enough, there are at least four directorates at the European Commission that have varying degrees of jurisdiction over media in member states: DGIV, DGX, DGXIll and DGXV. The last forty years have produced five free national channels, nine major pieces of legislation and ten organisations with regulatory powers.[1]
>
> Those in authority have always taken an interest in the mass media and this interest has always been ambivalent. On the one hand these media have always been instruments of great potential use to those in power; on the other their volatility and the scope which they have provided for the expression of ideas have made them dangerous. After early and abortive attempts to monopolise the media, however, they developed in most of the Western world without being entirely taken over by governments. Although the problem of freedom and control of the means of expressing opinions has engaged political theorists, moralists and literary men since the end of the eighteenth century, it was not until broadcasting arrived on the scene that governments throughout Western Europe decided that this medium was too important to be left to development by private enterprise, and to make policy decisions for its conduct by public enterprise.[2]

This is how George Wedell described the position at the time of the launching of radio in the 1920s.

That was quite different from the position of North America:

> Europe as a whole was slower to develop the broadcasting media than North America and the private enterprise systems of the

United States in particular provide a strong contrast to the European pattern. As the nations of Africa and Asia have developed their systems, they have found themselves torn between the existing models in Europe and North America. In whichever way they have decided to organise their broadcasting, they have attached high priority to its development. Much else is being deferred in many newly independent states in order to create the means of communicating with all sections of the population at a time of rapid social economic and cultural change.[3]

In the UK public, rather than government, policy has been the determining element, both because until the 1980s the broadcasting policy of the two major parties, with significant exceptions, was bipartisan and because, at an early stage, broadcasting was taken out of the immediate political arena. It has been the subject of the first large-scale attempts to exercise public control over a sector of the national life without making this control immediately subject to the government of the day. As Lord Reith recalled later,

> the determining reason for turning the British Broadcasting Company Ltd of 1923–26 into a public corporation was to achieve unencumbered, unembarrassed and unconditional *efficiency* – just that; the resolve to institutionalise a governing board for the first time in British or any other national constitutional history, with an executive staff responsible to it, for service at maximum efficiency, normally untrammelled by any political interference, by any delegacy, by any Civil Service procedures, by any political party expectations and claims, by any demands, by any impatient shareholders – not one factor of the kind that disquiets the life of most administrators and managers.[4]

Basically the stake is socio-political in character and origin, as are the arguments which govern public intervention in the other media of mass communication. In the case of broadcasting the arguments thought valid in the fields of publishing, the press, the theatre and the cinema, are reinforced by social and operational considerations not to the same extent present in the other media. The act of switching on a wireless or a television receiver, for instance, is only superficially comparable to the act of buying a book or a ticket. It is more like the act of turning on the water tap in the bathroom. This being the case any control, if it is to be effective, must be exercised at the point of production or transmission, and not left to be exercised at the point of sale. Added to these criteria there are technical considerations which are entirely confined to the field of broadcasting.

The public stake has, of course, by no means always been the determining factor in the control of the mass media by governments. The separation of the *public* interest from that of the *government of the day* which is enunciated in Lord Reith's description of the origins of the British Broadcasting Corporation was, as he says, relatively new at the time. It has been one of the ways in which the arrival on the scene of broadcasting has forced societies to look afresh at the relationship between their communication media and the function of government.

The main reason for this regulatory urge was the protection of the consumer from the influence of a monopoly franchise arising from restricted access to the airwaves. The main concern at that time was the prevention of undue influence on the part of political parties or others seeking to control the output.

Nowadays producers still prefer to have external control of this output. As recently as October 1999 Ian McBride, Granada Media managing director of factual programmes, told the participants of the Sheffield International Documentary Festival that 'the industry needs regulation to keep it honest'. He cited the Independent Television ruling against Carlton TV over *The Connection* as a reminder of the broadcaster's contract with the viewers. 'If there are no rules what takes their place?' McBride asked. 'Self regulation? What does it mean? It means a playing field that's not level any more. A 45 degree inclined pitch. If *you* don't cheat, then *someone else* will.' The outcome of the debate was that only 2 people out of 80 were in favour of the abolition of content regulations.[5]

This straw vote is significant in that it illustrates the lack of confidence which currently pervades the broadcasting industry. In particular it illustrates the lack of confidence of those producing the 'serious' output of programmes in their controllers. In the face of widespread pressure for cost-cutting and for audience maximisation those who control the broadcasting systems will respond, with varying degrees of grace, to legislative and contractual obligations. Within the confines of these, however, the trend to cut corners is pronounced, and those employees responsible for production of the 'serious' programmes seek the protection of third parties, such as Parliament, the government and contractual engagements inside the broadcasting industry to keep them honest.

Since the 1954 Television Act there has now been a steady stream of broadcasting legislation up to the 1996 Broadcasting Act. The BBC has increasingly been drawn into this legislation as the diversification of the television services has come to cover the area of cable, satellite and digital services.

Gradually the case for a unitary authority to take responsibility for all televisual media has gained strength. It is likely that the next generation of legislative instruments will grasp the nettle of the dual system, and create a single statutory authority to oversee the whole range of television services including the BBC.

The regulators

For the present the television industry not only has a multitude of regulators, but is hedged about with many and detailed codes and guidelines. The ITC alone issues 11 of them:

(a) programme code
(b) code of advertising standards and practice
(c) rules on amount and scheduling of advertising
(d) code of programme sponsorship
(e) technical performance code
(f) guidance on standards for subtitling
(g) code on sport and other limited events
(h) code of conduct on electronic programme guides
(i) code for text services
(j) code on subtitling, signing and audio
(k) description of digital terrestrial television[6]

The BBC's list of regulatory activities has grown over the years, and much of it is now consolidated into a 275-page book called *Producers' Guidelines*. Sir John Birt, the BBC's former director-general, claimed in his foreword to the second edition in 1993, that the book represents 'the most comprehensive and coherent code of ethics in broadcasting. [The Guidelines] draw on the experience and wisdom of BBC programme makers over seventy years. They take account of the needs of current legislation and of the various regulatory authorities.'[7]

The Producers' Guidelines, which originally were memoranda issued by the BBC directors of programme production and, as such, internal documents, now have to face both ways. They are, in the main, intended to offer a frame of reference 'aimed at helping our programme people make difficult judgements for themselves'. This is a significant statement since it affirms the autonomy of the independent judgement of the producer. It recognises the professional status of the producer who, even in a large and bureaucratic organisation like the BBC, retains his autonomy within the circumscribed framework of his or her programme. This can nowadays by no means be taken for granted. We return, in Chapter 10, to the important issue of professional autonomy.

At the same time this second edition of the *Guidelines* faces outward towards the viewers. The foreword claims that:

> For the public, the *Producers' Guidelines* offer more than just an insight into the way the BBC approaches its work. They constitute a measure against which viewers and listeners may judge our programmes. If what they see and hear belies the principles we claim to espouse, they will have a right to call us to account and we must expect them to do so.

The problem is that viewers are, on the whole, inarticulate in their criticisms; therefore the good intentions about sensitivity to viewer criticism only rarely issue in the satisfactory operation of the regulatory system provided by the *Guidelines*. Moreover 'it has increasingly been argued that the BBC governors are involving themselves too much in the internal management of the BBC, and by inference, are not looking after the public interest. . . . The role of the governors themselves was to be the surrogates for the public.'[8] In fact 'Dialogue with the public was seen as superfluous because the governors were the trustees of the public interest. Thus they become the means by which the BBC avoided genuine accountability.'[9] So the good intentions enunciated in the *Guidelines* need to be taken with a pinch of salt.

The problem of regulation continues to be aggravated by the expansion of television services. The regulatory work of the ITC falls into six areas:

(a) economic regulation
(b) licensing
(c) programme regulation
(d) advertising and sponsorship regulation
(e) technical quality, service planning and research
(f) cable and local delivery

The scale of the operation is by now such that for large areas such as cable and satellite the figures become approximate. Currently the ITC licenses 'over 400 television services for analogue and digital terrestrial television and for cable and satellite'.[10] The licensing of so many services is bound to become a matter of approximation, even though the Commission claims that it 'involves the detailed application of the broadcasting legislation and, with the growth of interactive services, consideration of the relevant European Community legislation'.[11]

The main difference between the ITC and its predecessor, the Independent Broadcasting Authority, is that it is not to the same extent in the business of content regulation, but much more analogous to the American Federal Communications Commission. It is responsible for the allocation of licences; beyond that it has only retrospective responsibility for watching over programmes. And yet, it cannot wash its hands of programme regulation entirely. In October 1999 Sir Robin Biggam told the ITV contractors that they had six months to improve their regional programming, which had suffered in the course of the reorganisation of the ITN's news bulletins. The warning was a signal that the Commission was not content with the killing off of *News at Ten* which was designed to allow the ITV companies to transmit more films and other entertainment programmes after the end of the family viewing period at 9 p.m.

The ITC noted that the ratings for regional programmes had suffered badly, especially for the all-important regional news magazines. The 6 p.m. regional news programmes inherited depleted audiences from the regional opt-out at 5.30 p.m. instead of the networked evening news which was transmitted at 6.30 p.m. instead of 5.40 p.m.

Sir Robin Biggam insisted: 'Ensuring that this regional service should continue to thrive was one of the conditions when we agreed to ITV moving *News at Ten* last April. We have made it clear to ITV that this trend needs to be reversed before the formal review next spring.' An ITV spokeswoman said: 'We understand the ITC's concerns and we are working with it to find out what we can do to improve matters.'[12]

This feeble exchange illustrates the emasculation of the relationship between the regulator and its contractors, which occurred during the latter years of the governments of Mrs Thatcher and Mr Major. Of course regional programming, which was largely pioneered by ITV and for which the structures were created by the regional characteristics built into the system in the 1960s and 1970s, was bound to decline when the network companies were allowed largely to absorb the regional companies. Of course the contractors abandoned their strong local roots at the behest of their metropolitan masters. Of course the ITV managers feigned pained surprise when their concentration on a schedule that would maximise their profits squeezed out the 'heart' of their regional programming. The tragedy of the wilful abandonment of the regulatory structures of independent television under the guise of regulation with a 'lighter touch' derives from the abandonment of the shared vision of the architects of ITV by the Conservative governments between 1979 and 1997. When the history of broadcasting of this period comes to be written those who allowed one of the most imaginative sociocultural success stories of the twentieth century to be abandoned will surely not escape blameless. The culprits will claim that the multichannel developments would have forced a change in any case. But the extraordinary stability of the terrestrial viewing figure will convict them. Unlike the American networks the British terrestrial channels have maintained their hold on viewers in spite of all cable and satellite offers. In 1999 these were: terrestrial 85.9 per cent; cable and satellite 14.1 per cent.[13]

The Broadcasting Standards Commission

The abandonment of the restraints which used to maintain the broadcasting system in the period 1979–92 and the expansion of television channels, caused the government of the day in 1988 to create two statutory bodies to oversee the maintenance of programme standards. The Broadcasting Complaints Commission dealt with complaints by individual viewers about the lack of fairness and privacy; and the Broadcasting Standards Council dealt with the portrayal of violence, sexual conduct, and matters of taste and decency. The Council was also given research responsibilities, essential to strengthen the credentials of its findings. Both bodies handled complaints from the public falling within their remits. These bodies, independent both of government and of the broadcasting organisations, added to the gallery of controllers of the broadcasting scene. As Colin Shaw, the first director of the Broadcasting Standards Council, has written:

> The confusion generated by the existence of two bodies led to the government's decision to merge them in a single Broadcasting Standards Commission [in 1997]. The Commissioners, now totalling 13, personally consider, with the help of small staff, the complaints sent to them. . . . When the Commission has reached its conclusions

. . . it has powers to require the broadcaster to publish them on the air or in the press.[14]

Lady Howe who was chairperson of the combined body until 1999 wrote in her last annual report that:

> The merger has been a success. It has provided a single statutory body, with a breadth of vision which enables all standards and fairness issues to be considered alongside each other, and consistent guidance offered to all broadcasters. That it is demonstrably independent helps to maintain public confidence in broadcasting.[15]

Public confidence is the key to the medium-term success of the newly combined Commission. Its role is of course a micro one, ruling on individual complaints rather than the broad field of television. The hope is that an accumulation of case law from individual complaints will build up into a critical mass causing the broadcasters to modify their practice on a broad front. More immediately the Commission offers to complainants a simple, speedy and no-cost alternative to redress through expensive legal action.

The role of the Secretary of State as champion of the viewer

So far, so good. The impact of the digital revolution has yet to be felt. The Secretary of State for Broadcasting, Culture and Sport, Mr Chris Smith, very sensibly has limited ambitions and time horizons. He is determined that the majority of viewers should not be disadvantaged by the switch from analogue to digital transmission of terrestrial signals. In 1999 he therefore set himself a target of between 7 and 11 years, i.e. between 2006 and 2010, as the period during which the abandonment of analogue transmissions might be envisaged. But he maintained his commitment to continue analogue transmissions as long as viewers require them.[16]

Thus the broadcasters will, incidentally, have time to develop their digital channels, and to sort out their financial implications. The BBC, for its part, has not been backward in stating its 'needs' if it is to make use of the new technological possibilities. In November 1999 it set out its requirements. It informed the government it would need to spend

> an extra £200 million in 2000/1 (8 per cent on current levels) rising to an extra £520 million by 2003/4 (21 per cent more) and an extra

£730 million by 2006/7 (31 per cent). You have to take a ruler to a
chart in the document to work out the figures for the years in
between to realise that the Corporation is asking licence payers to
come up with more than £3.5 billion between [1999] and 2006.[17]

The BBC claimed to need the money to launch interactive digital services for children, for an arts channel, for the creation of a chain of BBC
Open Centres in high streets across the country, and for the development
of a bank of digital educational content to support the national curriculum. The Corporation recognised that the take-up of digital was uncertain, and promised that BBC networks would cater for the 90 per cent of
the audience that might not have access to digital channels. Those who
have followed the rise of the licence fee over the last 40 years, and have
tried to relate this to the implementation of the Corporation's basic
commitment to provide education, information and entertainment,
may well wonder whether the new financial demands should not be
met within the basic licence fee as part of the evolution of general educational and cultural expenditure. As Mr Raymond Snoddy, a funda-
mentally sympathetic observer of the BBC over the years, concluded.
'The BBC proposals should be rejected as outrageous.'[18]

The difficulty of politicians in dealing with the Corporation is that
politicians come and go; the BBC accountants are there for a lifetime
career. So they are in a position to browbeat peripatetic politicians
without fear that these will remember the history of BBC demands
over the years, and the *actual* return that the Corporation has provided
over the years. The short-term approach by politicians to decision-
making is endemic in populist democracies. For British politicians the
planning horizon tends to be three or four years, depending on the
length of the life of a Parliament. Relatively few politicians even last
that length of time in the same ministerial post. Unless, therefore, they
have a strong-minded commitment to a particular post, they are likely
to continue, willingly, on the way 'up' the ministerial ladder or,
unwillingly, on the way 'down' at the next reshuffle.

This puts a heavy responsibility on the civil servants to maintain a
given policy long enough for its effects to become apparent. They have
not only to implement the policy agreed upon with their political
masters at the time, but also to persuade their masters' successors that
a policy which they have not envisaged themselves could have merit,
given time to mature. That is difficult enough if these successors are of

the same political persuasion as their predecessors; if they are of the other political party it becomes almost impossible.

The European dimension

The freedom of action of British ministers is tending to become more circumscribed as the process of convergence of the technological options gathers pace at the level of the European Union. Digital technology now allows both traditional and new communication services, whether voice, data, sound or pictures, to be provided over many different networks.

The European Commission's Green Paper of December 1997[19] initiated

> a new phase in the European Union's policy approach to the communications environment. As such it represents a key element of the overall framework put in place to support the development of an Information Society. It builds on the current strengths of the framework for telecommunications (launched by the landmark 1987 Green Paper on Telecommunications)[20] and for media (established by various Community legislative initiatives). The first step is intended to pave the way for the development of an appropriate regulatory environment which will facilitate the full achievement of the opportunities offered by the Information Society, in the interests of Europe and its citizens as the 21st century begins.[21]

The legislative instrument following up the Green Paper and the subsequent discussion is likely to be an EU directive which will have legislative consequences at national level.

The Green Paper was heavily criticised as failing to take cognisance of the legitimate requirements of consumers. Since the protection of consumers is a primary concern of legislation both at national and at the European level, consumer issues should be given priority in the formulation of policy by the EU Commission. There is a firm basis for such priority in the main legislation of the Community. Article 3[(s)] of the Treaty of Maastricht defines 'a contribution to the strengthening of consumer protection' as one of the designated activities of the Community in achieving its task. Further, Article 129 states that 'the Community shall contribute to the attainment of a high level of consumer protection through measures adopted pursuant to Article 100[(a)] in the context of the completion of the internal market'.[22]

The United States/UK comparison

Since the United States are a country with a written constitution all regulation, including the regulation of broadcasting, has to flow from the provision of that constitution. The communications element of the constitution is nowadays dominated by the First Amendment relating to the freedom of expression of American citizens. Over time the assertion of this freedom, rather than the way it is used, has become the focus of the attention of interpreters of the constitution. At the time of writing a great deal of discussion is going on in the United States about the way in which the technical transformations of broadcasting, and in particular of television, are affecting the First Amendment. We found little or no discussion of the way in which the freedom of the citizen to express views, and in this case it is almost exclusively confined to the expression of 'views' by the broadcasting providers, can or ought to be modified in the light of the new technology available to the broadcasters. It is claimed that 'three of the most significant characteristics of this transformation are that at each stage television: 1) increases its technical quality, presenting ever more realistic experiences to the audiences; 2) expands to choice of experiences; and 3) provides viewers with increasing control over the expanding choice.'[23] Mr Pepper of the Federal Communications Commission claims that the viewer likes these developments. He is right in so far as the United States is a continent and whereas in 1975 it had only three commercial broadcast television networks and no cable networks, today there are four national commercial broadcast networks and more than 100 national and regional cable networks. Cable is in fact the means whereby television has extended beyond the national scale and become responsive to the needs of local and regional communities. In 1998 cable was available to almost all the homes in America and more than 60 per cent of US television households subscribed to it because it often provided a better signal, it brought television down to the local scale and added the diversity that came from local programming.

It is interesting, at this point, to compare the fate of cable television in the United States with that in the UK because cable in America is the way in which satellite signals are brought to local communities. There has been little development of direct-to-home transmission of satellite signals to individual households. It seems unlikely that, even with the new satellite technologies, direct-to-home transmission will catch up with cable with quantitative terms.

In the UK the late arrival of cable, largely due to the unwillingness of British entrepreneurs to invest in the legislation when first passed, has resulted in a head start being given to direct-to-home satellite transmissions. It will be interesting to see what happens when the two expensive cable systems that have in recent years been laid in most conurbations in this country become fully operational.

The United States having adopted cable as the preferred transmission system has been able to extend the range of programming in formats which are of high interest to certain minorities and do not carry a heavy production cost. The coverage of Congress by the two 24-hour C-Span channels constitute a significant addition to the contribution which television can make to an informed citizenry. Ethnic channels for minority groups did not exist until the expanded capacity of cable made them possible. There is now black television, as well as two Spanish language channels and programming in Japanese, Korean, Chinese (both Cantonese and Mandarin), Hindi and Greek. There are also 24-hour channels providing news, information about the weather and information about sport. The size of the population of the United States means that quite a small proportion of the potential can yield an adequate income to make such programmes viable.

But of course there is only 100 per cent of the audience. Any percentage taken up by cable is bound to decrease the percentage available to the networks. So it is not surprising that the audience of the networks declined from 93 per cent in 1975 to only 61 per cent in 1992. Since then, of course, the addition of a fourth network, Fox Television, has increased the total viewing of the network programmes without increasing the percentage to any one of them.

In this way the decline of the 'network' share of the audience in the United States has been a good deal steeper than in the UK where the combined figures for cable and satellite reception have made only a modest dent on the reception of the five national services.

In terms of financial viability the scale is all-important. Whereas the 24-hour weather station in the United States can survive on a tiny audience share, the weather station created in the UK in 1997 had to close within a few months because of a lack of viewers. Even in the United States the profit margins of television stations have declined. Those in the largest 'markets' still do well. But in the smaller markets the chances of survival into the medium term are not good.

There is no doubt that in the United States viewers have benefited from the development of the multichannel market place. It is less certain whether this has been the case in the UK where the five 'general' services have in fact covered the sort of diversity of programming that has been accorded to the American audience only recently.

It is one of the dangers of the present situation that broadcasters in the UK compare themselves to closely with the broadcasters in the United States. They deduce from American experience that the UK is bound to move in the same way. This is only partly true. Scale is important, as has already been observed. Expectation as regards quality is also important; British viewers have to some extent been spoilt by the high quality of British output in the last 30 or so years. That is why the decline in quality and diversity observed in the last decade or so has been so widely remarked. There is no doubt that the diversity injected into the system by the provision of cable systems has improved the range of choices available to American viewers. It is not obvious that the availability of cable, or indeed satellite, channels significantly increases the range of real options available to British viewers. The high turnover in customers of the cable systems (rather inelegantly called 'churn'), suggests that many cable customers are disappointed by the fare that they are offered. The turnover of customers of encrypted satellite channels betokens a similar disappointment with their offerings. It is not to be taken for granted that the numerical increase in options will be pop popd into the exercise of more active choice.

The future of regulation

The building of ever larger and more detailed regulating edifices as mass communications expands has been a feature of the last decade or so. Governments of both the right and the left (whether old or new) have given deregulated freedom with one hand, and taken away room for initiative and personal choice with the other. As a result this country now suffers the worst of all possible worlds: a lack of vision masked by pernickety attempts to tinker with the system. It may be help is at hand.

The then Secretary of State, Mr Chris Smith, told the Royal Television Society at its Cambridge Convention in September 1999: 'It's your job to make the digital revolution happen. It's my job to make sure that it happens in the interest of the consumer.'[24] This suggests that the government, for one, recognises its role: to ensure that the ordinary viewer is served well by those who make a living from the television industry. Mr Smith appears to recognise that a more radical approach to regulation is needed which uses existing law as far as possible,

> based in the first instance on competition law with a reduced set of distinctive media rules only where strictly necessary . . . the time for a more fundamental reassessment is coming and I believe that we must be ready to contemplate a more radical approach, including major legislation early in the next Parliament.[25]

The heart sinks at the suggestion of yet more major legislation. But if it means better legislation and more consolidation with the existing law of the land, then the effort may be worthwhile. As television becomes a more diverse tool, useful to the ordinary citizen in daily life, it needs to take account of existing laws. One would hope that, as the convergent strands of evolving information and media technology come together, so the need for a distinct range of regulatory instruments and agencies may decline. Much will depend on the quality of the broadcasters themselves. The quality of the human resources of the television industry has been much diluted as a result of the rapid expansion and commercialisation of large parts of the sector. In Chapter 10 we turn to this determinant of the future of television.

10

Professionals in Search of a Profession

The people who work in broadcasting fall into two groups: the entrepreneurs, whether in the public or the private sector, who decide what goes and who is employed/promoted if 'reliable' or sacked if incompetent or independent. The other group consists of the objects of these decisions, the workers. In the days of the BBC monopoly it was literally a matter of doing as you were told, or being out of a job and unemployable in broadcasting in Britain. The power over professional life or death in the apocryphal story of the newsreader found flirting with a secretary when John Reith passed by illustrates the totality of the subservience of BBC employees. The eleventh-hour reprieve: 'you may stay, but you must never read the epilogue', reinforces the mercy necessary in an autocratic employment situation to avoid mutiny among the slaves.

Since the broadcasting employees have no professional status of their own, and no single professional body, they have no corporate standards to pit against those of the employers. There is a multitude of trade organisations, most of them doing the job of a trade union, but few, if any, exercising control of their professional standards: British Actors Equity Association, Writers' Guild of Great Britain, Musicians' Union, Amalgamated Engineering Electrical Union, Cine Guilds of Great Britain, under whose umbrella operate: Association of Motion Picture Sound, British Society of Cinematographers, Guild of British Camera Technicians, Guild of British Film Editors, Guild of British Film Production Accountants and Financial Administrators, Guild of Film Production Executives, Guild of Location Managers, Guild of Special Effects Technicians, Guild of Stunt and Action Coordinators, Advertising Film and Videotape Producers' Association, Directors' Guild of Great Britain, Guild of British Animation and International Visual Communication's Association.[1] They therefore remain at the mercy of their employers, and the standards of conduct of their employers who are usually, in their turn, at the mercy of the broadcasting regulators.

For all this broadcasters have only themselves to thank. If they could bring themselves to identify unified standards of their own, and ensure that they and their colleagues observed these, they could begin to create a professional counterweight to their employers.

But broadcasting is a cut-throat business. Given the chance a broadcaster can on occasion be found who will, for the sake of employment, promotion or financial gain, do something that his or her predecessor refused to have anything to do with. Thus a particularly nasty act of violence or the rigging of a panel game can be arranged for the sake of the ratings. The *courage civil* to refuse is rare, because there is no well-thought-out position of principle on which it can be based, nor any group loyalty based on hard values. When, for example, researchers have been discovered booking fake guests to appear on a show, the reason has been that they were in insecure employment (freelance, on a fixed term contract, or frightened of losing their jobs), had an impossible job to do and needed to cut corners to do it in time. And they did so without complaining because they felt that if they complained, or failed to supply sufficient guests, they would not be hired again. So broadcasters are in the hands of their employers; they will mutter but in the end they will comply.

Russian roulette seems to have become a stock-in-trade of increasing competition. The producer who can with impunity go one better (or worse, more infamous or irresponsible) than the producer dealing with a comparable situation last time may win the acclaim of his or her peers and, no doubt, the approbation of the employers. It is remarkable how easily normally responsible people fall into this trap. And that is, as we have pointed out, because they have no corporate standards of their own. Bodies such as the Royal Television Society, the Producers' Guild, the British Academy of Film and Television Arts spend much time devising mutual admiration mechanisms which allow them to award each other prizes. They spend next to no time on the development of independent professional standards which would give backbone to their members vis-à-vis their employers. So the human resources of the industry are not helped to achieve levels of professional conduct which can stand up to the pressures of the organisations in which they are employed. In a confrontation with their employers producers therefore find themselves sliding down the slippery slope to compromise, relativism and half-truths.

What is to be done?

As the multiplication of channels, video and other outlets proceeds, the public control organs, as we have seen in Chapter 9, progressively lose their teeth. New, longer and ever more detailed codes are produced for political and public relations purposes. A large proportion of broadcast material is totally impervious to their existence, since it is produced outside the country. The exigencies of the schedules often render nugatory even those codes that *are* applicable. It is therefore essential that the broadcasters themselves, and here we refer to producers, directors, scriptwriters, editors and line managers in the production process, identify what they stand for, and achieve a consensus on what that position is. Will they, or will they not, produce or allow to be produced a particularly disgusting act of violence for the sake of attracting a few more viewers? Will they, or not, add a particularly vulgar twist to a sitcom with the same objective? Time after time in long careers concerned with the media we have come across people who are ashamed of the standards to which they expose their viewers, but nonetheless do so because they have no corporate culture to reinforce their own sound human instincts.

The extension of the role of the organisations of the broadcasters into the field of professional conduct is long overdue. If they were to recognise their responsibilities in this field, and do so energetically and comprehensively, they would transform the climate in the broadcasting and film industries. They would astonish and disconcert their employers. The presentation of a united front is as essential as it seems to be difficult. There will always be mavericks. But if the big battalions could agree, and persist in their argument, employers would have to take notice.

Much would be achieved if broadcasters could be given the right start. Broadcasting has always been an industry where people have learned on the job. The start as a production assistant led to the job of floor manager, on from there to the directing of programmes and the producer's responsibility. Moving up the line of promotion thereafter depends on a combination of conformity and luck, if not nepotism.

The BBC has been more disposed to spend time and money on training its staff. Although the start was late, and the scope limited, John Arkell, the then director of administration, in 1954 launched a General Training Scheme intended to attract a small number of highly promising university graduates to the BBC. These graduates were recruited by the same selection process as that by which entrants to what was then the Administrative (i.e. senior) Class of the Home Civil Service were recruited. This meant that those likely to deal with the BBC from the government side were selected on much the same criteria as the future heads of the BBC. They were likely to share the same assumptions about the role of the 'mandarins' in managing the country: high-minded, politically neutral and inbred with a strong conviction about the rightness of their views.[2]

Independent television never had an agreed training policy. At the BBC both Leonard Miall and Grace Wyndham Goldie complained that

ITV had failed to institute any training schemes. The companies were signing on BBC staff and broadcasters at higher salaries than they had ever been paid before. 'Why should we bother to train staff' was ITV's attitude: 'The BBC will do that for us.'[3] Granada was the exception here as in other fields. A comparable scheme to recruit able young graduates was instituted, although its emphasis was more on programme production than at the BBC.

One of the reasons why training has been so slow to develop is the absence of a clearly defined understanding of what broadcasting is about. Thirty years ago George Wedell wrote: 'As the medium grows up, it wants to assert a right to its own autonomous professionalism. This right is challenged by those who regard broadcasting as little more than a linking device between the *really* creative people and their public.'[4] John Wain, the writer, in the 1960s pleaded for

> a more sceptical attitude towards that professionalism that makes 'the medium' a value in itself. Television producers are understandably anxious to put a high technical gloss on their work, to produce beautifully finished programmes that use the medium to the full. But this anxiety can grow into a tyranny. If television is determined, as it seems to be, to challenge radio on its own ground, to become the mass medium that handles everything, then it will have to learn not to insist on remaking everything in its own image . . . what is this 'television' that has the lofty power of imposing its own nature on every kind of material?[5]

John Wain's scepticism of professionalism in television was extended by Barbara Wootton to sound radio.

> In sound radio the professionalism of the spoken-word producers is a tribute more to Professor Parkinson than to anyone else; and for *The Times* to write, *à propos* of the Reith Lectures that 'the talks producers can play almost as important a part in the success of the broadcasts as the lecturer' is deplorable nonsense.[6]

These views represented the intelligentsia's position vis-à-vis the broadcasters a generation ago. Thirty-five years later we have the impression that, on the whole, serious people have largely lost interest in television. Probably the converse is also true: television people have given up on serious people. This does not mean that television people are not serious: there are lots of competent people working in television. It is merely that their frames of reference have changed.

Two examples will serve: Tim Gardam, director of programmes at Channel 4, and Dawn Airey, director of programmes at Channel 5. Mr Gardam describes the role of Channel 4 as being

> to connect the most creative and surprising minds in Britain to an audience that is increasingly restless for new ideas. It has at its heart the belief that talent and creativity in Britain is, and always has been, anti-institutional. The best producers remain outsiders, often a pain in the neck to work with, but this conviction and obsession are at one with the claustrophobia they would feel in a corporate culture.[7]

Channel 4 was only a gleam in the eye of the pioneers of television in 1955. The model which they took for granted was the corporate culture created by John Reith for BBC Radio, adapted for BBC Television after the Second World War, and retained to a surprising extent for independent television in the mid-1950s. It was the creation of Channel 4 following the opening of a second channel by the BBC that opened the way for serious concern with minority interests. It has to be admitted that some of the interests the channel has followed up, such as American football and bungee-jumping, were not what the founders of the channel had in mind.

The contrast between the role of Channel 4 and the use of the remaining VHF frequencies to provide a fifth service accessible to about 80 per cent of viewers of terrestrial television could not be more marked. Channel 5 has no intellectual pretensions. It exists in order to use available frequencies. As Ms Dawn Airey, the channel's director of programmes, explains,

> I am in the commercial broadcast business. Channel 5 is there to make money for share holders, to return value on their investment and to ensure that the company they invested in is highly capitalised. I am not bound by Reithian aspirations. I am not a traditional public service broadcaster and I am not about aiming above people's heads – a little lower is more my style.[8]

One has the impression that Ms Airey has a fair amount of tongue-in-cheek in her description of her programme decisions.

This recent description of the role of Channel 5 raises some interesting points. Of course, the channel has a licence from the ITC, and has therefore to conform to the same basic requirements as the other independent television channels. Moreover, the qualifications of those responsible for Channel 5 should be of the same order as those responsible for the other independent television channels. The ITC should have satisfied itself that Channel 5 would have resources adequate to compete with the other ITV channels. And so forth. But it may well be that the ITC in the event never pursued the questions related to the comparability of standards. The government should insist on identifying the qualities of those permitted to control the television services in this country. Lord Reith had no doubt about the importance of the moral fibre of those being 'allowed' to work for the BBC. Over time the standard was relaxed, as it was bound to be in order to deal with the expansion of BBC services. But, as mentioned above, the senior staff of the Corporation are recruited on the same assumptions of moral rectitude as that expected of the senior branch of the Home Civil Service.

The Pilkington inquiry

The breaking of the monopoly in 1955 made it necessary to appoint contractors to conduct the independent television companies. The members of the ITA had to be fairly flexible in the standards they required of the applicants for television franchises. The question of 'fitness' to become a contractor to the Authority was answered entirely in terms of the financial competence of the applicant. Little, if any, attention was paid to the identification of the applicant with the area in which it wished to hold the monopoly franchise. That consideration came later, under pressure from investigations by the Pilkington Committee.[9] The terms of reference of the Committee were

> To consider the future of broadcasting services in the United Kingdom, the dissemination by wire of broadcasting and other programmes, and the possibility of television for public showing. To advise on the services which should in future be provided in the United Kingdom by the BBC and the ITA. To recommend whether additional services should be provided by any other organisation. To propose what financial and other conditions should apply to the conduct of all these services.[10]

The significance of the Pilkington inquiry derives from the fact it was the first undertaken since the creation of independent television. Its report was critical of the way in which the ITA had gone about the creation of the system. There was an element of consensus among the educated classes that the attitude of the Authority had been too lax and relativist. This attitude was criticised by Sir Robert Fraser, the first director-general of the Authority, in an address to the Manchester Luncheon Club in 1960.

If you decide to have a system of people's television, then people's television you must expect it to be. It will reflect their likes and dislikes, their tastes and aversions, what they can comprehend and what is beyond them. Every person of common sense knows that people of superior mental constitution are bound to find much of television intellectually beneath them. If such innately fortunate people cannot realise this gently and considerately and with good manners, if in their hearts they despise popular pleasures and interests, then of course they will be angrily dissatisfied with television. But it is not really television with which they are dissatisfied, it is with people.[11]

This criticism did not carry conviction with the 'people of superior mental constitution', who took a less dismissive attitude to ordinary people. Richard Hoggart, a prominent member of the Pilkington Committee, took the view that ordinary people deserved the best the broadcasters could provide, and needed continually to be encouraged to exercise a choice. Sir Kenneth Clark, who had been the first chairman of the ITA, wrote to Sir Harry Pilkington that '. . . more control will be needed to prevent a Gadarene Descent'.[12]

In the 40 years or so since the Pilkington Committee deliberated the problem of identifying standards in television has not gone away. Not only the identification of standards, but the means of maintaining them, have eluded the broadcasting policy makers over the years.

Where should the standard be fixed?

Is the relativism of Sir Robert Fraser (and his successors) the attitude that should be adopted, or is some more normative standard required? There is no doubt that the norms of civilised society should apply. To abandon these threatens a decline into cultural anarchy. A professional organisation based on its own standards would be in a much better position than the trade unions to stand up to the employers in the television industry.

In 1993 the late Sir Karl Popper[13] became concerned about the role in society of the relativism of those controlling television. He contributed to a colloquium of the European Institute for the Media held in the council chamber of Broadcasting House, London. Owing to his deafness his contribution took the form of a dialogue on video tape with George Wedell.[14] The following is the text of the dialogue.

> *Professor Wedell*   Sir Karl, I suggested that you might be willing to contribute to our colloquium because I know that you have become increasingly concerned in recent times about the effects of television on children. In answers to questions put to you in January of this year by Italian television, you said: 'I believe that the effect of television on a child can be immense. A child grows up in a world to which it must adjust itself. For this it is most important whether the world is friendly or hostile, loving or hating, gentle or violent, helpful or threatening.' Would you care to expand on this statement from your background as both a biologist and a philosopher?
>
> *Sir Karl Popper*   I shall say something as an educationalist. From 18 or 19 on I worked with difficult children. I actually started under Alfred Adler,[15] in a clinic he ran in Vienna, and I can say that the most difficult children with whom I had to work came from houses in which they had been exposed to violence (mainly due to beer, the excessive consumption of which was a Viennese working-class habit). The typical background from which you would get difficult children to deal with, including criminal children, was one in which the father would lose his temper and maltreat the mother; today, however, there is violence in every house, or in almost every house. In almost every house there is a box – the television set – which describes and brings violence into the house, into the home of the child.
>
> *Professor Wedell*   So, would you say that it is very important for someone to do an element of selection for the child, and for children's programmes especially to be directed to particular objectives connected with the learning process of children?
>
> *Sir Karl Popper*   Not the learning process; although one could be very successful in using television for this purpose, it is unlikely that one will see it happen to any great extent because of the

element of advertising in television, which makes development in that direction improbable.

Professor Wedell   One could argue that advertising has an informational value to it.

Sir Karl Popper   It also has a disinformational value.

Professor Wedell   Yet I think that most people would accept that the television programmes which are watched by children ought to have an element of direction to them.

Sir Karl Popper   I would – for the moment at least – be happy enough if there were no element of misdirection.

Professor Wedell   Moving on to the subject of television for adults, this aspect of television is often neglected on the grounds that grown-ups should be able to make up their own minds about what they watch. The attitude of the broadcasters themselves ranges from the views of most commercial broadcasters – that the doctrine of demand and supply applies in television as it does elsewhere and that it is their duty to give the public what it wants – to the view of the public service broadcasters who try to hang on, however tenuously, to the Reithian concepts of the provision of education, information and entertainment. At this end of the spectrum there has traditionally been quite a strong directive streak, although this has been weakening in recent years in the face of competition, mainly from the commercial channels. Would you, Sir Karl, comment on this range of options and indicate where, if anywhere, the responsibilities which ought to be exercised by the broadcasters on behalf of their viewers lie?

Sir Karl Popper   I perceive the whole situation much more radically than you. What is the direction to our society? The preservation of civilisation. Civilisation is the driving out of violence for our society. If we fail in this task, civilisation will decay and we shall have more and more violence; so what we have to aim at is the reduction of violence and what we have to be afraid of is an ongoing increase in violence. As I see it, the situation is much more urgent than one might deduce from what you say. It is a question of whether we educate our children to violence or not. I was around when television started, and nobody can deny that when television started it was more peaceful and more friendly. I think we have used the competition within television of which you were speaking to edge ourselves and others towards the presentation in ever greater volume of things that were better not presented, especially violence.

Professor Wedell   The question therefore arises of what you feel ought to be the way in which the public interest in the maintenance of civilisation is given expression. We have talked in the past about an equivalent to the Hippocratic oath which defines the responsibility of medical practitioners, but applied to media practitioners. In view of what you have said, how do you see this as being a possible solution to the problem of the responsibility of the broadcaster towards the public?

Sir Karl Popper   I have worked out the following plan: doctors can easily kill people, but they are prevented from doing so by a medical board which watches over them and threatens to deprive them of their powers if they do something they are not supposed to. Exactly what they are supposed to do is either obvious or difficult to define in the short time we have available to us. I believe that television has more power than doctors. It is the most powerful institution existing at present in our society; I also think that in a democratic society such a powerful institution has to be self-controlled. When I say 'self-controlled', I envisage a system such as that used by the doctors, who are answerable to a board of their peers, which is elected by them and perhaps by some others.

Professor Wedell   You have made a very important point about the management of this Hippocratic commitment, which is that it is managed by the doctors themselves. In television, there has always been an element of public intervention and public control, but it seems that you are saying that it would be better if the broadcasters could control themselves.

Sir Karl Popper   What I am thinking of is a method of licensing similar to that which applies to the doctors, and a certain course in public responsibility which all television people should undergo; they must be made aware that if things go on as they are now, they will – unwittingly because of competition and such factors – destroy civilisation.

Professor Wedell   Thank you, Sir Karl. You have made a very helpful contribution to the thinking of the Institute on a subject with which it is much concerned at the present time.

Professor Popper's proposal for the institution of a 'Hippocratic oath' for broadcasters has evoked echoes in media circles since he made it in 1993. The proposal was circulated to the participants in the Royal Television Society's Convention in Cambridge in 1995. It appears to have been published in the United States.[16] It may be that the time has come to take up the proposal in a context where the expansion in the number of television outlets renders effective public accountability less and less feasible.

But first the nature of the Hippocratic oath. It runs as follows:

> I swear by Apollo the physician, and Æsculapius, and Health, and All-heal,[17] and all the gods and goddesses, that, according to my ability and judgment, I will keep this Oath and this stipulation – to reckon him who taught me this Art equally dear to me as my parents, to share my substance with him, and relieve his necessities if required; to look upon his offspring in the same footing as my own brothers, and to teach them this art, if they shall wish to learn it, without fee or stipulation; and that by precept, lecture,[18] and every other mode of instruction, I will impart a knowledge of the Art to my own sons, and those of my teachers, and to disciples bound by a stipulation and oath according to the law of medicine, but to none others. I will follow that system of regimen which, according to my ability and judgment, I consider for the benefit of my patients, and abstain from whatever is deleterious and mischievous. I will give no deadly medicine to any one if asked, nor suggest any such counsel; and in like manner I will not give to a woman a pessary to produce abortion. With purity and with holiness I will pass my life and practise my Art. I will not cut persons labouring under the stone, but will leave this to be done by men who are practitioners of this work. Into whatever houses I enter, I will go into them for the benefit of the sick, and will abstain from every voluntary act of mischief and corruption; and, further, from the seduction of females or males, of free men and slaves. Whatever, in connexion with my professional practice, or not in connexion with it, I see or hear, in the life of men, which ought not to be spoken of abroad, I will not divulge, as reckoning that all such should be kept secret. While I continue to keep this Oath unviolated, may it be granted to me to enjoy life and the practice of the art, respected by all men, in all times! But should I trespass and violate this Oath, may the reverse be my lot.[19]

It is, of course, a product of its age and a full exposition of the text is not possible here. Suffice it to say that Hippocrates was a Greek physician. He is thought to have lived from about 460 to 377 or 359 BC. He was the most celebrated physician of antiquity; he was born and practised on the island of Cos. His oath derives from his experience as a doctor and teacher, and it is relevant to a consideration of his practice to know that he was not an altruistic do-gooder. He taught for money, and earned his living in that way. The Hippocratic oath is, as we have seen, an oath stating the obligations and proper conduct of physicians, formerly taken by those beginning medial practice. Parts of the oath are still used in some medical schools.

How transferable is the concept of such a professional commitment to people working in broadcasting, an industry which contains a variety of workers with widely different occupational profiles and levels of education? It would be important to identify those to whose conduct professional commitment of this kind would make a difference.

There are two specific areas in which it would be useful. The first is in influencing the quality of the output. Anyone committed to avoid causing harm to his or her patients (= viewers) would evidently be willing to take part in the production of some programmes and not others. The refusal to undertake some assignments might well lose them work which would be given to others with no such professional scruples. Thus the success of a professional scheme on Hippocratic lines would depend on the extent to which all those with a given professional profile were willing to subscribe to it.

In such a context the role of a professional body or learned society would be decisive. If the Royal Television Society (RTS) or the British Academy of Film and Television Arts, for example, decided to make admission to membership subject to a judgement about professional competence, and a commitment to a specific code of conduct, then it might bring about a significant raising of the sense of responsibility of the profession. At present, as far as we are aware, neither the Society nor the Academy has such a requirement. The Society's mission statement begins its priority areas by stating that it aims 'to strengthen the reputation of the RTS, provided as a "learned society", as an "academy" for the industry as it approaches the 21st century'.[20] The use of these terms from the academic vocabulary is appropriately put into inverted commas, because the Society does not seem to understand what they mean or what disciplines they presuppose. If the Society were to take these two concepts seriously, this might well reduce the number of members eligible to join. At the same time the knowledge that the Society applied specific professional criteria to its members might significantly improve its influence on the industry. Action by the Society might encourage the ITC to take its one regulatory role more seriously.

The British Academy of Film and Television Arts (BAFTA) has a production, rather than, in the case of the RTS, an engineering background. So it is arguable that the Academy operates according to less tangible criteria than the RTS, closer perhaps to its neighbour across the road in Piccadilly, the Royal Academy consisting of painters and sculptors. BAFTA is at present aiming to help starters in film or television. 'When you start out in television', Jan Clarke the chief executive has explained,

> you are craving an opportunity to continue learning, but you haven't got the support structure anymore of a college. So you've got a lot of fragmented individuals, just starting out in the industry, wanting to feel connected to a network. BAFTA is the place for them. I want them to become members. There's a snag however . . . they've got to have a track record, a minimum of three years. I want them gradually to come to events and then after two or three years . . . to join.[21]

The second beneficial effect of taking such Hippocratic commitments seriously would be to ensure for the workers in the industry a point of reference independent of their employers. As Janice Turner editor of the journal of BECTU, the principal trade union of the broadcasting industry, has pointed out, the effect of market liberalisation has been to weaken the position of the workers in the industry:

> The search for more and ever greater returns to investors and the deliberate weakening of union power has led companies to more and more rounds of cost-cutting and redundancies, thus adversely affecting output and quality, not to mention the quality of the workers' lives – despite the fact that in many cases the company concerned is already very profitable. This has also caused widespread attempts to circumvent corporate obligations towards employees. Now only 40 per cent of the workforce is in tenured, full-time employment; another 30 per cent are insecurely self-employed, involuntarily part-time, or casual workers; while the bottom 30 per cent are unemployed or working for poverty wages.
>
> In the BBC, market forces were introduced under the aegis of the policy of Producer Choice. The idea was that instead of the Corporation working as one united whole, it was broken down into small business units, apportioned a percentage of overheads, and all the units were told to buy and sell services from one to another. Producers were theoretically able to 'choose' whether to use the BBC's own staff and facilities or hire them from outside the

Corporation. However, absurd calculations of overheads for BBC departmental budgets, coupled with essential BBC expenditure on public service duties which are not carried by independent companies (e.g. maintaining an orchestra), mean that if price alone is the criteria, there is no choice at all. The observation that no normal company would give its workforce the choice of not using the company's own quality facilities appears to have been lost somewhere along the line.

The situation in ITV has also deteriorated. The last franchise round produced new publisher-broadcasters, making hardly any programmes themselves. So in previously profitable programme making franchises, especially the former Thames franchise, mass lay-offs resulted. Across the network, profitable companies sacked thousands of staff between them before the new franchises were awarded, with the excuse that they needed to build 'war chests' to finance their bids.

Afterwards the redundancies continued, but with little justification. At LWT, redundancies were carried out while the top 44 managers participated in a share scheme, which ultimately netted them upwards of £70 million. (Contrary to their claims, the nature of the scheme was such that there was hardly any risk attached. Their share options, set up *before* the outcome of the franchise bids was known, at pre-franchise share prices, only had to be taken up *after* the announcement on whether they had won their new franchise.)

More recently, when MAI took over Anglia, the 1992 profits had increased by more than 100 per cent. MAI's first move was to announce the redundancy of one-third of the staff, many of whom were hired back as freelances. And in December 1995, when ITN was reportedly in line for record profits, staff at the company balloted for strike action after management had turned down a demand for a pay rise and sought to cut other benefits and derecognise the unions. This had followed a two-year pay freeze accepted by staff on the basis that ITN was having financial problems. It was discovered from company accounts that during the first year of the pay freeze, directors had awarded themselves increases in remuneration of 64 per cent, and increases in their pension contributions of 70 per cent.

Working hours in ITV and ITN are as bad, if not worse, than those at the BBC. The concept of annualised hours, where an employee is contracted to work a number of hours per year, effectively allows companies to work their employees at unacceptable levels of hours per day or week, with little compensation for it in overtime pay.

Towards the end of 1999 ITN proposed the introduction of night working for all staff, resulting in increased levels of stress and a damaging effect on home lives through seeing families less often. ITN maintained that total flexibility is necessary if ITN is to remain competitive.

The impact of this casualisation, not to say exploitation, is much against the public interest.

(a) Much of the training in the broadcasting industry has been through the apprenticeship system. Make-up and hair artists, riggers, painters, carpenters, wardrobe and wigs etc. have all learned their skills by watching how the industry's most accomplished professionals work. Since these grades have been casualised, including at the BBC, there is now little chance of apprenticeship training so the skills base and quality of the workforce is being diminished. Recent research from *Skillset* shows how fast our skilled workforce is disappearing: the average age of workers in the set construction grades is middle aged and rising, and these grades have the greatest proportion of people over 50.

(b) When large companies or corporations, such as the BBC, close down departments and contract out the work, it ends their interest in developing new technological innovation in these areas. Small companies with uncertain income are often unable or unwilling to put money into this, either because they don't have enough, or their future prospects are too uncertain to finance such investment – or even that they prefer to make larger profits now. The case of the special effects sector in the film and broadcasting industry is a case in point. The BBC's job (and that of ITV) as a public service must be to keep our industry at the forefront of technology.

(c) The industry is totally dependent on ideas. It is a creative industry. Therefore it depends on its workforce first and foremost. Unfortunately the majority of its current workforce is made up of people in a state of what may be termed 'permanent instability'. These people have little idea where their next job is coming from; their freelance/casual employment status makes it difficult to obtain a mortgage, house and other insurance, or loans. Their fear of upsetting their employers and thus not being rehired forces them to work all the hours they are told. Working 60–90 hours in one week is fairly common. Many dare not complain of risky health and safety practices, or poor treatment. People in this state of instability are hardly in a position to give of their best, no matter how deep their commitment to the programme.

(d) These same conditions give rise to breakdowns in people's family life. They lead to increased levels of ill-health through higher rates of stress-related illnesses such as heart attacks; alcohol or drug-related illness; accidents at work or traffic accidents due to over-work (falling asleep at the wheel). BECTU now wins around £1 million in compensation for its members every year.

(e) Casualisation is losing the industry its most valuable workers – those with years of experience. There is discrimination against hiring workers over 50 – in fact, there is increasing anecdotal evidence of discrimination against people over the age of 40. One producer/director says: 'Most people over 35 are considered to be "geriatric" by those running production companies. Younger people are cheaper – a decided advantage in these days of ultra-low budget productions in which quality is no longer considered to be of prime importance.'[22]

An industry to be proud of

The developments described above are likely to have affected the levels of job satisfaction of those that remain in television. But it is not only the shrinking of job opportunities and the casualisation of employment that have produced the disease which now pervades the people working in television.

The cuts reducing the numbers employed in independent television from about 15 000 in 1990 to just over 8000 in 1996[23] have evidently left their scars. Of course, some of these jobs have been transferred to the independent production companies. Having, moreover, been content to run a high-cost industry during the golden age of the duopoly, any thinking person would not have expected this comparatively affluent condition to go on for ever.

Yet the same carelessness that allowed overmanning and excessive staffing, coupled with the absence of clearly identified standards of qualification and experience, allowed an element of nepotism to creep into the history, as Mr John Willis, son of Lord (Ted) Willis, pointed out in a speech to the RTS in 1999. He said: 'We need to make sure there is a healthy, diverse and trained intake. Otherwise only kids with well-off parents and good contacts need apply. It is not a healthy industry when only our own children and their friends can get a job.'[24] The old boy 'network' among programme makers was disclosed in the early results of a survey of entrants to the television industry conducted by the British Film Institute. According to this, 30 per cent of respondents in the 41–50-year age group said that they had secured their jobs through personal contacts, this percentage rose to 44 per cent for entrants in the 21–30-year age group. Families such as the Grades have dominated show business; the Dimblebys current affairs; the Magnussons news and current affairs; and so forth. In fact Mr Willis's wife Janet is the co-author of the Television Industry Tracking Study, which has drawn attention to this state of affairs.

For those not blessed with family connections in television the burgeoning non-discipline of so-called media studies is thought to provide a means of access. There are few universities which have not succumbed to the temptation to launch first degree courses in the subject in the course of the inflation of university numbers of the last decade. The lead was taken by the polytechnics and further education colleges, which began to provide degree courses in the 1980s and 1990s.

We resisted these pressures in the University of Manchester, believing that the value of a first degree depended on the discipline required to master a well-defined field of study with a clearly delimited subject matter such as English, history, mathematics, philosophy, sociology or economics. We were, moreover, persuaded by practical experience that good broadcasters need well-trained minds schooled in careful analytical methods and, preferably, a good grounding in the humanities. On such a basis we believe it is possible to build a professional postgraduate course which, with carefully structured practical experience, prepares a limited number of candidates for one or other branch of the broadcasting profession.

Alas, our diagnosis of ways of preparing potential broadcasters has so far fallen on stony ground. As one lecturer in the subject has admitted, 'The hardest thing about running a media course is preparing all those young for jobs that don't exist.'[25] The institutions that offer such courses incur a heavy responsibility in misleading impressionable young people at an important point in their career development.

It may be that the disappointment experienced by many of the present generation of graduates in media studies will engender a healthy realism in the academic area. 'There are signs', one media studies lecturer has written,

> that the mood is changing. One consistent complaint has been that media studies courses are too wide-ranging, so the newer ones have become more specialised . . . prejudice will be broken down if the industry knows what the students are learning and if the teaching staff have the respect of the industry.[26]

In the European Institute for the Media we have had a steady demand
from broadcasters with between 5 and 15 years of practical experience
for attachment, individually or in small groups, to our research projects. This has worked to the benefit of both sides. It has brought into
the Institute people with significant experience in the industry; and it
has exposed broadcasters to some of the fundamental questions with
which they have to grapple if television is to be a blessing rather than a
curse of modern society. In particular one colleague from the television
industry found it helpful to catch up on the reading of significant
texts. Those in directing positions need from time to time to refresh
their criteria of judgement. We are inclined to adopt the list of required
reading for members of the 1997 Nolan Commission on Standards of
Conduct in Public Life:

Aristotle: *Ethics*
Max Weber: *Politics as a Vocation*
Michael Oakeshott: *Rationalism in Politics and Other Essays*
Conor Cruise O'Brien: *The Great Melody*
Sir Lewis Namier: *The Structure of Politics at the Accession of George III*
*Report of the Royal Commission on Standards of Conduct in Public Life,
1976*
John Grigg: *Lloyd George*
Leo Amery: *Thought on the Constitution*
Peter Riddell: *Honest Opportunism: the Rise of the Career Politician*
Julian Critchley: *A Bag of Boiled Sweets*

People in the television industry are, whether they recognise this or
not, guardians of the public philosophy of our age, those who set the
tone of the discourse of the people. Hence the argument of this chapter
links with Chapter 3, 'The Accountants Drive out the Guardians' and
with Sir Karl Popper's discourse on our civilisation. The books on the
Nolan list will leave their readers with not only more understanding of
the motivation of our common life but also of the profound origins of
that motivation, and of the sense of humour which keeps it going.
They will also ensure a proper understanding of the relationship
between freedom and control. Our common life, having achieved this
delicate balance, is once again in danger of succumbing to the dictates
of authoritarian managers. Both at the BBC and in independent television the effect of intense competition has been to turn their managing
staffs into what has come to be called control freaks, i.e. people who
believe that they must control all aspects of their operations if their

well-meant designs are to come to fruition. Mercifully such control can rarely be sustained for any length of time.

The abandonment by the last three governments of the carefully constructed network of independent television companies derives from a centripetal tendency, which threatens to destroy the imperfect and yet creative diversity of the service. So it was not surprising that ITV's three major shareholders, the heads of Carlton, Granada and United News and Media, did not like some of the views expressed by the ITV chief executive, Mr Richard Eyre, in his McTaggart Lecture in Edinburgh in the summer of 1999. If they understood the nature of their roles they would have recognised that their chief executive was entitled to exercise the freedom deriving from his post. Instead one of the board members of ITV informed him 'You are entitled only to the opinions we allow you to have.'[27] The consequence followed as day follows night: Mr Eyre resigned and the key appointment in independent television once more fell vacant. The control freaks are once more at a loss.

11
Television at the Crossroads: Which Way to Turn?

Moving the goalposts

The previous chapters have illustrated the choices which television is facing. As a dynamic aspect of our common life it has been, and will continue to be, in crisis. But since this is being written just before the end of the millennium, not to mention the *fin de siècle*, the options before us are perhaps rather more fundamental than they have been for some time. Moreover, the 18 years of Thatcherism and neo-Thatcherism with its thoughtless pursuit of the market paradigm have put in question verities which in 1979 were regarded as relatively established. The advance of information technology has added to the climate of flux which currently dominates thinking about the communications industry. It has unsettled the BBC; and it has put the commercial broadcasters off their well-established target of providing good quality television for the population of their coverage areas while making a more than adequate return. The goalposts are being moved and nobody quite knows where they will be repositioned. The government is taking an understandably short view: let us get digitalisation out of the way in the next decade, and then think again.

The commercial sector is pushing hard for a global market. The specious argument that only players on the global scale will survive in the new millennium has persuaded politicians to abandon the well-established regional structure of ITV. The people who matter, the viewers, are as usual conservative and in the main hold on to the range of five terrestrial channels. Even Channel 5 has had problems in establishing itself. The poor take-up of cable and satellite channels demonstrates that there is little hunger for more choice; indeed the use of television appears to be declining.

On the assumption that, the old framework having been destroyed, some new structure has to be designed, two organisations, the Institute for Public Policy Research (IPPR) and the Campaign for Quality Television, have tried to think creatively about possible new dispensations. *The Third Age of Broadcasting* report of the IPPR[1] and *The Purposes of Broadcasting*[2] both make sensible proposals, which do not involve the wholesale scrapping of existing structures. They concentrate on the output: what can be done to give viewers a reliable television service? As such the proposals are at least operating in the right ballpark. They are properly concerned with the central issue: quality television.

Outside those concerned with this issue, most of the entrepreneurs seem to succumb to the financial opportunities which the present confusion offers. Typical of these seems to be a Mr Jeffrey Berg, chairman and chief executive of International Creative Management who, in a lecture on media companies and the creation of value at the London School of Economics in 1998, announced that media companies 'were now interested in all aspects of communication including the Internet. Far from concentrating on movies and television, media companies would be focussing more in future on "new media" and "e-commerce".'[3]

Touching on government regulation, Mr Berg distinguished between the attitude to culture in this country and the USA: 'Culture, basically, in the UK is a political phenomenon; in the United States it's purely a commercial phenomenon.'[4] The difference certainly exists. We know the history of American mass communications is essentially commercial. Over here culture belongs to the community at large, and governments of different political persuasions have taken a positive attitude to it. At best they have taken the view that culture, like broadcasting, should be supported from public finds without making it subservient to political considerations. At present the clearly contrasted attitude which has defined the British view of culture is at risk due to deregulation of broadcasting in the UK. The massive economic dominance of the US media system, as well as the sharing of a common language, means that we are much more exposed than other European countries to American influence. It remains to be seen whether we can retain the cultural autonomy necessary to prevent the total Americanisation of our mass media. This requires firm control of television in the public interest, and the underpinning of facilities for national and regional television production. Support for the creative elements of the industry is at present more important than censorship of what limited output there is.

Needs must when innovation drives

As we point out in Chapter 2, development in television has in the past been technology-led. Viewers did not know they wanted television until technological innovators showed them what was possible. Now of course, it is in the interest of the television entrepreneurs to demonstrate the growing dependence of a proportion of the population on what television can offer. Its future will be determined by viewer demand. Having begun as a public service system in the 1920s, the Corporation until recently maintained a primacy which has outlived the breaking of the monopoly in 1954 and the arrival of the technology innovations of the 1980s and the early 1990s.

There is by now some evidence of an element of viewer resistance. The take-up of satellite and cable is slower than expected, and of digital terrestrial services marginal, in spite of the improved picture and sound quality which is promised. The recommendation by the Broadcasting Select Committee in December 1999 that the BBC should not be granted an additional licence fee of £24 in respect of digital services had not, at the time of writing, been assured by the Secretary of State for Culture, Media and Sport. If he follows the Committee's advice, the development of digital broadcasting will be put back.

This in turn will affect the adoption of other innovations. The development of television equipment which takes up less space in the home is likely to be the next urgent requirement. Flat-screen technology may well be the preferred answer of the conservative television viewer. And although few exercise a wide range of choice, the electronic programme guide may follow.

A technical obstacle which has so far been imperfectly overcome is the language barrier. This has reinforced the dependence of the broadcasters on American programmes. The costs of dubbing, subtitling or voice-over transfers into English still render the use of non-English language programming prohibitive and cumbersome.[5] Non-English language services have come to build the cost of dubbing (in the larger countries) or subtitling (in the smaller countries) into their programme production costs. The sheer volume and the effective marketing of Hollywood products have given American products economies of scale which have strengthened their hold on the market. Attempts to create a comparable European market in programmes have come to grief largely on the diversity of languages in use, and on the lack of a Europe-wide marketing strategy.

The lack of innovative technology to overcome the language barrier has seemed to reinforce the primacy of Hollywood. As the number of daily broadcasting hours increased, and finally filled the whole day, the demand for material outstripped supply. More and more films came to be used. This reinforced the role of Hollywood. Pressure was exerted on the American regulatory authorities by the media interests, to change the law inhibiting the monopolistic tendencies of the media industry. Since the 1970s US Federal rules, which were designed to protect the big Hollywood studios, prohibited the broadcast networks from owning the entertainment production enterprises. In the mid-1990s these rules were repealed at the insistence of those who wished to combine the television and film branches of the industry. This resulted in Walt Disney buying the ABC network; the News Corporation set up its own fourth network while buying the Fox film studios; and, more recently Viacom bought CBS. Only NBC, part of General Electric, is still looking for a partner in the production side of the industry.

In the UK there has only recently been any attempt to separate production from broadcasting, particularly in the BBC. But other elements of regulation, such as the rules of public service broadcasting, have prevented the BBC from engaging in a similar global outreach to that of the American media giants. Now it is argued that the US trend to tie together production and distribution is an inevitable development which other countries must follow. In this country it is argued that the inevitable consequence is the privatisation of the BBC, so that the Corporation can develop its brand on a global scale. This leads to the key question: for whom is a broadcasting service provided? As *The Independent* argued in an editorial headed 'Another reason to privatise the BBC',

> Across the industrial spectrum 'vertical integration' – the tying together of product and distribution – has once again become the corporate end game. The merits of this process are at best debatable, both from a public interest perspective and in terms of commercial benefit to the new partners. But there seems to be no stopping it now. In the US, both business leaders and policy makers share a common vision: the creation of media Goliaths which will allow domination of one of the world's fastest growing industries.[6] This trend should be firmly resisted by the UK television industry, if it wishes to survive.

The accountants drive out the guardians

The Reithian concept of the guardians of broadcasting derived from the concept of the public corporation invented during the First World War. It required the Corporation to use the trilogy of entertainment, education and information in the service of the public. While the monopoly lasted this was not challenged. Anyone who did was doing him or herself out of a job and, given the monopoly control of BBC employment, out of a livelihood. Now all this has changed. The guardians have to compete with the commercial sector. Following the introduction of accountants the neo-classical model of economics began to be used. The concept of producer choice in the BBC forced the accountants to estimate the cost of such choice. They effectively took over the decision-making role.

The effect of the accountants on content is already there for all to see. The decline of home-produced drama, of news and current affairs coverage which costs money. The peak-hour reliance on crime (whether on tape or on film) and on game shows which rely on cash prizes to attract audiences means that television is deprived of most programmes that would be worth seeing.

If viewers are not progressively to vote with their remote control equipment, then responsibility for content will have to revert to some kind of guardian, whose interest is in the service of the public. They will be accountable, but in the context of broadcasting for the UK, not for the global media market. The service of national and regional audiences will be their first responsibility, and they will not be diverted from that by specious arguments of management consultants.

That's all we have time for: news and current affairs

The controversy about the timing of Independent Television News in the course of 1999 has to some extent obscured the changing role of news bulletins on British television. News and current affairs has retained from its role during the Second World War an aura of priority. It is assumed that viewers will want the news, whatever else they are prepared to forgo. And in the course of duty the weekly current affairs slot is retained by the regulators as an obligation.

We regard news and current affairs as an obligatory commitment of all those who aspire to control a general service television licence. In practice, as we recount in Chapter 4, television news is now so pervasive, both in the general programmes and in the 24-hour news services, that the BBC1 news, the lead programme in the genre, no longer holds the primacy it once enjoyed.

The issue is no longer when and where to place a news bulletin, but its content. Will it provide adequate coverage of domestic and foreign news? Will the news element of the bulletin be given more attention than sport, or gossip? What is the place of parliamentary coverage? These are the issues which will claim attention in the twenty-first century. And these issues lead into the financial basis of news gathering and the resources appropriate to news bulletins of the major terrestrial channels.

Similarly the seriousness with which current affairs is treated is a yardstick by which the quality of a general service channel should be measured. The temptation is great to treat current affairs as part of the entertainment output; to deal with themes that attract audiences instead of leading viewers to a better understanding of the major issues of the day.

Sport: does the tail wag the dog?

A serious outcome of television sports coverage is that sports performance and competition are losing their autonomy. Although one accepts that contractors, broadcasters and advertisers wish to maximise audiences and profits their capacity to manage audience share currently envisages behind-the-scenes bargaining and manipulation in fixing long-term contracts for coverage. Attempts to gain monopolistic contracts are particularly important for football and other major sports with considerable attention to timing, duration and even rules of the game, like one-day matches in cricket. The use of combined contract packages, which bundle minor sports, may be of some assistance to them, but the viewer has no say in this. While television is primarily an important part of the wider entertainment industry, increasingly promoters make financial investment in major clubs, with effective determination in contracts of numbers of games, length of season and even earnings of players. The promoters also control payments for the promotion of sports goods, clothing and other lifestyle features. Sport is thus losing its symbolic and traditional national image by being subordinated to the requirements of the broadcasters.

The issues discussed in Chapter 5 tend to turn on the economics of sports coverage as much as on sport itself. Football has become the predominant television sport, and is by far the major preoccupation of the sports entrepreneurs. Minor sports, by definition, attract less attention, even though they fill the schedules of the minority channels, particularly in off-peak hours.

The battle for ratings: peak-hour schedules

Since the arrival of 24-hour television the costs of continuous operation have grown. For reasons known only to the broadcasters themselves, the urge 'never to close' has led to the filling of schedules with low-cost programmes in off-peak hours. But even these hours have to be paid for, even if audiences are meagre. The opportunities for profit remain largely in the peak hours. Peak-hour programmes, therefore, consist largely of well-tried uncontroversial material, mainly in crime series, soap operas and game shows. Assuming peak hours run from 6.30 to 10.30 p.m. on weekdays and for seven hours at weekends, the main income accrues during about 34 hours each week. Variety during these hours is therefore unlikely: 11 hours of crime series (including films), 11 hours of soap operas and 11 hours of game shows make up the peak-hour genres. Regular high-quality programming is virtually ruled out by the economics of 24-hour operation. The need to keep a number of audiences on board means that crime series must have a romantic subplot to attract different segments of the audience.

The exploitation of emotion

In the main programme services violence and sex have currently achieved an agreed element of self-censorship. The more explicit treatment of both genres tends to be relegated to video cassettes which can be viewed in private. The eight categories of the British Board for Film Classification cover a wider range of brutality, horror and sexual exploitation than before. In addition the Board is currently experimenting with the acceptance of visual images which were automatically prohibited before. The fact that a single board provides classification of video recordings as well as of films for both television and film exhibition, has established a measure of uniformity in the treatment of these areas which is beneficial. But the temptation to play Russian roulette remains, particularly in the area of violence.

Minority programmes: a major problem

The breadth of the programme genres covered in Chapter 8 is vast. It ranges from programmes for children to what is now called the History Zone: two clearly distinguished programme streams. The worry which has beset children's programming persists. It concerns its general decline; the exploitation of the easy option of the use of cartoons; the conflict between cheap animation and expensive production of *Blue Peter*-type educative programmes; the failure to engage the full potential of ethnic creative talent; the temptation to regard downloading in the small hours as equivalent to programme provision; and so forth. It may well be that digital thematic channels will resolve the current competition for airspace.

Programmes for children have been shown as highly vulnerable in the quality stakes. Some are so trivial that they frequently lose audiences, as certainly they do in summer when children discover more active and educational experiences with their friends and playmates. There are few observers who would defend the present pattern of provision. But it is not just programme content. The capitulation to cartoons and adult-dominated presentations, drawing to a large extent on imported materials, is a betrayal of children and an affront to the talented programme makers in this country. The targeting of children by advertisers betrays a cynical abuse of them as a captive audience. The growing concern about this in the European Union may bring about the ending of this abuse.

Shoring up the stable door: the limits of regulation

The television industry has now reached a stage of diversification where the management of regulation becomes difficult. As Ian McBride of Granada is cited in Chapter 9, 'the industry needs regulation to keep it honest.'[7] This state of affairs requires prompt action. Is it realistic to pile more regulatory efforts on each other, even if the chance of their being heeded is small? What is the alternative?

The alternative is to recognise the limitations of the system and not to expect it to bear a load which it cannot sustain. We need to modify the regulations in such a manner that what remains is relevant and enforceable. This is a job for the government. The regulators, the BBC and the ITC, the BSC, and, of course, the programme providers must be helped to simplify their codes and requirements. The best way of ensuring compliance is to make sure that the programme providers appointed, whether in the public service or the commercial sectors, understand clearly what is required of them and exercise their responsibility to their viewers. For example, there are the obligations on regional programming. The contractors need to understand that this is a *sine qua non*, without which their contracts become null and void. The system needs to return to a situation where contractors do not sign contracts if they have no intention of observing them. We need to achieve a situation of full and willing compliance, which does not require constant policing.

This presupposes a mindset in which all broadcasters pull together. It may be that the historical split between the BBC and ITV, not to mention the other channels, militates against the cooperation essential for the television industry. It may be that the only way in which a common mind and will are achieved is the creation of a single broadcasting authority to which all broadcasters will be accountable.

Any proposal of this kind is likely to raise hackles, at least in the BBC, which will appeal to its special status deriving from the Corporation's royal charter. The rest of the broadcasting system derives its legitimacy from the relevant legislation. But a single regulator makes sense to the viewers because their interest is in what appears on the screen, not in the juridical status of the broadcasters, which harks back to a historical accident.

In a McTaggart Lecture at the 1999 Edinburgh International Television Festival the then head of the ITV secretariat, Mr Richard Eyre, asked the question, 'Is there a post-Reithian model of public service broadcasting?'[8] His answer to the question was:

> Public service broadcasting will soon be dead . . . because it relies on an active broadcaster and a passive viewer . . . it relies on regulators who will in time no longer be able to do a comprehensive job. . . . Have we reached that point when we're obliged to let the market decide? And does that mean it's all over for quality television? . . . Well, no because it is not true to say that broadcasters can thrive without reference to the public interest.[9]

Mr Eyre suggests that we should employ the formula 'broadcasting in the public interest' rather than 'public service broadcasting', and postulates that all will be well if that is done. In practice, without careful definition of *how* that is done, the substitution of one term for another will be a distinction without a difference. Mr Eyre claims that the job of regulators 'in the next five to ten years will become impossible. Effective regulation needs teeth and an ultimate sanction.'[10] That, as we have already pointed out, is agreed. But how is it to be done? Mr Eyre does not explain how it is to be done. Without some agreed basis for action his forecast will come true: 'It is a fact of life that future broadcasters will push the boundaries of taste and decency and some people will be very uncomfortable.'[11] At that point both ITV and the BBC will fail their audiences unless their controllers have a clear understanding of the civilisation in which we all share, and to which Sir Karl Popper refers in Chapter 10. Civilisation, according to the *OED*, is 'an advanced stage or system of social development'. It confers freedom under the law on all citizens. It expects from the citizen conduct which is enlightened and educated. Such conduct includes the ability to distinguish between civilised behaviour that recognises rules supporting enlightened relations between individual citizens, and uncivilised behaviour which takes no account of the sensibilities of fellow citizens, particularly when pursued for personal gain.

All citizens are expected to contribute to the maintenance of a civilisation just as all citizens benefit from it. It is not permissible for anyone to exercise authority unless he or she subscribes to the support of that civilisation. That, as they say, 'goes without saying'! If such a shared civilisation is no longer subscribed to by all reasonable people, civilisation is in danger of disintegration. In broadcasting the effect of disintegration can be fast and pervasive.

Professionals without a profession

The plea by Sir Karl Popper in Chapter 10 for a professional commitment, analogous to the Hippocratic oath of doctors, to be undertaken by broadcasters is very powerful. Anyone who has followed the analysis of trends in television in this book cannot but have sympathy with Sir Karl's proposal. The question is whether the proposal is practicable, given the structure and history of the television industry.

The introduction of thresholds of admission to the industry would close access to what has been a theoretically open system. Although entry to the BBC effectively closed the system in its early days, it has become much more open since the creation of the commercial system and the creation of satellite and cable channels. The addition of the world wide web has effectively removed even such inhibitions as existed. As we argue in Chapter 10, the insistence on professional standards and discipline for workers in television could, not to put it more strongly, replace the progressively less effective regulatory machinery which is currently in place. If there existed a corps of television professionals whose standards would not allow them to degrade the content of television programmes beyond a given level, then the need for controllers and censors (even of the feeble type provided by the ITC) might become largely superfluous. The professionals would (as to some extent they do already) establish codes of conduct and of practice of their own which would satisfy most, if not all, their clients (who are the viewers).

So this is worth considering, even if in the short term it will be difficult to achieve. On the way to such a development the quasi-professional organisations such as the RTS and BAFTA should consider ways and means of identifying unacceptable practice in the same way as they already reward acceptable, if not always distinguished, practice. If this were done, and members of these bodies were suspended for unacceptable standards, the argument would move in the right direction. In any case these bodies should establish means to identify poor quality output, and take active notice of this tendency in the industry.

The training of entrants to the television industry and, indeed, the further education of people working in it, should receive much more active consideration than it has done. Many of the professional bodies in other sectors (lawyers, doctors, teachers) already insist on continuing professional education than the practitioners in television. The rapid expansion of first degree courses in university-level institutions referred to in Chapter 10 needs the support of those leading the television industry to strengthen their links with the trainees. Such training should not be limited to technical competence. It should have as an integral part education in the social philosophy and ethics of television and the identification of professional standards. Active engagement by those purporting to lead the television industry could, over the medium term, significantly improve its performance. Indeed it would not be too much to assert that it might help in the affirmation of the civilisation we all share.

Notes

Foreword

1. E. G. Wedell, *Broadcasting and Public Policy*, London, Michael Joseph, 1968.

1 Moving the Goalposts

1. W. A. Robson, *British Government since 1918*, London, Allen and Unwin, 1950, p. 96.
2. Asa Briggs, *The Golden Age of Wireless*, London, OUP, 1965, pp. 418–19. Briggs here also gives a useful account of the way in which A. V. Dicey's views on state management influenced the thinking of all three political parties.
3. Lord Reith, 'Facade of Public Corporations', *The Times*, London, 29/03/66.
4. *Report of the Committee on Broadcasting 1926*, Cmnd 2599, London, HMSO, 1926.
5. A. Briggs, *The Birth of Broadcasting*, London, OUP, 1961, pp. 276–7.
6. *Media Ownership, The Government's Proposals*, Cmnd 287, London, HMSO, May 1995.
7. Ibid., para. 5.1.
8. Ibid., para. 5.3.
9. Conversation with Mr L. P. Wright, Head of the Broadcasting Branch of the Department of National Heritage, 05/06/95.
10. K. D. Bracher, *Turning Points in Modern Times*, Cambridge, Mass., Harvard Univ. Press, 1995, p. 115.
11. Ibid.
12. Conversation with Professor Ronald Preston, Professor of Moral and Pastoral Theology in the University of Manchester.
13. Broadcast on BBC Radio 4 on 08/10/95 at 7.30 p.m.
14. Quoted in Anthony Smith, 'The Public Interest' in London, *Intermedia*, June–July 1989, Vol. 17, No. 2, p. 15.
15. Ibid.
16. Ibid., p. 12.
17. Quoted in P. Fiddick, 'Reinventing the Wheel' in *Television*, London, Royal Television Society, February–March 1995, p. 11.
18. *Broadcast*, 10/11/92, p. 2.
19. *People and Programmes*, BBC, 1994, p. 25.
20. Ibid.
21. Ibid., p. 26.
22. Marginal quotation in *People and Programmes*, op. cit., p. 25.
23. *Media Ownership*, op. cit., p. 17, para. 5.10.
24. Charles Curran, *A Seamless Robe*, London, Collins, 1979.
25. *Media Ownership*, op. cit., p. 1, para. 3.

26. Ibid.
27. Ibid., p. 5, para. 1.11.

2   Needs Must When Innovation Drives

1. Martin Jackson, 'Digital: a Warning from History', *Broadcast*, 09/01/98, pp. 18 and 19.
2. 'Cable Services Pass Ten Million Homes', ITC press release, 09/12/97.
3. Leading article in *The Spectator*, 16/01/98.
4. Edward Briffa, Controller of the BBC On-line and Interactive Dept, reported in *The Observer*, 05/10/97, Business p. 7.
5. See Alexander Garrett, 'Wrestling for the Source of the Internet', *The Observer*, 05/10/97.
6. Ibid.
7. See report by Dataquest, December 1996.
8. See *European Digital Television*, Baskerville Communications, London and Los Angeles, December 1996.
9. Continental Research.
10. Data monitor.
11. The report of the Pace research project is quoted by Emily Bell in *The Observer* on 22/02/98.
12. *The Economist*, 24/08/96, p. 59.
13. Quoted in *The Observer*, 28/01/96.
14. See Helen Sage, 'Your Guide to the Digital Future', *Broadcast*, 15/05/98, pp. 18–19.
15. Ibid.

3   The Accountants Drive out the Guardians

1. The quotation is from unpublished lecture notes given to me by my colleague, Dorothy Emmet, Professor of Philosophy in the University of Manchester 1946–66, and author of several seminal works in the field of political philosophy, such as *Functions, Purpose Powers*, 1958, second edn. 1974, *Rules, Roles and Relations*, 1966, *The Effectiveness of Causes*, 1984, *The Role of the Unrealisable*, 1994, etc.
2. The Laodiceans living in Asia Minor, according to Revelations 3: 14–16 were 'neither cold nor hot: I would thou wert cold or hot. So then because thou art lukewarm and neither cold nor hot, I will spew thee out of my mouth.'
3. Ray Fitzwalter, 'The Money Men Are in Control of the I.T.C.', *Broadcast*, 20/03/98, p. 16. Ray Fitzwalter is also chairman of the Campaign for Quality Broadcasting.
4. Ibid.
5. 'Resources Privatisation: the Sinking of the BBC', *Stage, Screen and Radio*, March 1998, p. 8.
6. Charles Curran, *A Seamless Robe*, London, Collins, 1979.
7. Ibid.
8. Ibid.

9. Ibid.
10. Richard Collins, 'The Media Market', *LSE Journal*, Spring 1998, pp. 10–11.
11. Ibid.
12. Cardinal Basil Hume, 'Changing Hearts and Minds', lecture in Oregon, USA, 07/08/97, p. 14.
13. Quoted from the leaflet for the 1997 Royal Television Society Convention.
14. See also Chapter 9.
15. See B. Sendall, *Independent Television in Britain*, vol. 2, *Expansion and Change 1958–68*, London, Macmillan – now Palgrave, 1983, Ch. 9, note 10, p. 378.
16. Ibid., p. 88.
17. Ibid., p. 87.
18. Pilkington Report, vol. 1, Appendix E, Paper No. 252.
19. Sendall, op. cit., p. 351.
20. Ibid.
21. *The Times*, 26/11/99.
22. *The Times*, 27/11/99.

4   That's All We Have Time for: News and Current Affairs

1. In *Broadcast*, 11/08/99 supplement on *ITN at Forty*, p. 3. Sir David Nicholas joined ITN as a sub-editor in 1960. He rose through the ranks to become chairman. He retired in 1961.
2. There is agreement among the broadcasters that all viewing up to 9 p.m. should be suitable for the whole family. Films with adult themes or treatment have not, on the terrestrial channels, begun until after the family viewing period.
3. Report by John Plunkett in *Broadcast*, 06/11/98, p. 16.
4. Emily Bell, 'When the Telly is No Longer an Event', *The Observer*, 24/01/99.
5. 'The Bias against Understanding', in Peter Jay, *The Crisis for Western Political Economy and Other Essays*, London, André Deutsch, 1984, on pp. 189–218 are reproduced four articles which appeared in *The Times* in 1975. The first was written by John Birt, the other three jointly with Peter Jay. Birt and Jay had collaborated on the programme *Weekend World* contributed by London Weekend Television to the ITV network.
6. Ibid., p. 194.
7. Interview in *Broadcast*, 27/10/95.
8. Report in *The Times*, 28/08/99 on John Humphrys' *Devil's Advocate*, London, Hutchinson, 1999.
9. Martin Bell, MP, 'The Journalism of Attachment', unpublished paper, 1998.
10. Report in *The Times*, 20/09/99.
11. Quoted by Tony Hall, at that time chief executive, BBC News, *The Times*, 20/09/99.
12. Ibid.
13. Report in *The Guardian*, 25/01/99.
14. Ibid.
15. Ibid.
16. See 'Tonight with …', *Television*, April 1999, pp. 43–4.
17. Brenda Maddox, 'TV is a Medium where Every Edit is a Lie', *The Times*, 27/08/97.

18. Ibid.
19. London, Michael Joseph, 1968.
20. At that time television critic of the *Daily Mail*.
21. Professor Jacob Bronowski, a popular science broadcaster at the time.
22. Stephen Coleman, *Electronic Media, Parliament and the People*, London, Hansard Society, 1999.
23. Ralph Negrine, *Media Coverage of Parliament: a Cause for Concern?*, London, Royal Institute for International Affairs, Briefing Paper No. 47, July 1998.
24. *The Guardian*, 19/07/99.
25. *The Economist*, 17/07/99, p. 29.
26. Ibid.
27. Negrine, op. cit.
28. Jon Snow in *The Guardian*, 19/07/99.
29. Ibid.
30. Ibid.
31. Negrine, op. cit.

5   Sport: Does the Tail Wag the Dog?

1. *Annual Reports*, BBC and ITC 1997 and 1998.
2. National Heritage Select Committee, House of Commons, *Sports Sponsorship and Television Coverage*, Report and Minutes of Evidence (3 volumes), 1994.
3. *Report of the Broadcasting Committee 1949* (the Beveridge Committee), Cmd 8116, HMSO; *Annual Reports* of the BBC.
4. Ibid.
5. Asa Briggs, *Sound and Vision History of Broadcasting in the United Kingdom*, vol. 4, p. 843, Oxford University Press, 1979.
6. *Annual Reports*, BBC.
7. *Annual Reports*, BBC and ITC.
8. P. Slater, *The Origins and Significance of the Frankfurt School*, Routledge and Kegan Paul, 1977.
9. National Heritage Select Committee, op. cit.
10. Ibid., vol. 2, p. 178.
11. Tina Mistry, 'The Price Isn't Right', *Broadcast*, 10/3/98, where she used calculations from Howard Nead.
12. Paul Bonner, *Independent Television Britain*, vol. 5, *ITV and IBA 1981–92. The Old Relationship Changes*, London, Macmillan – now Palgrave, 1995, pp. 114–15.
13. Ibid., pp. 110–15.

6   The Battle for Ratings: Peak-Hour Schedules

1. D. Hobson, *Crossroads: the Drama of a Soap Opera*, Methuen, London, 1982.
2. Pilkington Committee, *Report of the Committee on Broadcasting*, HMSO, 1962.
3. *Annual Reports*, BBC and IBA/ITC.
4. Ibid.
5. M. Young, head of BBC Drama Services, on BBC2 13 October 1999.

6. Ibid.
7. *General Household Survey Reports*, HMSO. Triennial analyses of leisure activity.
8. Bonner, op. cit., p. 334, quoting research used by the Peacock Committee, *Report of the Committee on Financing the BBC*, HMSO, 1986.
9. Ibid.
10. *Annual Reports*, BBC and ITC.
11. Calculated from data in *Annual Reports* of BBC and ITC, and *Annual Abstract of Statistics*, HMSO.
12. From widely trailed promotions at time of Davies Report, autumn 1999.
13. C. Smith, Secretary of State for Culture, Media and Sport. Address given at Royal Television Society Conference, Cambridge, 1999.
14. Statement at Annual Meeting of Mirror Newspapers Ltd, 1956.
15. *Marketing Pocket Book*, Annual issues, NTC Publications, London.

7   The Exploitation of Emotion

1. P. Bonner, *Independent Television in Britain*, vol. 5, London, Macmillan – now Palgrave, 1998, p. 351.
2. C. Shaw, *Deciding What We Watch*, Oxford University Press, Oxford, 1999, Chs 5 and 6.
3. Broadcasting Standards Commission, *Annual Monitoring Report*, No. 7, London, 1999.
4. R. Woods and M. Wroe, 'Beyond Laddism', *Sunday Times*, 17/10/99.
5. ITC, *Annual Review of Programmes*, London, 1999.
6. BBC, *Producers' Guidelines*, London, 1997 and ITC, *Television Programme Code*, London, 1995.
7. Shaw, op. cit., p. 98.
8. British Board of Film Classification, *Draft Guidelines and Memorandum for Classifying Films and Videos*, London, 1999.
9. B. Woffinden, *Hanratty: the Final Verdict*, London, Macmillan – now Palgrave, 1997.
10. ITC, *Annual Report for 1998*, London, 1999.
11. T. Stammers, 'A University General Practice Tutor', *The Times*, 20/10/99.
12. S. Alinsky, *Reveille for Radicals*, New York, Vintage Books, 1969, and S. Freud, 'Jokes and Their Relationship to the Unconscious', in *The Psychological Works*, vol. 8, London, Hogarth Press, 1955.
13. Home Office, *Crime Statistics* (Annual) and *National Crime Surveys* (Annual), London, sometimes give rather divergent evidence.
14. BBC, *Producers' Guidelines*, op. cit.
15. ITC, *Television Programme Code*, op. cit.
16. ITC, *Spectrum*, No. 24, Spring 1997, and *The BBC and the Reporting of Crime*. Report of BBC Governors' Seminar, June 1994.
17. G. Noble, *Children in Front of the Small Screen*, London, Constable, 1975; W. Belson, *Adolescents, Violence and Television*, Stockholm, Akademilitteratur, 1980, and *Television Violence and the Adolescent Boy*, London, Saxon House, 1978.

8 Minority Programmes: a Major Problem

1. J. Humphrys, *Devil's Advocate*, Hutchinson, 1999.
2. *The Guardian*, 24/05/99.
3. *Broadcast*, 11/06/99.
4. B. Luckham and J. M. Orr, 'Educational Broadcasts and Book Borrowing', in *Library and Adult Education Studies*, Public Libraries and Adult Education Committee for the North West, Manchester, 1973.
5. K. Popper, *The Logic of Scientific Discovery*, Hutchinson, London, 1959.
6. E. Rea, 'Faith in the Future: Religious Broadcasting for a New Millennium', Lecture at the University of Manchester, November 1999.
7. S. Livingstone, 'Screen Entertainment for British Children', Paper given at the 30th Manchester International Broadcasting Symposium, 1999.
8. J. G. Blumler and D. Biltereyst, *The Integrity and Erosion of Public Television for Children*, Centre for Media Education, Washington, USA, 1997.
9. Calculated from data in BBC *Annual Reports*, 1990–98.
10. *Performance Review of Independent Television*, ITC, 1999.
11. *General Household Survey Reports*, 1977–96 and Advertising Association, Annual Media Pocket Books.
12. Ibid.

9 Shoring up the Stable Door: the Limits of Regulation

1. Nigel Walmsley, 'Getting it Right', *Television*, Journal of the Royal Television Society, January–February 1998, p. 13.
2. E. G. Wedell, *Broadcasting and Public Policy*, London, Michael Joseph, 1968, p. 19.
3. Ibid., p. 20.
4. Lord Reith, 'Façade of Public Corporation', *The Times*, 29/03/66.
5. Walé Azeez, 'Document Makers Agree TV Can't Be Trusted', *Broadcast*, 29/10/99.
6. ITC Fact file 1999, J. Dugdale, *The Guardian*, 06/01/92, p. 16.
7. *Producers' Guidelines*, BBC, 1993.
8. See Jeremy Mitchell and Jay G. Blumler, *Television and the Viewer Interest* (Media Monograph No. 18 of the European Institute for the Media), London, Montague and Rome, John Libbey, 1994. The UK chapter of this survey contains a careful study of the relations between broadcasters and their audiences by Naomi Sargant.
9. J. Dugdale, *The Guardian*, 06/01/92.
10. See ITC, *Annual Report and Accounts 1998*, p. 23.
11. Ibid.
12. *The Times*, 24/10/99.
13. *Broadcast*, 29/10/99, p. 31.
14. Colin Shaw, *Deciding What We Watch*, Oxford, Clarendon Press, 1999, p. 56.
15. Broadcasting Standards Commission, *Annual Review 1998–99*, Chairman's statement, p. 4.

16. Vide the Secretary of State's speech at the convention of the Royal Television Society in Cambridge, September 1999.
17. Raymond Snoddy, 'Money Talks at the BBC', *The Times*, 05/11/99.
18. Ibid.
19. *Towards an Information Society Approach* (Green Paper on the Convergence of the Telecommunications, Media and Information Technology Sectors, and the Implications for Regulation), Brussels, the European Commission, COM(97)623, 3/12/97.
20. COM(87)290 final.
21. *Towards an Information Society Approach*, op. cit., Conclusion.
22. We are indebted for this analysis to the article by Jeremy Mitchell on 'How the Green Paper Fails the Consumer' in the March 1997 issue of *Commercial Communications*, pp. 4–7.
23. Robert Pepper, 'Broadcasting Policies in a Multi-channel Marketplace' in Charles Firestone (ed.) *Television for the 21st Century. The Next Wave*, Washington DC, Aspen Institute, 1993, p. 119.
24. Chris Smith, 'The Big Switch', *Television*, Journal of the Royal Television Society, October 1999.
25. Ibid.

10   Professionals in Search of a Profession

1. British Film Commission, Check Book 3: *Film Maker's Companion*, London, annually.
2. Asa Briggs, *History of Broadcasting in the UK*, vol. V, *Competition 1955–74*, Oxford and New York, Oxford University Press, pp. 383–4.
3. Ibid., p. 289.
4. E. G. Wedell, *Broadcasting and Public Policy*, London, Michael Joseph, 1968, p. 174.
5. J. Wain, 'The BBC's Duty to Society – V', *The Listener*, 22/07/65.
6. B. Wootton, 'The BBC's Duty to Society – VI', *The Listener*, 29/07/65.
7. T. Gardam, 'What is Channel 4 for?', *Television*, November/December 1990, p. 10.
8. Dawn Airey, 'Channel 5 with Money, a Commercially Driven BBC', *Television*, November/December 1999, p. 14.
9. The decision to set up the Pilkington Committee was taken on the basis of a memorandum by the Postmaster General, Mr Reginald Bevins MP, *Broadcasting in the United Kingdom* of 16/03/1990 (PRO CAB 129, vol. 100, c(60)50).
10. Cmnd 1753 (1962), *Report of the Committee on Broadcasting 1960*, p. 1.
11. On 17 May 1960. See B. Sendall, *Independent Television in Britain*, vol. 1, London, Macmillan Press – now Palgrave, 1982.
12. Letter of January 1961 quoted in the *Report of the Committee on Broadcasting*, vol. 11, appendix E, paper 232.
13. Sir Karl Popper (1902–94) was professor of philosophy at the London School of Economics from 1949 to 1969. His books include *The Open Society*

and its Enemies (1945) and *The Poverty of Historicism* (1957). He always linked his philosophical thinking with the practical issues of government.

14. The videotape was made by Superchannel in association with the European Institute for the Media. The text of the dialogue was published in *The European Citizen and the Media* (proceedings of a colloquium) in the *Mediafact* series of the European Institute for the Media on 4 June 1993.

15. Alfred Adler (1870–1937) pioneer Austrian psychiatrist. He opened the first child guidance clinic in Vienna in 1921.

16. In W. W. Bartley II (ed.), *Realism and the Area of Science*, publisher and date unknown.

17. Apollo, in the mythology of the Greeks and Romans, was regarded as the healing god. In this capacity he appears in the very beginning of the *Iliad*, as the divinity who causes and removes the pestilence; and in the Homeric Hymn to Apollo he is introduced in the same capacity. Hence the epithet 'healing' is applied to him by Sophocles (Ed. Tyr., 154); and its synonym, 'the healer' *or* 'the physician', by our author in this place. The beautiful lines of Ovid, in reference to the healing power of Apollo, are in everybody's mouth: 'Inventum Medicina meum est; opiferque per orbem Dicor, et herbarum subjecta potentia nobis.' (Met. i. 521) Æsculapius was universally represented as the son of Apollo, according to Pindar, the contemporary of our author, by the nymph Coronis (Pyth. iii); but according to the later myths, by Arsinoe (Apollodor. Bibl. iii, 10). I need scarcely say that he was the patron god of the Asclepiadæ, or priest-physicians, to which order Hippocrates belonged.

18. There has been considerable difference of opinion about what the two kinds of instruction are to which Hippocrates adverts here. See Zuinger, Foës and Littré. The most probable supposition appears to be that the former applies to general precepts and the latter to professional lectures. Of the one we have a good specimen in the Hippocratic treatise entitled the *Præcepts* and of the other in the *Auscultationes Naturales* of Aristotle. That our author delivered public lectures in the cities he visited there can be no doubt, for he is so represented by his contemporary, Plato, in his *Protagoras*. It will be seen, however, from this piece, that he confined his instruction to his own family and that of his teachers, and to such pupils as were bound by a regular stipulation *or* indenture.

19. See F. Adams, *The Genuine Works of Hippocrates*, London, The Sydenham Society, 1849, pp. 779–80.

20. See RTS Handbook for 1998–99, p. 6.

21. Peter Keighron, 'Clarke of Works', *Broadcast*, 17/04/98, p. 19.

22. Janice Turner in a personal communication.

23. See 'ITV Barons Block out 7000 "Unsuitable" Jobs', *The Observer*, 28/09/97, p. 4.

24. Quoted by Nicholas Hellen, media correspondent, *The Sunday Times*, n.d. in 1999.

25. Quoted in 'I Want to Be in the Media' by Henry Bonson, *The Times*, 08/10/1997, p. 23.

26. 'Courses Are no Open Sesames' by Sandy Parker, *The Times*, n.d.
27. See Emily Bell, 'Saint who Squared the Circle', *The Observer*, 07/11/1999, p. 7.

11   Television at the Crossroads: Which Way to Turn?

1. David Boulton, Social Policy Paper No. 3, IPPR, 1997.
2. The Campaign for Quality Television, 1998.
3. Jeffrey Berg, 'Media Companies and the Creation of Value', *LSE Journal*, 1999, p. 34.
4. Ibid.
5. See G. M. Luyken and others: *Overcoming Language Barriers in Television*, Manchester, European Institute for the Media, 1993.
6. *The Independent*, September 1999.
7. See Chapter 9, p. 174.
8. 'Eyre's Vision for the Future of TV', *The Guardian*, 28/09/99.
9. Ibid.
10. Ibid.
11. Ibid.

Bibliography
(Books published since 1990)

Adler, R. P. (rapporteur), *The Future of Advertising*, Washington, The Aspen Institute, 1997.

Baran, S. & Wallis, R., *The Known World of Broadcast News*, London, Routledge, 1990.

Barnett, S., *Funding the BBC's Future*, London, BFI, 1991.

Barnett, S. & Curry, A., *The Battle for the BBC*, London, Aurum Press, 1994.

Biltereyst, D. & Blumler, J. G., *The Integrity and Erosion of Public Television for Children*, Centre for Media Education, Washington, USA, 1997.

Blumler, J. (ed.), *Television and the Public Interest*, London, Saga, 1992.

Blumler, J. & Mitchell, J., *Television and the Viewer Interest*, London, John Libbey and European Institute for the Media, 1994.

Bogart, L., *Commercial Culture: the Media System and the Public Interest*, OUP, 1995.

Brown, D. R., Firestone, C. M. & Michiewicz, E., *Television/Radio News and Minorities*, Washington, The Aspen Institute and Atlanta, Georgia, The Carter Centre of Emory University, 1994.

Buckingham, D. et al., *Children's Television in Britain*, London, BFI, 1999.

Caterall, P., *The Making of Channel Four*, London, Frank Cass Books, 1999.

Collins, R., *Television: Policy and Culture*, London, Unwin Hyman, 1990.

Collins, R. (ed.), *Converging Media? Converging Regulation*, London, Institute for Public Policy Research, 1996.

Collins, R. & Murroni, C., *New Media, New Policies*, Cambridge, Polity Press, 1996.

Congdon, T. et al., *Paying for Broadcasting*, London, Routledge, 1992.

Congdon, T. et al., *The Cross-Media Revolution: Ownership and Control*, University of Luton Press, 1995.

Cox, G., *Pioneering Television News*, University of Luton Press, 1995.

Crisell, A., *An Introductory History of British Broadcasting*, London, Routledge, 1997.

Cummings, B., *War and Television*, London, Verso, 1992.

Curran, J. & Seaton, J., *Power without Responsibility*, London, Routledge, 1995.

Dizard, W. P. Jr, *Old Media, New Media*, New York, Longman, 1994 (second edn 1997).

Dizard, W. P. Jr, *The Coming Information Age*, London, Longman, 1989 (third edn).

Docherty, D., *Violence in Television Fiction*, London, Broadcasting Standards Council, 1990.

Dries, J. & Woldt, R., *The Role of Public Service Broadcasting in the Information Society*, Düsseldorf, European Institute for the Media, 1996.

Eldridge, J., *Mass Media and Power in Modern Britain*, OUP, 1997.

Firestone, C. M. (ed.), *Television for the 21st Century: the Next Wave*, Washington, The Aspen Institute, 1993.

Firestone, C. M. & Mickering, E., *Television and Electronics*, Washington, The Aspen Institute and Atlanta, Georgia, The Carter Centre of Emory University, 1994.

Franklin, B., *Televising Democracies*, London, Routledge Chapman & Hall, 1992.

Gauntlett, D., *Moving Experiences: Understanding Television's Influences and Effects*, University of Luton Press, 1991.

Gerbner, G., 'Why the Culture Environment Movement?', *Gazette, The Internet Journal for Communication's Study*, vol. 60, No. 2, April 1998, London, Sage Publications, 1998.

Gow, B. et al., *Bosnia by Television*, London, BFI, 1996.

Graham, A. et al., *Public Purposes in Broadcasting: Funding the BBC*, University of Luton Press, 1999.

Groombridge, B. & Hay, J., *The Price of Choice: Broadcasting in a Competitive European Market*, University of Luton Press, 1995.

Gunter, B. & McAteer, J., *Children and Television*, London, Routledge, 1990.

Gunter, B. & Wober, M., *Television and Social Control*, London, IBA, 1988.

Hill, J. & McLoone, M. (eds), *Big Picture, Small Screen*, University of Luton Press, 1995.

Humphrys, J., *Devil's Advocate*, London, Hutchinson, 1999.

Ishikawa, S. (ed.), *Quality Assessment of Television*, University of Luton Press, John Libbey, 1996.

Izod, J. & Kilborn, J. R., *An Introduction to Television Documentary*, Manchester University Press, 1997.

Jankowski, G. F. & Fuchs, D. C., *Television Today and Tomorrow*, OUP, 1995.

Lange, B. P. & Woldt, R., *Television Requires Responsibility*, Gutersloh, Bertelsmann, 1995.

Levy, J. & Setzer, F., *Broadcast Television in a Multi-channel Marketplace*, Washington, Federal Communications Commission, 1991.

McDonnell, J., *Public Service Broadcasting*, London, Routledge, 1991.

McIlroy, B., *Shooting to Kill*, Trowbridge, Flicks Books, 1998.

McQuail, D., *Media Performance*, London, Sage, 1993.

Milwood Hargrave, A., *Sex and Sexuality in Broadcasting*, London, Libbey and Broadcasting Standards Council, 1992.

Morley, D., *Television Audiences and Cultural Studies*, London, Routledge, 1992.

Morrison, D., *Television and the Gulf War*, London, Libbey, 1992.

Mulgan, G. (ed.), *The Question of Quality*, London, BFI, 1989.

Murroni, C. et al., *Conveying Communications*, London, Institute for Public Policy Research, 1996.

Negrine, R., *Television and the Press since 1945*, Manchester University Press, 1998.

Palmer, M. & Tunstall, J., *Media Moguls*, London, Routledge, 1991.

Pines, G. (ed.), *Black and White in Colour*, London, BFI, 1992.

Price, M. E., *Television, the Public Sphere and National Identity*, Oxford, Clarendon Press, 1995.

Price, M. E., 'The Market for Loyalties: Electronic Media and the Global Competition for Allegiance', *The Yale Law Journal*, vol. 104, No. 3, December 1994.

Raboy, M. (ed.), *Public Broadcasting for the 21ˢᵗ Century*, University of Luton Press, 1996.

Ross, K., *Black & White Media*, Cambridge, Polity Press, 1996.
Rushton, D., *Citizen Television*, London, Libbey, 1995.
Seymour, C., *British Press and Broadcasting since 1945*, Oxford, Blackwell, 1991.
Shaw, C., *Deciding What We Watch*, Oxford, Clarendon Press, 1999.
Shaw, C. (ed.), *Rethinking Governance and Accountability*, London, BFI, 1993.
Silverstone, R., *Television and Everyday Life*, London, Routledge, 1994.
Tulloch, J., *Drama: Agency, Audience and Myth*, London, Routledge, 1990.
Twitchin, J. (ed.), *The Black and White Media Book*, London, Trentham, 1992.
UNESCO, *Public Service Broadcasting*, Paris, 1996.
Woffenden, B., *Hanratty: the Final Verdict*, London, Macmillan – now Palgrave, 1997.
Yorke, I., *Television News*, London, Focal Press, 1995.

This list does not include publications by the broadcasting organisations.

Index